# Reorganizing
# Roosevelt's Government

# Reorganizing

# Roosevelt's Government

## THE CONTROVERSY
## OVER EXECUTIVE REORGANIZATION
## 1936–1939

Richard Polenberg

HARVARD UNIVERSITY PRESS

CAMBRIDGE·MASSACHUSETTS

1966····

For Marcia

# Preface

In April 1938 more than one hundred Democratic congressmen deserted President Roosevelt to defeat the Executive Reorganization Bill by a vote of 204 to 196. Defeat of the measure followed six weeks of acrimonious debate in both House and Senate. Congressmen who opposed reorganization contended that it would create a presidential dictatorship, and scores of newspapers echoed this sentiment. Many Americans were apparently disturbed by these accusations; hundreds of thousands of letters and telegrams poured into Washington, and a group of "modern Paul Reveres" descended upon the Capital to demand defeat of the measure. Nearly all observers agreed that the President suffered a major setback in the recommittal of the bill; Roosevelt himself seemed stunned by the vote. In addition, the impact of the defeat seemed to dampen prospects for the future of the New Deal as a reform movement. For this reason, one Republican Congressman jubilantly termed the defeat of the Reorganization Bill "about the biggest political event which has taken place since 1932."

The controversy over reorganization raises several important questions. Why did Roosevelt attempt to reorganize the government, and what significance did his decision hold for administrative developments under the New Deal? What were the sources of support for reorganization? Why did the plan arouse so much angry contention among special-interest groups and the public at large, and how was this opposition expressed? What explains the defeat of the bill and what were the implications of the struggle for the political history of the New Deal? This study seeks to answer these questions.

In writing this book I have been helped by many persons, and I am happy to record my gratitude to them. I wish to thank William E. Leuchtenburg of Columbia University for his advice, encouragement, and many valuable suggestions concerning the organization of this study. I am also indebted to Robert D. Cross of Columbia University and Don K. Price of Harvard University for many critical suggestions. Any errors that may remain are, of course, my responsibility.

I am indebted to Clifford Hope, Alfred M. Landon, and Lindsay Carter Warren for granting me access to their papers. I should also like to thank Mrs. Caroline Werner Gannett for permission to use the Frank E. Gannett Papers, and Allan Nevins for the use of the James Truslow Adams Papers. Herbert Emmerich kindly permitted me to examine his papers. Louis Brownlow, James A. Farley, and Henry A. Wallace graciously consented to be interviewed.

I am particularly grateful to Elizabeth B. Drewry and the staff of the Franklin D. Roosevelt Library for their assistance. Librarians at the University of Oklahoma, University of North Carolina, Duke University, University of Virginia, Columbia University, Cornell University, Indiana University, New York Public Library, Library of Congress, and National Archives proved most helpful. State librarians and archivists in Kansas, Alabama, Minnesota, Wisconsin, and Colorado also aided my research. My thanks go to Earl Latham of Amherst College for aiding me in the use of the Joseph B. Eastman Papers and to Joseph Riggs of Memphis State University for guiding me through the Kenneth McKellar Papers.

I should like to thank the editors of *Agricultural History* and the *Journal of American History* for permission to use material which has appeared in a different form in their journals.

The book is dedicated to my wife, who helped in more ways than she can know.

R.P.

# Contents

PART ONE

# The Background

# CHAPTER I

# The Origins of Executive Reorganization

## 1933–1936

LUTHER Gulick, a chief architect of Roosevelt's plan of reorganization, once remarked that the program was "not a daring new and original compound of untried theories," but was based on time-tested ideas of proven merit.[1] Indeed, every president since Theodore Roosevelt had called for reorganization, and business groups had strongly supported the application of modern management techniques to government. But if the President's proposals drew on the past, they owed even more to his experience in the White House. His scheme of reorganization represented a concrete solution to the administrative problems which arose during the 1930's. In part, this was because Franklin Roosevelt brought to the Presidency an understanding of reorganization markedly different from that of any of his predecessors.

### 1

The earliest proposals for reorganization emanated not from the President but from Congress. In the thirty years following the Civil War, Congress sponsored four important investigations into departmental management. In each case the objective was to promote economy through the introduction of improved working methods, and the underlying assumption was the responsibility of the administrative system to the Legislature. Of these early attempts, only the Dockery-Cockrell Commission, created in 1893, made a significant contribution to the cause of efficient management. These investigations, Leonard D. White has concluded, "reveal the incapacity of Congress to think in terms other than detail. For twenty years members of Congress acted as amateur organization and methods analysts, but they failed to rise to higher levels."[2]

Although Congressional efforts during these years proved inadequate, no president responded by initiating executive studies designed to improve administration. When, in 1905, Theodore Roosevelt appointed the Keep Commission to study departmental procedures, responsibility for administrative reform passed from Congress to the President. Since few of its recommendations were enacted, the Commission had little impact upon administrative operations. Following this, President Taft created a Commission on Economy and Efficiency, which recommended the consolidation and abolition of certain agencies. Although the Commission's report did not lead to the creation of the Labor Department in 1913, Congress did pass an act authorizing the President to bring about needed transfers.[3]

As a close student of public administration, Woodrow Wilson had a firm commitment to improve governmental organization. His program, however, was blocked by several Cabinet members who feared a possible loss of authority. Josephus Daniels, Wilson's Secretary of the Navy, later recalled that the President had strongly favored redistribution but that Secretary of the Treasury William McAdoo "kicked like a steer even at the suggestion of taking health service and building post-office buildings away from the Treasury, and most Cabinet officials opposed any plan by which they might lose a bureau." Ultimately, spurred by the war emergency, Congress approved the Overman Act which gave Wilson broad power to redistribute the functions of executive agencies. This authority expired at the end of the war, and Wilson's transfers had little permanent effect upon the administrative structure of the government.[4]

If the drive for reorganization depended upon active presidential interest, it also enjoyed the support of business groups who urged adoption of up-to-date management techniques to reduce waste and promote efficiency. During the 1920's the movement may have been sustained by this latter impulse, for neither Harding nor Coolidge proved a vigorous advocate. President Harding's suggestion for a comprehensive plan of reorganization in 1923 fizzled out. "When his Cabinet and Bureau Chiefs began to squabble, and Congressmen put in objections to this or that, he threw up his hands," recalled one observer. Harding had also endorsed the creation of a Joint Congressional Committee to study the problem, but its report in June 1924 calling for a more rational assignment of agencies received only mild support from Coolidge and was scotched by Congress early in 1925.[5]

With the onset of the depression in 1929, the demand for reorganization became intense. There existed a universal desire to impose some order upon a "crazy-quilt" governmental structure. This, it was hoped, would save money and stave off budget deficits. "The immense and unwieldy Government bureaucracy fairly cries aloud for reduction and recasting," asserted the *New York Times*. Herbert Hoover responded to the challenge with a determined effort to secure a redistribution of functions and nearly reached his goal. In February 1932 he stated that "the absolute necessity for the most drastic economy makes the problem of government reorganization one of paramount importance."[6] Hoover urged the use of Presidential authority to achieve the traditional ends of economy and efficiency.

As a result, in June 1932 Congress passed the Economy Act which enabled the President to regroup agencies, subject to a veto by either house within sixty days. But by December, when Hoover proposed a sweeping reassignment of bureaus, he had been defeated in his bid for re-election. The Democratic majority in the House of Representatives rejected all of his recommendations on the grounds that President-elect Roosevelt should be free to implement his own program. "After March 4 we will do some real reorganizing," said one Democrat confidently.[7]

## 2

Several days after his inauguration Franklin Roosevelt replied to a senator who proposed a reorganization plan: "Your ideas are not any more revolutionary than some of mine." Most observers believed that the new President would rapidly implement a far-reaching program. As a candidate he had pledged that his efforts in this area would "constitute a chapter to be written in action."[8] He had recruited Daniel Roper as Secretary of Commerce by emphasizing the urgency of reorganization. At his first press conference Roosevelt announced that reorganization would have top priority: "It has got to proceed as fast as the law will let us." Roosevelt's commitment to improve governmental administration was total.[9]

In part this commitment stemmed from Roosevelt's experience under Woodrow Wilson. Wilson's ideas on administration powerfully influenced his admirers, and to many the New Deal offered an opportunity to consummate his program. Some tried consciously to emulate their former chief. Josephus Daniels assured Roosevelt that "Wilson wanted to do what you are doing, but I do not think he would have taken the bull by the horns. . . ." Bernard Baruch explained to the President that Wilson had faced very similar problems of administration fifteen years earlier.[10] Senator McAdoo based his support for reorganization during the 1930's upon the insight gained as a member of Wilson's cabinet. Another friend wrote Roosevelt wistfully: "Our old chief, Woodrow Wilson, were he here, would be proud of you and what you have done."[11]

Roosevelt's career as Governor of New York confirmed his Wilsonian training. Alfred E. Smith had successfully reorganized the executive departments of the state in 1927, but Roosevelt continued to call for modernization of the archaic system of local government. Toward the end of his second term he requested the

Institute of Public Administration to examine local government in the state and to suggest a general program of reorganization. In February 1932 he asked the legislature to create a "commission of practical experts," composed of businessmen and students of government, to propose extensive revisions. Reform of government administration at all levels was never far from Roosevelt's mind.[12]

What distinguished Roosevelt's conception of reorganization from that of his predecessors was his objective rather than the means he employed. Other presidents had considered reorganization an Executive responsibility, but their aim had consistently been the reduction of expenditures. Roosevelt disagreed. He believed that the true purpose of reorganization was improved management, which would make administration more responsive to the national interest and better able to serve that interest. Although Roosevelt favored a balanced budget, he realized that this could only be achieved by trimming expenditures, not by shifting bureaus or agencies. In this appraisal of reorganization the New Deal marks a sharp break with tradition.

Unfortunately, Roosevelt's outlook has been distorted by certain of his 1932 campaign addresses, when, under sharp attack from Hoover he succumbed for a time to conservative fiscal advisers and bracketed reorganization with economy. At Pittsburgh, on October 19, he declared: "Before any man enters my Cabinet he must pledge . . . complete cooperation with me looking to economy and reorganization in his department." Just before the election, in Brooklyn, he asserted that large savings could be achieved by abolishing useless commissions and "consolidating many activities of the government." Indeed, the candidate went on to attack Hoover's failure to reorganize the government in the interests of economy.[13]

This campaign oratory reflected a temporary aberration, not Roosevelt's real beliefs. As Governor of New York he had pointed to the unfortunate consequences of promising monetary savings through reorganization. No amount of reorganization could offset the cost of increased public services: "The chief result of administrative reorganization has been that which has been urged by advocates of reorganization for so many years . . . —centralization of executive and administrative responsibility."[14] "We have got to get over the notion that the purpose of reorganization is economy," he told Louis Brownlow and Luther Gulick in 1936, "I had that out with Al Smith in New York. . . . The reason for reorganization is good management."[15]

The President took the same position at press conferences in the spring of 1933. When, on May 31, newsmen inquired about the potential savings to be gained through reorganization, Roosevelt answered that the transfer of agencies "isn't going to save such an awful lot of money." Minor overhead expenses might be somewhat reduced, but "the importance of it isn't so much the financial saving as it is the better supervision of things." Two days later he elaborated: ". . . It is awfully erroneous to assume that it is in the reorganization of Departments and Bureaus that you save money. That is a very easy fallacy to fall into. Where you save money is by lopping off debts and lopping off employees and stopping the spending of money." Savings through reorganization, at best, would be "a drop in the bucket."[16]

Considering Roosevelt's conviction that reorganization would improve management, his first administration failed notoriously to live up to expectations. Although the Economy Act of 1933 conferred broad reorganization authority upon the President for two years, he used it sparingly.[17] In all, he issued seven executive orders which brought about minor changes: the Office of National Parks and the Division of Territories were established in the Department of the Interior, and the Bureau of Mines was transferred from the Department of Commerce to Interior; the U. S. Geographic Board and the Office of Alien Property Custodian were discontinued and their duties transferred to other departments; and the U. S. Shipping Board and the Federal Employment Stabilization Board were abolished.[18] The President himself did not consider these to be of great importance. By the end of 1934 many feared that reorganization had been indefinitely postponed.[19]

Why did the President not use his power to a greater extent? The most obvious explanation is that his concern with the critical problems of relief and recovery took precedence and shunted reorganization aside. His press conferences during 1933 illustrate grandiose schemes giving way to meager achievement under the stress of the emergency. On March 22 Roosevelt admitted that he had been too preoccupied with other matters to discuss reorganization: "You will not get to it until after the emergency?" "No," he replied. A week later he confessed that the Cabinet had not considered it: "We had many other things to talk about." Pressure did not ease in the following months, and on May 19 he conceded that he would take up reorganization with Lewis Douglas for the first time on a boat excursion during the next two days. Upon his return the President reported ruefully: "I had grand intentions and that is as far as we got. We brought down a large package with all the figures and all the departments and bureaus and we brought it ashore unopened. . . We haven't touched it yet."[20]

Not only did the grave problems of the depression command Roosevelt's time and energy, but they also forced him to adopt unorthodox administrative formulas. Very often the swiftest way to deal with a situation was to bypass the existing administrative structure and create a special agency. "We have new and complex problems," he once told Frances Perkins: "Why not establish a new agency to take over the new duty rather than saddle it on an old institution? . . . If it is not permanent, we don't get bad precedents. . . ."[21] The emergency agency became an essential instrument in Roosevelt's administrative technique. Although the President believed, in theory, that these agencies should be brought under one of the major departments, he was impelled to create a myriad of autonomous bodies and rely upon special coordinating boards to impose some order on the rambling structure.

Roosevelt's own administrative habits also militated against reorganization. He preferred a competitive approach to administration. Encouragement of overlapping jurisdictions may have seemed poor administrative theory, but it often spurred government officials to greater achievement. He was influenced, too, by purely personal considerations. The Director of the Budget Bureau once complained that the President permitted his view of personalities to affect his objectivity toward organization.[22] For example, he would not abolish the unnecessary Battle Monuments Commission while General Pershing lived. Moreover, the merits of redistribution very often could be argued equally well on both sides: "Should the Park Service go into the Department of Agriculture or should the Forestry Service go into the Department of the Interior. Well, it is probable that at this particular time I won't do anything on that. I want to have a little more argument on it during the summer."[23] To resolve such an issue might embitter subordinates and stir dissension; to postpone it might preserve the rivalry that was so conducive to imaginative administration.

In addition to the nature of the problems he faced, and his own administrative temperament, Roosevelt may have been aware of the political dangers posed by reorganization. When, in December 1936, a visitor told Henry Morgenthau that reorganization was a scientific process, the Secretary smiled: "Well . . . I think the only time new consolidations can be made is the second time you're President; then you can be scientific, but you can't be scientific the first time. The second time—the second time very scientific. You take in Customs, for instance. . . We have a fairly big office in Des Moines, Iowa. Why should we have a Collector of Customs in Des Moines, Iowa? But before election try to close that up; it's just impossible. Now we can be very scientific. . . The only chance to do it is the second time, if the President has to decide."[24] The President, too, recognized the perils implicit in reorganization. In 1933 Dan Roper prepared a "radical and far-reaching" plan and, after discussion with Roosevelt, suggested that the "utmost care" be taken to forestall the "concerted opposition" which they both feared. Congress, said Roper, should be allowed to approve each feature of the Executive Order separately, without having to accept or reject an entire package. Roosevelt jotted on Roper's memorandum: "Can we separate the controversial from the non-controv.? in the Exec Order?"[25]

Nevertheless, Roosevelt retained his belief in the need for administrative reorganization. He seemed somewhat dismayed at the multiplication of semi-autonomous regulatory commissions, which not only did violence to his strong historical sense of unity and continuity in the Presidency, but threatened to become a dangerous political liability. He once remarked that administration was the most vulnerable aspect of his first term but, fortunately, the Republicans had not hammered at it in 1936.[26] When the pressure of the emergency abated, the political situation appeared promising, and the opportunity presented itself, Roosevelt would undoubtedly consider anew the problem of reorganization.

### 3

If President Roosevelt was willing to defer systematic administrative improvement, other New Deal sympathizers regarded it with more urgency. One of them, Louis Brownlow, was typical of the many men of energy and ability who flocked to Washington in the heady atmosphere of March 1933. Born in Buffalo, Missouri, in 1879, Brownlow had been educated at home by his parents. At the age of twenty-one he took a job as a newspaper reporter in Nashville, Tennessee, and followed a journalistic career for fifteen years. In 1915 Woodrow Wilson appointed Brownlow a Commissioner of the District of Columbia. When World War I ended, he became city manager of Petersburg, Virginia; in 1924 he went to Knoxville, Tennessee, in the same capacity. During the late 1920's his interest came to center upon improving the techniques of governmental administration. Brownlow recalled that "a dream had captured my imagination, a dream that I, in my own way, might contribute . . . to the business of improving the administration of government. It was . . . an essentially humanitarian, egalitarian, and libertarian dream."[27]

In 1931 Brownlow helped found the Public Administration Clearing House (PACH) in Chicago and became its director. Supported by a grant from the Spelman Fund, PACH became a center for disseminating information about governmental administration. Two years later, in Washington, Brownlow was drawn into the early recovery efforts of the New Deal. Although he declined an offer of a position as Assistant Secretary of Commerce, Brownlow was recruited by Harold Ickes and Harry Hopkins as an unofficial adviser to aid in the development of various public works and relief projects. Meanwhile, on behalf of PACH, Brownlow offered to provide funds for any Cabinet member who wished to consult experts on problems of administration. PACH would proffer no advice on its own account, but would merely make available the results of private research. The President consented, and in the following years several Cabinet officers made use of the service.[28]

Brownlow's attempt to improve governmental administration received the eager support of his friend Charles E. Merriam. Raised in Hopkinton, Iowa, Merriam had studied political science at Columbia University and at Berlin; in 1900, at the age of twenty-six, he had moved to the University of Chicago. A student of political theory, Merriam did not neglect the practice of politics. In 1911 he ran as a Progressive candidate for Mayor of Chicago but was defeated. In 1924 he founded the Social Science Research Council, a federation of academic societies which included economists, political scientists, psychologists, sociologists, and historians. Merriam hoped to place academic research at the disposal of the government. To this end the Social Science Research Council helped persuade President Hoover to appoint a Research Committee on Social Trends in 1929. Hoover hoped that this committee would point out "where social stresses are occurring and where major efforts should be undertaken to deal with them constructively." The committee was financed, in part, by the Rockefeller Foundation. As a director of the Spelman Fund, founder of the Social Science Research Council, and Vice-Chairman of the Committee on Social Trends, Charles Merriam exemplified the academic specialist in the role of government consultant.[29]

This position was enhanced after Franklin Roosevelt took office. Appointed to the National Resources Committee by Harold Ickes, Merriam urged the adoption of a "plan for a plan" to coordinate all of the emergency activities. When, in the summer of 1935, Roosevelt expressed serious concern with the problem of integrating the emergency agencies into the regular departments, Merriam acted swiftly. He prepared a statement that stressed the need for development of the administrative role of the Executive Branch. A study promoting "more effective over-all management in the Federal Government, a better integration of the activities of the administrative departments and agencies, and a reduction of . . . jurisdictional conflicts" would be of great value. Suggesting that the Public Administration Committee of the Social Science Research Council undertake the project, Merriam stipulated that its report be withheld until after the 1936 election so that "it might have a non-political setting and effect."[30]

The Chairman of this Public Administration Committee, Merriam's collaborator Louis Brownlow, had taken care to obtain its approval for such a study, pending a presidential request. In the fall of 1935, when Merriam's suggestion received the blessing of the National Resources Committee, Roosevelt appeared to indicate definite interest.[31] Brownlow's group confidently awaited the summons from the White House. On December 16 Brownlow and several colleagues agreed upon the composition of an "ideal committee" and prepared an extensive outline of the proposed study to submit to the Public Administration Committee at its meeting in Atlanta.[32] There, during the last week in December, they anxiously awaited the presidential nod, but it never came. On December 28 Brownlow received word that the President still had not made up his mind; preparations would have to be canceled.[33]

Roosevelt's reservations were based upon considerations of political expediency. He wanted to be sure that the committee would not bring in a report which, if he could not endorse it, might prove politically damaging. The President explained his requirements to Merriam at a White House conference on February 20, 1936. It was only by accepting certain limitations that Merriam dispelled Roosevelt's doubts and gained his endorsement. "I had quite a discussion," Merriam informed his colleague, "but believe it will come out all right."[34]

From the start the President made clear his opposition to bringing in the Social Science Research Council, since it was partially supported by a Rockefeller Foundation grant. Roosevelt feared that "politically the name of Rockefeller in connection with such a study would have a bad effect upon the Hill." A special presidential committee would avoid this stigma. In addition, the President hesitated to sponsor a study without some assurance that its final recommendations would be to his liking. He conveyed this sentiment quite bluntly. Discussing one possible reform, "he remarked that he would not wish Mr. Brownlow's committee to recommend adoption of that procedure . . . because he [Roosevelt] might have another idea." Roosevelt wished to preclude the possibility of discord because "the public effect of a disagreement would make impossible any action . . . ."[35] Merriam described Roosevelt's outlook to Brownlow: "The President seemed apprehensive that recommendations might be brought in of a kind which might embarrass him in the development of some alternative plan of his own."[36]

Seeking to reassure the President, Merriam pointed out the numerous advantages of an outside report. It might take a more advanced position than the President could. "If the President himself discussed these matters, it would almost inevitably be interpreted as a reach for more power for himself."[37] Merriam suggested that Brownlow be permitted to indicate more exactly the scope and aim of the study. Brownlow hastened to comply, drafting a statement which largely prefigured the finished report of the Committee. His first sentence could not have failed to impress the President: "The primary object of the study should be to discover and invent ways and means to give the President effective managerial direction and control over all departments and agencies of the Executive Branch of the Federal Government commensurate with his responsibility."[38]

By March 4 Roosevelt had decided to name a committee. On that day, Brownlow discussed the details of the study with Roosevelt: "[We] found ourselves in quite close agreement as to the nature of the problem," he recalled.[39] In the following weeks they considered the membership of the Committee, and on March 20, 1936, the President sent letters of appointment to Brownlow, Merriam, and Luther Gulick. Gulick, the youngest of the three men, had been born in Japan in 1892 of missionary parents. Upon graduation from Oberlin College, Gulick did not enter the ministry but took up the study of political science at Columbia University. An outstanding expert on budgetary and fiscal management, Gulick had been director of the Institute of Public Administration in New York since 1921.[40]

Brownlow and his associates did not believe that acceptance of Roosevelt's terms marred their commitment to objectivity. Merriam claimed that the Committee "had an absolutely free hand, without any direction or pressure whatsoever, by President Roosevelt or anyone else." Brownlow emphasized that he and his colleagues fastidiously avoided communicating with the President before the election. Unavoidably, Merriam came in contact with him; but "care was exercised that . . . no word concerning the work of our committee was uttered."[41] Once Roosevelt won re-election, however, the Committee felt no reluctance to discuss its recommendations with him or to modify them slightly to conform with his views. It would have done the same for the Republican candidate, Alfred M. Landon.[42] Nevertheless, according to one student of the Committee, its members understood "that the President's wishes were the controlling factor in their assignment."[43]

The very choice of the Committee's personnel ensured that its report would receive Presidential approval. Brownlow, a life-long Democrat, shared with Roosevelt the common bond of association with Woodrow Wilson. Merriam, formerly a Progressive Republican, had come to support the New Deal not only because it offered a chance to fulfill the program of the New Nationalism, but because it gave power to old Bull Moosers like his good friend Harold Ickes. Merriam was always "Uncle Charley" to both Roosevelt and Ickes. Luther Gulick, too, had deserted the Republican party by 1933. All three men sympathized with the New Deal, ardently admired the President, and valued his friendship.

Their political views closely corresponded to those of the President. They were convinced that the American Presidency represented the most reliable bulwark against the tide of totalitarianism, that it was "the institution around and behind which democrats might rally to repel the enemy." They were dismayed by the expansion of European Fascism and the violence that accompanied it. To demonstrate that freedom and efficiency were linked, that democratic societies could act with promptness and vigor, the President must be given authority to match his responsibility. Congress should concentrate on setting down general principles; the President should be free to execute the laws and administer the government.[44]

To assist the President in achieving freedom and abundance, social planning by the government was necessary. "The indispensable condition of success of the New Deal . . . is effective and unified planning," which would encourage the use of "social intelligence in the determination of national policies."[45] Effective planning, asserted members of the Committee, hinged upon skillful administration. Proper management was "the great lubricator of human relations"; it was essential for the continued success of the New Deal.[46] To be truly effective, administration must be based on scientific principles. Although science provided no ultimate solutions to society's problems, it offered the most rewarding approach to them. To perfect "human engineering" and "adopt and apply a truly scientific spirit" would bring a better world that much closer.[47]

The Committee eventually took on a staff of twenty-six experts under the direction of Dr. Joseph P. Harris. More than half had doctoral degrees and more than two thirds held academic positions. Indeed, Harris feared that the disproportionate number of professors might have a damaging effect on public opinion.[48] The staff worked diligently through the summer of 1936, while Brownlow and Merriam traveled abroad. The members interviewed government officials, prepared papers on various aspects of administrative management, and submitted progress reports to Harris. During the fall Brownlow, Merriam, and Gulick met with each of the staff members to discuss their proposals. But the staff reports had, at best, only an indirect effect upon the Committee's final recommendations. "The real value of the research group was in their service as staff aides, advisers, and stimulators to Committee thinking," recalled one participant. The studies varied considerably in value; many were disregarded entirely. Although some were published with the Committee's report, Merriam always referred to them as "non-supporting documents."[49]

The Committee's approach to its task emerged clearly at a staff meeting held May 9–10 in New York City. Brownlow explained why the President had created the Committee and what he expected it to do. It was to study "top management" rather than the transfer of particular agencies or bureaus. Brownlow reported: "The President hoped that the Committee would not get lost in detail . . . [He] asked that principles be set up and not methodology worked out. It is not a question of whether the Forest Service should be transferred to the Department of the Interior." Brownlow suggested that the criterion be, "what gives the President more effective managerial control." Whatever did would fall within the purview of the Committee.[50]

Moreover, Brownlow cautioned, the President would in no way be bound by the Committee's report. He would be entirely free to accept it or reject it as he wished. The President might prefer to disregard its advice "because of political considerations." Brownlow continued: "He may wish to say that he has never seen the report and in that way not commit himself in regard to the suggested policy. . . Remember that if the President wants to turn down his experts' report because of short-term considerations, he cannot be put in the position of facing a public battle if this results, or else, in order to protect himself, he will never look at a planning report again." Staff members would therefore have to relinquish all proprietary rights to their reports. Nothing could be done that might compromise Roosevelt's political position.[51]

Because of this, strict secrecy had to be preserved. "Many people will be interested in learning of the work of the Committee," warned Brownlow, "we must guard ourselves." One influential aide feared that "if any word got out [about] the possible recommendations of the committee, the Administration would have to walk out"; therefore, any staff member who failed to observe certain precautions would be dismissed.[52] The stress upon secrecy was to have far-reaching implications, especially as it conditioned the relations between the President's Committee and Congress.[53] At the meeting on May 9, one staff member warned: "I can not see how you can make plans . . . unless you bring the leaders of Congress into it before you submit the final plan to Congress."[54] This advice was not heeded. Brownlow presumed that congressmen would cooperate with his Committee, and for a time this belief seemed well-founded. Unhappily the atmosphere of amiable agreement soon gave way to mutual mistrust.

The House of Representatives had appointed a Select Committee on Government Organization at the invitation of President Roosevelt, who believed that since the Senate had created its own committee it would be wise to include the House.[55] Brownlow disagreed, but failed to dissuade the President. Brownlow candidly disparaged Congressional participation. He admitted that Roosevelt's scheme would establish presidential initiative and "deprive the dictatorship school of critics of any opportunity to say that the President was undertaking the reorganization of the

Government without consulting Congress." But the plan, Brownlow argued, was full of danger. The House Committee, "unless very carefully selected and instructed by the Speaker, might decide to hold public hearings between now and the election"; and it might engage different advisers, thereby "breaking the chain of collaboration." Above all, the President "would be under considerable pressure from members of both Houses, either to disclose interim progress reports of the study or to compel members of the President's Committee and its staff to engage in conversations with members of the Congressional Committees, which could not result in anything but half-baked premature disclosures."[56] Brownlow warned that the Congressional groups might hamper his committee "which will more particularly reflect the point of view of the Executive."[57]

Brownlow's fears were quickly confirmed. The House Committee, under Representative James Buchanan of Texas, differed sharply with Roosevelt's advisers. Unlike Brownlow, Buchanan considered reorganization a Congressional function. He wanted to approach it gradually; he thought it ought to aim at saving money; and he resented the insistence of the President's Committee upon secrecy. Buchanan, a southern conservative who believed strongly in a balanced budget,[58] had a shrewd sense of political realities. He believed that "considerable economies may be accomplished,— preferably through the consolidation, rather than abolition, of Bureaus, because consolidations are easily put through Congress, where it is hell to abolish."[59]

As chief adviser, Buchanan imported a fellow-Texan, Colonel Clark C. Wren, who accurately reflected the Congressional point of view. Wren believed that past attempts at reorganization had failed because "too much was attempted at one time."[60] No comprehensive program could possibly succeed: "Any such general attempt tends to affright the heads of all departments, bureaus and agencies, so as to bring to them all the desire to 'gang up' in opposition to the general scheme." The best hope lay in small, painless doses. "Reorganization by piece meal . . . will cause no such general opposition and, although a much slower process, is less apt to result in injury."[61] Wren also warned that presidential representatives had tended to dominate Congressional committees concerned with reorganization, and hoped that Buchanan might be able to prevent this. Certainly Wren did not consider the approach of the President's Committee very promising.[62]

Brownlow and Buchanan disagreed about the nature and purpose of reorganization; Brownlow's emphasis upon secrecy reinforced the lack of agreement. Harris had taken every precaution to prevent premature leaks. He even asked the staff to submit confidential data orally to avoid the danger of Congressional inspection.[63] On November 14, the very day that the President's Committee discussed the outline of its report with Roosevelt, Wren admitted that he knew little about its intentions. By late December he had learned little more. He complained that "the President's Committee feels that it is not privileged to disclose anything as to what will be the scope of its report beyond saying . . . that it will deal with the principles to be observed to attain good administrative management, rather than with recommendations as to specific changes."[64] This concealment may have been unavoidable but it tended to alienate Congressional sentiment.

### 4

"One hundred per cent!" exclaimed the President, banging his fist on the desk, when Brownlow and Gulick presented their recommendations on November 14, 1936. He agreed fully with their underlying assumption that managerial direction and control of all executive agencies should be centered in the President. Roosevelt offered only two serious criticisms. His experts had tentatively suggested that a "White House Secretariat" under an Executive Secretary be created. Roosevelt balked at this. "You can't have just one Executive Secretary. The damn columnists would never let him alone. They are always looking for the 'white-haired boy.' "

The President also seemed rather disappointed that no concrete plan regarding the independent regulatory commissions had been offered. "Is that all you can say?" he asked sourly.[65] In both cases the Committee revised its proposals to suit the President. A month later, when Roosevelt read the final draft, he beamed: "I think that is grand."[66]

The report of the President's Committee spoke eloquently. "There is but one grand purpose," it declared, "namely to make democracy work today." The authors rejected the totalitarian claim that democracy inevitably dissipated its energies in futile debate. The key to making democracy effective was vigorous executive leadership. Far from breaking with tradition, such leadership would restore the concept of the Presidency found in the Constitution. "Those who waiver at the sight of needed power are false friends of modern democracy," wrote Gulick. "Strong executive leadership is essential to democratic government today."[67]

The Committee proposed to strengthen the President in five ways. First, furnish six executive assistants to lighten the intolerable personal burden upon him. Second, reinvigorate the civil service by expanding the merit system and raising government salaries, and by replacing the ineffectual Civil Service Commission with an energetic administrator. Third, improve fiscal management by encouraging budget-planning, by restoring control of accounts to the Executive, and by providing Congress with an independent audit of all transactions. Fourth, establish the National Resources Planning Board as a permanent central planning agency to coordinate government programs. Fifth, reorganize the government by creating two new cabinet posts and by bringing every executive agency, including the independent regulatory commissions, under one of the twelve major departments.[68]

This program accurately represented the administrative theories of the Committee members; students of government had urged similar reforms for many years. But the recommendations also reflected a concern with concrete issues that arose during the

1930's. The Committee's counsel neatly catalogued the major administrative problems which plagued President Roosevelt. The proposals offered were meant to ease his way and reflected the New Deal perspective of the authors. The report represented the happy circumstance of theoretical perceptions dovetailing with political preconceptions.

This can be clearly seen in the Committee's recommendations concerning the civil service. During Roosevelt's first term the merit system suffered a major setback. More than four fifths of the 250,000 government employees hired were exempted from civil service requirements. The Administration deliberately bypassed the civil service because New Deal emergency agencies needed to be organized swiftly and manned by sympathetic, specialized personnel. The Civil Service Commission, swamped with applicants, behind in its work, subject to veterans' preference, and mired in obsolete registers, too often failed to recruit men of marked ability.[69] New Dealers preferred not to burden their creations "with the kind of civil service system we now have."[70] Rexford Tugwell asserted that the system had become a way "of making certain that, barring revolution, war or economic disaster, the chosen dullards could have a long, uneventful, thoroughly secure working life." Members of the President's Committee admitted privately that their task was to raise civil service above the dead level of mediocrity.[71]

The Committee believed that the inadequacy of the civil service could, in large part, be traced to the inherent administrative incompetence of boards and commissions. The much-heralded bipartisanship of such bodies was grossly exaggerated; not only did members serve at the mercy of the president, but the minority representative failed to provide an effective safeguard against partisan control. Commissions spent too much time bickering over trivia; only a single administrator could bring unified, energetic, responsible leadership and make possible a creative civil service program.[72] Gulick believed that abandonment of the merit system had been less the fault of President Roosevelt than of the Civil Service Commission itself. He was not persuaded that it would be desirable to extend the civil service unless it could at the same time be imbued with new vigor and flexibility.[73] Replacing the antiquated system with a highly trained, competent personnel director would revitalize the civil service system and at the same time place it at the disposal of the New Deal.

Even more aggravating to the Administration was the stubborn obstruction by the Comptroller-General. Established in 1921 to serve as the fiscal agent of Congress, the Comptroller-General prescribed the rules and regulations governing expenditures by the Executive Branch. He also was expected to provide Congress with an audit of all government transactions. In practice, the real power of the Comptroller-General derived from his function of pre-audit. In order to avoid controversy and possible disallowance, cabinet officers sometimes requested a pre-audit to determine the legality of an expenditure. By deferring administrative action until the Comptroller reached a decision, they could substitute rejection before payment for possible disallowance afterward, with its attending embarrassment.[74]

John R. McCarl, a Republican, had been appointed to a fifteen-year term as Comptroller in 1921. McCarl, who had come to Washington as George Norris's personal secretary, soon came to embrace fiscal conservatism. In two articles published just before the election of 1936, he bitterly assailed the New Deal. Considering stern retrenchment the only solution to the depression, he had, for a brief period in 1933, looked upon Roosevelt hopefully. McCarl recalled: "With Douglas watching for waste in estimates and with my opportunities to help . . . accomplish economies . . . it seemed almost too good to be true." But this interlude soon passed. New Dealers, the "ultra-intellectuals," the "dreamers," seduced Roosevelt from his Jeffersonian moorings and convinced him to try to spend his way out of the depression. Unable to resist the lure of patronage, inspired by the "Santa Claus" motive, congressmen violated their pledges and joined the orgy of spending. "Public money was literally flowing in the Washington streets." McCarl protested, but his hands were tied. The "pathetic Congressmen" could not be stopped. Ever since, the country had been "traveling downhill" steadily, heading straight for a worse crash than that of 1929. Inevitably "a careless . . . and extravagant government induces a like effect upon our people." McCarl's point was plain: the people must repudiate at the polls those who had betrayed their trust.[75]

New Dealers fully reciprocated this hostility. They denounced McCarl as a petty tyrant who indulged in legal hair-splitting, arbitrarily held up needed funds, and snarled administration in reams of red tape. They complained that McCarl harassed the TVA and failed dismally to provide Congress with an intelligible account of government operations.[76] Administrators muttered that McCarl was "a reactionary Republican," surrounded by a "group of red-tape artists" whose "officious intermeddling" caused great damage.[77] In June 1936 Roosevelt told Henry Morgenthau that he was considering Harold Ickes as McCarl's successor, but added: "I would make him give me a letter in writing that on all legal questions he would ask for the opinion of the Attorney General." Tugwell has recalled that the "infinite delays and infinite personal prejudices of McCarl became a New Deal legend."[78]

Brownlow and Merriam shared the New Dealers' estimate of McCarl and made this plain to Roosevelt. In February 1936, when Merriam persuaded the President to appoint the Committee, he had argued that it could attack "the arrogation of policy powers by the Comptroller-General." Two years later Brownlow urged Roosevelt to appoint a "strong man" as Comptroller: "If immediate action is not taken here there is grave danger that any spending and recovery program that you may initiate may be quite effectively sabotaged by the present inimical regime in this office."[79] The Committee's proposals were designed to replace "administrative paralysis" with speed, vigor, and decision. By separating control and audit, giving control of expenditures to the Executive and providing Congress with an independent post-audit, government fiscal policy would be brought into line with modern accounting practice, and the New Deal would be preserved in the process.[80]

George Washington supervised nine executive agencies, Abraham Lincoln eleven, and Franklin D. Roosevelt sixty-three. Perhaps the administrative problem that most worried the President was how to control this sprawling structure. Roosevelt often voiced his concern. In 1933 he told Roper: "I'd like to see all the independent commissions brought under the general supervision of Cabinet officers." A year later, he wanted Bernard Baruch to head a special board to consider the conundrum.[81] By 1935 the President complained that it had become almost impossible for him to give adequate attention to every department and commission head.[82] The Brownlow Committee echoed his anxiety. Gulick believed that the multiplication of independent bodies threatened to cripple the power of the Executive. This, in turn, gravely imperiled the social objectives of the New Deal. The existence of a great many independent boards and commissions, Gulick concluded, tended to block the implementation of an effective social program.[83]

As a remedy the Committee suggested creating two new Cabinet positions—Public Works and Welfare—changing the name of the Department of the Interior to the Department of Conservation and giving the President full authority to transfer agencies.[84] The report went on to brand the independent commissions a "headless 'fourth branch' " of government which produced "confusion, conflict and incoherence." Exercising power without responsibility, they left the President responsibility without power. Even worse, they violated the clear constitutional mandate for a tripartite division of powers.[85] Recognizing that these commissions exercised judicial as well as administrative power, the Committee proposed to divide them into corresponding sections. The administrative section would be a regular departmental bureau; it would formulate rules, initiate action, investigate complaints, and prepare case records. The judicial section would be "in" the department merely for administrative housekeeping. It would be an independent body making impartial decisions on the basis of the evidence presented, or might serve in an appellate capacity. Such a scheme would at the same time guarantee administrative responsibility and preserve judicial independence.[86]

Just as the Committee's civil service, fiscal, and departmental proposals represented solutions to the administrative dilemmas facing the Roosevelt Administration, its social philosophy was in accord with the ideology of the New Deal. "The gains of civilization are essentially mass gains," the report declared. "They should be distributed as fairly as possible among those who created them." Reorganization would benefit all segments of society, but especially the underprivileged: "For they need the help of government in their struggle for justice, security, steadier employment, better living and working conditions, and a growing share of the gains of civilization."[87]

With respect to government planning, the Committee took a position beyond that of President Roosevelt, recommending creation of a National Resources Planning Board to collect data concerning both human and physical resources. Harris's directions to the staff indicated the Committee's outlook: "We may assume that the nature of the problems of American economic life are such as not to permit any political party for any length of time to abandon most of the collectivistic functions which are now being exercised. . . . We must roughly plot the areas of social control within our social system upon which the National planning structure may be predicated."[88] "We can not escape planning," Brownlow informed his colleagues.[89]

A powerful president equipped with the personnel, planning, and fiscal control necessary to implement his social program—this was the Committee's aim. But success ultimately hinged upon the caliber of administration. The Committee assumed that men of exceptional ability would be readily available for government service. It characterized the six presidential assistants as men of "high competence, great physical vigor and a passion for anonymity."[90] The same point recurred throughout the report. The Civil Service Administrator "should be highly competent, should possess a broad knowledge of personnel administration, and should be a qualified and experienced executive." In the Bureau of the Budget, "division chiefs of high competence should be appointed." The head of research activities should be a man "possessing in unusual degree imagination, vision, creativeness, and analytical insight. . . The research division must be staffed with persons of unusually high competence." The central planning agency would need "men of undoubted competence."[91] In part, the conviction that such personnel could be found grew out of the earlier success of the New Deal in attracting highly talented government servants.

The movement for executive reorganization during the New Deal was founded on an alliance between the President and a group of professional administrators. Their aim was to strengthen the Chief Executive and help him realize his objectives by overcoming the administrative obstacles which stood in his way.[92] Still, if "The Heavenly City of the 20th Century Public Administrators"[93] was to be brought into being, it would have to be through the political process. Prospects could not have been brighter than during the winter of 1936 when Roosevelt's career had reached its apogee, and a thoughtful appraisal of the Committee's report submitted by one New Deal official may not have attracted the attention it deserved. The report had many merits, the official agreed, but he noted: "It does not take adequate cognizance of the caprices of members of the House and Senate."[94]

# CHAPTER II

# The Progress of Reorganization during 1937

CONGRESS greeted the reorganization plan submitted by President Roosevelt in January 1937 with sullen silence. Reporters described congressmen as "shocked," "flabbergasted," and "knocked breathless" by the daring nature of the proposals. "Congress appears in a stupor," stated the *New York Times*.[1] But before any action could be taken, Roosevelt offered his ill-fated plan to enlarge the Supreme Court, and reorganization was largely forgotten. The Court controversy held center-stage until midsummer, stalling all other legislation. Nevertheless, events during 1937 powerfully influenced the direction and outcome of the reorganization controversy.

### 1

Never did President Roosevelt more convincingly demonstrate his political craft than in his presentation of the reorganization program. On Monday, January 11, the President explained the project at a press conference lasting several hours. Roosevelt, whose knowledge of the structure of the federal establishment was extraordinary, had thoroughly mastered his Committee's recommendations. In his most engaging manner he anticipated the objections he knew would be raised and tried to dispel them. He stressed the proposals he thought most popular and played down those which might prove dangerous. He presented the plan as one consistent with the best American traditions of efficiency and accomplishment. Some reporters remained unconvinced, or even cynical,[2] but the general clarity of their stories was, in part, a tribute to Roosevelt's presentation.

The President repeatedly stressed one major theme: reorganization was consonant with the American tradition of good management. He believed that his proposals resembled what "a farmer on an old farm would do." Faced with great expansion the hypothetical rustic would build an addition on the main barn, move in the scattered machinery, and "tear down the old shacks, tool-sheds, lean-to's. . ." The proposal to create two departments, move in various activities, and "wipe out all of the old machinery" amounted to much the same thing.[3] "I hope you will use the word management a great deal in any stories you may write," he suggested. "The word 'management' is a thoroughly clear American word. . . If we say our wives are good managers, everybody understands what we mean. If a small gasoline station is working out well and making money, what do we say about the owner? We say, 'He is a good manager.' . . What we are trying to do is to put a good management into the government in exactly the same sense of the term."[4]

Roosevelt also attempted to appease those officeholders who objected to any plan which threatened the status quo. "What we need is management rather than drastic change," he said soothingly. He firmly denied that any specific transfer had been contemplated. He advised reporters to discount rumors: "Keep away from saying that this is going to be transferred there and the other thing somewhere else, because, heavens, we haven't even approached that and haven't a thought on it."[5] Considerable study would be necessary before any final decisions could be made: "In other words, you ask me, 'Where is X Bureau going?' I say, 'The Lord only knows, I don't.' That is a thing I will not say anything about. I will keep a completely open or blank mind, if you choose, until after the bill is passed. And guesses will be, as usual, 90% wrong. [Laughter.]"[6] The President hoped, by disclaiming any immediate intention to shift bureaus, to allay bureaucratic suspicion.

Repeatedly, Roosevelt denied that the proposals increased his own power. The independent post-audit would, he insisted, provide Congress with an effective check upon the Executive.[7] The various independent regulatory commissions would "remain independent agencies so far as their judicial work is concerned"; only their administrative work would be affected.[8] The purity of the merit system would be preserved by a Civil Service Administrator chosen for proven ability.[9] The six assistants would provide "legs" for the President and allow him added time for contemplation. "How would you answer the charge that it gives you too much power?" asked a reporter. "It doesn't give me any more power than I have today," asserted Roosevelt staunchly.[10]

This strategy, at first, seemed highly successful. Public reaction to the proposals ranged from mildly sympathetic to highly enthusiastic. No one questioned the desirability of reorganization, and most applauded the Committee's plan. The League of Women Voters extended full support. Prominent Republicans such as Will Hays and Frank Lowden expressed hearty approval.[11] Nicholas Murray Butler solemnly termed the Report "the most important utterance on any question affecting the organization and efficiency of our government which has come from the White House in my memory."[12] Political scientists hailed the Committee's contribution to administrative theory.[13] Most newspapers, led by the *New York Times,* offered firm editorial support.[14] There were, of course, dissenters; but they were in a distinct minority. No one seemed more surprised by the widespread conservative acclaim than Roosevelt, who quipped: "I am reminded that a member of the family rushed in the other day and said, 'We are all wrong about the Child Labor Amendment; we shall have to reverse our position—former President Hoover has endorsed it.' "[15]

Observers unanimously predicted that reorganization would face rough sledding in Congress. Even those disposed to be sanguine knew that the President would have to press hard to achieve his objective, and some feared that the possible political damage might offset the anticipated advantages. "No one will ever be able to say that this Roosevelt is not himself an enthusiast for the strenuous life," commented Walter Lippmann: "There he is . . . the most successful chieftain of the most powerful political organization this country has ever seen, and the first program he offers to his devoted followers is one which strikes deeply at their dearest prerogatives, privileges and perquisites."[16]

## 2

Senator Harry Flood Byrd of Virginia loomed as one imposing obstacle to reorganization. Byrd acceded to Administration policy throughout 1936, and his continued support might have ensured the plan's success. But in January 1937 he broke with the President. From then on, in press releases, at Committee hearings, and on the floor of the Senate, Byrd sharply attacked reorganization. He played a decisive role in the eventual defeat of the bill. By the fall of 1937 the man who had helped deliver the Virginia delegation for Roosevelt at the 1932 Democratic convention was criticizing those who had "become obsessed with the mania for Roosevelt."[17]

Byrd's hostility to government reorganization caught New Dealers off guard. As Governor of Virginia he had driven through a brilliant plan of reorganization which rather closely resembled Roosevelt's program. Urging that the governor be made "the real executive head of the state," with all important agencies responsible to him, Byrd had boldly proclaimed: "There is little danger in this concentration of executive authority."[18] Virginia's reorganization plan had been drawn up by Luther Gulick, who became a close friend of the Governor. Moreover, Byrd served as a trustee of Gulick's Institute of Public Administration and Brownlow's Public Administration Clearing House. For many, Byrd had symbolized the kind of creative executive leadership that recognized the value of the public administration profession, sought its advice, and enlisted its aid.

Openly admiring their administrative talent and accomplishments, Byrd had cooperated freely with Brownlow and Gulick during 1936. He had asked Brownlow to advise his Senate Committee, and assured him that he favored "a serious scientific study."[19] He wanted Gulick's Institute for Public Administration to take on the research for his Committee, and looked elsewhere only because Gulick's organization had committed itself to another project.[20] Roosevelt solicited Byrd's suggestions in drafting his letters to Congress announcing the appointment of the President's Committee. Byrd even seemed to be a valuable Congressional ally; when Buchanan's House Committee proved uncooperative, Harris asked Gulick if he might not telephone or write the senator to solicit his support.[21] Although Brownlow and his colleagues regarded the Senator's study of reorganization with genuine misgivings, they hoped to "bring Byrd's latent executive attitude to the forefront" and hold his support.[22]

Writing to Roosevelt late in November 1936, Gulick described his efforts to "bring the Senator into line with your plan of action." With some satisfaction, Gulick recounted the concessions he had obtained. Byrd recognized that Roosevelt alone would "draw up the program and . . . lead off in its public presentation." Specifically, Byrd promised to "lie low," and "do nothing . . . to step out in front or make trouble." He agreed not to give any interviews to the press, not to release the findings of the Senate research group until after the President's message, and to withhold an article for the *Saturday Evening Post* which stressed his own role in the reorganization movement, "because he wants you to understand that he is in line and will follow your lead." In return, Gulick made only one promise, "namely, that you would see him . . . and discuss next steps and legislative plans." Gulick also hinted that Byrd might be allowed to sponsor the bill if the President was "satisfied with his position in the whole affair." "In coming along," Gulick reported, "he wants to be assured that a real reorganization is contemplated and not merely a piece of 'window dressing.' "[23]

Byrd had evidently accepted these limitations with the understanding that he would have an opportunity to examine the proposals and offer his own suggestions. But the President's Committee intended to play its cards close to the chest. Gulick told the President that he gave Byrd "no specific information whatsoever regarding the program we presented to you," and concluded: "I feel sure that the Committee should not give him any specific material until after you have seen him in December. We shall, however, have to discuss some things with him in the meantime to keep the pot aboiling."[24] Brownlow concurred; secrecy was essential to maintain the integrity of the recommendations. The Committee confidently expected that "Byrd can be brought along all the way."[25]

Byrd's attitude toward reorganization early in January 1937 was still conciliatory. The *Saturday Evening Post* of January 2 carried an interview with him in which he implied that "pruning" government agencies would promote savings and demanded that reorganization offer "substantial economies and a definite contribution to budget balancing possibilities."[26] The Senator, however, did not attempt to pre-empt the President's role, and declared presidential direction essential to effective reorganization. In a radio address on January 11 Byrd again welcomed Roosevelt's leadership: "No top-to-bottom reorganization of any State has ever been accomplished without executive leadership of a governor."[27] The points dividing Byrd and Roosevelt still seemed less important than the wide area of agreement between them. But on January 13 Byrd informed the President that he could not support the plan.[28]

Differences over government spending appear to have caused Byrd to desert the President. To Byrd a balanced budget was an article of faith, and reorganization should be geared to achieving it. To Roosevelt a balanced budget was a much-desired economic expedient, but reorganization was a wholly different matter. As early as March 1936 Byrd informed Brownlow that he disagreed with Roosevelt's spending policy.[29] Most, though not all, of Byrd's objections to the reorganization plan reflected his suspicion of Roosevelt's loose fiscal policy. He complained that the President had not only failed to abolish bureaus when he had the power but

had created many new ones. The proposed Department of Public
Welfare might prove to be a back door to perpetual federal relief.
He distrusted the plan to abolish the office of Comptroller-General,
which had been "virtually the only restraining influence on reckless
public spending for the last few years."[30] Not only did the President's reorganization program fail to promise savings; it actually
paved the way to increased spending.

Ironically, Roosevelt also wanted to reduce government expenditures and came close to balancing the budget in 1937. He refused,
however, to promise savings through reorganization. As in 1933,
he maintained that bureau shuffling had only a marginal effect upon
expenditures. Only "careless people," he said, failed to realize that
a balanced budget could be achieved by curtailing functions, and
that the true purpose of reorganization was to make government
function smoothly. The President resented news stories which
insinuated that he had sacrificed economy: "Of course that is rot,
just plain tommyrot," he snapped.[31] Roosevelt, indeed, hoped that
reorganization would produce minor savings. Central planning
would save money by establishing a priority of projects and eliminating reservoirs of unauthorized projects. Also, he would have
liked to include in the bill a provision to put government services
on a self-supporting basis.[32] But economy was not the chief end of
reorganization, nor the justification for it.

If Byrd's opposition was sparked by the economy issue, it was
confirmed by the Committee's failure to consult him before announcing the plan, as he had expected. The President presented the
report to the Democratic Congressional leaders on Sunday,
January 10; it was released to the press Monday afternoon. Byrd
had telephoned Brownlow in Chicago on Saturday, but was not
shown the proposals until Monday morning, a few hours before it
was made public. Brownlow wished to "show it to Byrd *before* the
President talks to the newspaper men and *after* the talk with the
Congressional leaders Sunday afternoon."[33] Byrd explained his
reaction in a letter to Roosevelt on January 13, announcing his

opposition: "It was my understanding . . . that either Mr. Brownlow or Mr. Gulick would call to see me . . . so that I could understand more in detail the proposals recommended by them. Due, I have no doubt, to the pressure of their work I did not see them until Monday of this week, and this was too late to see you before the recommendations were made. I regret this as I would like the opportunity to discuss certain details of the report."[34] Roosevelt evidently did not see the Senator until January 22; a few hours later he told the Cabinet that he did not want Harry Byrd to be a member of the Joint Committee on Reorganization.[35]

Luther Gulick had written Byrd a personal letter in a last-minute effort to prevent his defection. In it, he asserted that the proposals of the President's Committee were essentially the same as those Byrd had supported in Virginia.[36] Byrd would not be moved. Not until after Roosevelt's death in 1945 did the Senator revert to the stand he had taken as governor and come out for broad executive authority to reorganize the government.[37] But Byrd never deviated from the view that savings should be the foremost aim of reorganization. He had supported Roosevelt in 1932 on a program of retrenchment and remained true to it. "I can still say I am the last of the old New Dealers," Byrd told his constituents thirty years later, "Roosevelt changed, but I did not."[38]

### 3

Opposition to the reorganization plan was quickened by the recommendations of the Brookings Institution. As an organization specializing in the appraisal of governmental administration, Brookings had been employed by both the Senate and House Committees in the spring of 1936. Despite good intentions and certain precautions, its study overlapped that of the President's Committee in crucial areas. As the realization grew that conflicting findings might result, sporadic efforts were made to avert an open break. Finally, frustrated by the fruitless negotiations and prodded by its Congressional sponsors, Brookings released a report that sharply challenged Brownlow's recommendations and provided a store of ammunition for Senator Byrd and other critics. Roosevelt's position—that of merely endorsing what "experts" had proposed—was badly undermined by his opponents' ability to summon their own, contradictory, "expert" opinion.

No one expected that this rupture would occur. Brownlow has recalled that in the beginning extremely cordial relations existed between his group and Brookings. Lewis Meriam of Brookings had played an active role in the creation of the President's Committee and seemed wholly sympathetic with its purposes.[39] Designated as "contact man" between Brookings and the Committee, Meriam maintained communications between the two groups during 1936. He offered friendly critiques of some of the drafts of staff reports, and the Committee's director even rebuked one staff member for failing to obtain Meriam's counsel.[40] Indeed, the President's Committee hoped to use Brookings' reports as a foundation for its own appraisal.[41] Joseph Harris, as well as Fred Powell, acting director of Brookings, fully expected that their studies would be complementary.[42]

Collaboration between the two groups hinged upon a division of labor agreed upon at the outset. The President's Committee would study executive management. Viewing administration from the perspective of the President, it would seek ways to improve his control of government operations. The Brookings Institution would study overlapping and duplication. Concentrating upon particular agencies, it would seek ways to simplify government operations and render them more efficient and economical. Both sides believed this demarcation would satisfactorily preclude rivalry; Luther Gulick considered it "practical and realistic."[43] Given the friendly relationship, the provisions for liaison, and the strong sense of professional solidarity, there seemed little reason to think otherwise.

For the most part this agreement effectively barred duplication of effort. But it collapsed at the very point in which Senator Byrd was most interested—fiscal management. Both groups insisted that government accounting practice properly fell within its orbit, and brought in experts to study the subject. When, in April 1936, Brookings employed a specialist in financial administration, Harris spoke to Powell to ward off any possible transgression. Powell firmly rejected the suggestion that Brookings omit a consideration of accounting and civil service from its report.[44] When Harris discussed this with Brownlow, "it was decided to do nothing further in the matter."[45] The conflict simmered during the summer of 1936, when Brownlow and Merriam were in Europe, and both staffs continued their inquiries. One or two conferences were held, but no agreement could be reached until each side prepared its final recommendations.[46]

The first full-scale attempt to avert a conflict occurred on September 23, 1936, when Byrd met with the President's Committee and the Brookings staff. Fred Powell understood that the meeting had been arranged "to consider the extent to which the President's Committee was overlapping work which belongs within our field."[47] Apparently Byrd pointed out that conflicting recommendations could seriously damage the prospects for reorganization and suggested that the President's Committee restrict the scope of its inquiry.[48] The meeting produced no formula of agreement. As Harold G. Moulton of Brookings admitted: "Much of the discussion was of an irrelevant character." Oddly, the issue of financial administration did not even arise during the conference, although Powell mentioned it to Brownlow afterward. The two groups of experts then lunched together and "had a very amicable discussion." Powell told Representative Buchanan that he "did not see much, if any, evidence of conflict and the only cases of overlapping—financial administration and possibly planning—seem to be consistent with the Resolutions and the instructions of the President."[49] During October Harris made several putative efforts to induce Brookings to abandon its study of fiscal management. Unfortunately, the rapid pace at which the Committee worked during November and December prevented another meeting to resolve differences.[50]

On the same day that the President's Committee released its report to the public Gulick took steps to forestall Brookings' opposition. He informed Moulton that the problem of financial management had been "squarely at the center" of the Committee's assignment, and pressed for an early conference.[51] Moulton agreed to talk over differences and assured Brownlow a few days later that Brookings had no immediate plans to release its study of accounting.[52] When Brownlow and Moulton became ill, the conference had to be postponed. Finally, on February 17, 1937, Moulton met with Brownlow, Merriam, and Gulick. Although he did not consent to withdraw from the field of financial management, Moulton promised to send all Brookings reports to the Committee at the same time that they went to Byrd, to furnish the Committee immediately with a tentative draft of the report on finances, and to withhold the final report to Congress "until it was specifically called for." On Friday, February 19, a preliminary draft of the Brookings report was delivered to Brownlow.[53]

From then on, Congressional pressure increasingly directed events. On February 26 Moulton informed Brownlow that both Byrd and Colonel Wren had urged Brookings to submit its report. Although Moulton had parried, "Our final conclusions have not yet been matured," Byrd would not accept refusal.[54] Since Brookings had provided Brownlow with a tentative draft, the Senator insisted upon equal courtesy. Moulton obliged, but pointed out that since the conclusions were still subject to modification they must not yet be made public.[55] Finally, confronted with real danger of a leak, the experts conferred on March 8. The President's Committee failed to convert Brookings to its position. Brownlow's urgent plea for unity went unheeded; the meeting only reinforced Moulton's conviction that their differences were of an "irreconcilable character."[56] Brookings would stand by its recommendations, though Moulton promised to refrain from any direct attack upon the Brownlow Committee.[57] Brookings presented its report to Congress on March 23; within a week it had been made public and representatives of Brookings were clashing with Brownlow and Gulick before the Joint Congressional Committee.

Fiscal management was the issue which had caused the rupture. The President's Committee held that the Comptroller-General had proved a sorry failure, that the purely executive function of financial control must be separated from audit, that by obscuring this distinction the pre-audit destroyed administrative responsibility and prevented a true reckoning of accounts. Brookings, on the other hand, argued that the defects of the Comptroller-General were remediable, and that a distinction could be made between executive control to promote efficient management and legislative control to prevent illegal transactions.[58] Gulick wished to create an independent auditor who would simply report malfeasance to Congress; Meriam wanted the auditor to have the power to approve contracts and disallow payments. The key difference concerned where the control should be located to prevent an illegal expenditure. Meriam believed that this control should be exercised by an independent agency responsible to Congress rather than by an executive department.[59]

Unfortunately, personal animosity soon displaced dispassionate analysis. Accusations of ineptitude, duplicity, and political prejudice were made which tended to obscure the large area of agreement between the two groups on other questions.[60] The outlook of the Brookings' experts was not that of Senator Byrd. Lewis Meriam sharply criticized the idea that reorganization would bring substantial savings.[61] Meriam still believed that "the major defect in the executive branch is the absence of a fully developed, effective, permanent, coordinating agency under the President, acting as his staff to aid him in . . . the management of the executive agencies."[62] Brookings accepted the concept of the President as a "general manager" and admitted that the existing system failed to provide him with adequate fiscal control. To a considerable extent, Brookings and the President's Committee spoke the same language.[63]

Nevertheless, the much-publicized conflict arose out of clearly disparate assumptions. Brookings questioned the validity of any single theory of reorganization. It denied that a "single controlling principle" existed; reorganization must be pragmatic.[64] "I must say that I am not one who believes a great deal in principles of public administration just as flat principles," admitted one spokesman.[65] Different situations demanded different solutions: "How can you work it out?" was the important question. Logically, therefore, the soundest approach to reorganization lay in a detailed study of particular agencies. "A satisfactory plan of organization can be arrived at only by proceeding from the particular to the general, from the parts to the whole." Brookings announced that its study would deal "with facts rather than theories."[66]

The major source of dissension, however, was a conflict in attitudes over the proper balance between the executive and legislative branches of government. Whereas Brownlow exalted the Presidency, Brookings feared that political requirements might vitiate the Executive's administrative reliability. Whereas Brownlow diluted the Congressional role in administration, Brookings enhanced, or at least preserved, that role. In part this may have resulted from the divergent political sympathies of the two groups.[67] In part it indicated Brookings' realization that reorganization would have to obtain Congressional approval. Meriam warned that the President's Committee should "give careful consideration to any recommendations that look toward diminishing the control of Congress, because I think such recommendations . . . will jeopardize the chances of any other recommendations that require legislation."[68] Certainly the Brookings staff was inclined to cater to Congressional sensibilities. Nothing illustrated this better than Brookings' relationship with the adviser to the House Committee, Colonel Wren. Brookings provided a private office for him, arranged for his use of its library, dining room, and social facilities, and regularly turned over drafts of its report for his perusal. A director asked if anything could be done to make him more comfortable. "Perfection cannot be improved upon," replied Wren.[69]

When the break between the President's Committee and Brookings had appeared imminent, Brownlow had hastily written a note to Moulton which revealed obvious agitation: "In this situation it seems to us of the utmost importance that the 'doctors' do not disagree on technical matters, as this disagreement will be used by oponents [sic] of any reform to confuse the issue. This is not a responsibility which can be passed off lightly. It may be that the reputation of government research . . . for scientific impartiality is at stake."[70] Although this statement was later omitted, it indicated Brownlow's understanding of the larger implications of the split. Submitting opposite findings might lead to a loss of confidence in the use of experts, or even to public ridicule. Happily, this prediction did not come true, in part because of the esoteric nature of the issue. Moreover, the increasing complexity of life had accustomed the public to such disputes, and no acceptable alternative to the use of experts existed. The disagreement in 1937 did, however, bring into focus fundamental conflicts among students of public administration, and, as Brownlow had foreseen, fortified the opposition to reorganization.

### 4

The Democratic party dominated the Seventy-fifth Congress. In January 1937, for the first time in more than a century, one party controlled three fourths of the votes in House and Senate.[71] And yet this Congress killed or brutally emasculated almost every Administration effort to expand the New Deal. Many explanations have been offered for this phenomenon. As one of Roosevelt's major objectives during 1937, the Reorganization bill offers a case study in presidential impotence despite overwhelming legislative majorities.

On Sunday, January 10, 1937, the President, flanked by the Brownlow Committee, handed his reorganization program to the Congressional leaders. All who gathered in the White House study were southerners: Vice-President John Garner of Texas, Senator

Joseph Robinson of Arkansas, Senator Pat Harrison of Mississippi, Speaker William Bankhead of Alabama, Congressmen Robert L. Doughton of North Carolina, Sam Rayburn and James Buchanan of Texas. The President distributed the draft of a bill prepared at his suggestion by Brownlow. He tried hard to drum up support by appealing to personal interests and Congressional pride, but he had little luck; his legislative lieutenants remained skeptical. They objected to raising the salaries of Cabinet members to $20,000, and to placing the independent regulatory commissions within an executive department. Roosevelt patiently explained his goals, but he harbored no illusions about his success. Drawing Brownlow aside after the Congressmen had left, he remarked: "You see, Louis, what I am up against. This was quite a little package to give them this afternoon. Every time they recovered from a blow I socked them under the jaw with another."[72]

The leaders had been shocked not only by the substance of the proposals but by the manner of presentation. Roosevelt had not consulted any congressmen in advance; instead, he had submitted a finished product that he did not want modified. As with the Supreme Court proposal four weeks later, the President insisted on secrecy and made no effort to elicit meaningful suggestions from Congress. That this procedure aroused antagonism seems certain. Discussing reorganization some months earlier, Middleton Beaman, a legislative adviser to the House of Representatives, had outlined Congressional expectations: "Congressional leaders want to feel that they have influence in the development of Administration policies. They accordingly should be consulted before Administration measures are sent to Congress, although most of them do not insist on being apprised of all the details. Administration proposals should seldom if ever be presented to Congress with the idea that they are not to be changed." And he added: "In unusual cases measures can be bludgeoned through Congress, but there is always much resentment."[73]

The special message which Roosevelt sent to Congress on

January 12 was written by Luther Gulick. After vividly describing the need for reorganization, it promised that adoption of the proposals would "prove to the world that American Government is both democratic and effective." "The great stake in efficient democracy is the stake of the common man," claimed Gulick. "This program rests solidly upon the Constitution and upon the American way of doing things." The plan was not a presidential grab for power, but an attempt to provide the "tools of management" he so desperately needed.[74] Congressional response was guarded, however. Some Administration leaders had lukewarm praise for the plan, but Democrats on the whole seemed reluctant to comment for publication. Privately, party leaders admitted that reorganization would meet with a great deal of opposition.[75]

As the immediate reaction subsided, the wheels of the legislative mechanism began slowly to turn. During February, March, and April the Joint Committee created by Congress scheduled sporadic hearings with the President's Committee. In the meantime, having foisted legislative responsibility for reorganization upon his son James, the President devoted his efforts to the Supreme Court struggle.[76] On February 26 he admitted: "I haven't discussed reorganization with anybody for three weeks, I think."[77] By March public attention was so firmly fixed upon Court-packing that one columnist complained, "It seems as futile as hollering down a rain barrel to call just now for public examination of the reorganization plan."[78] Roosevelt still assumed that reorganization would go through, but while hearings continued he had to mark time.[79] The hearings of the Joint Committee afforded excellent insights into Congressional attitudes.

The President's Committee had called for a sharp increase in governmental salaries. Recruitment of the skilled personnel demanded by the revamped administrative structure hinged upon this reform. Yet it was the first to be yielded. At the Committee hearings Senator Robinson reminded Brownlow that he himself had expressed strong reservations at the White House conference, adding·

"It is a great mistake to confuse the question of increases in salaries with the question of reorganization." A leading Democratic member of the House chimed in: "Before you got through you would have a bill raising the salaries of all Government employees rather than a reorganization bill, you had better remember that." The Congressmen promptly pared the proposed salary increase from the bill.[80]

The proposals concerning the independent regulatory commissions aroused even more antagonism. At the White House meeting Rayburn had inquired if the Interstate Commerce Commission might not be permitted to remain outside an executive department. Roosevelt replied firmly: "There will be no exceptions, not one."[81] Brownlow, at the hearings, attempted to explain the dangers of an irresponsible fourth branch of government, but promised that the ICC would retain a semi-autonomous status. He converted few congressmen to his point of view. Representative John Cochran of Missouri forced Brownlow to concede that the bill, as drafted, would permit the President to abolish the regulatory commissions, or to place them in a department under an assistant secretary. Even an Administration stalwart like Representative Pat Boland of Pennsylvania predicated his support on the belief that the independence of these commissions would be preserved.[82]

Luther Gulick was quick to recognize the prevailing sentiment. On January 20 he informed Brownlow that "substantial and intelligent opinion" would demand a modification of the proposals concerning the independent agencies. He suggested that "in order to strengthen our position," the bill should prescribe the President's power to turn over such quasi-judicial activities to an executive officer. Specifically, Gulick proposed that the independent status of the ICC be guaranteed and that the Federal Reserve Board be exempted from transfer, even though this might establish a poor precedent.[83] In Washington, Joseph Harris relayed this message to James Roosevelt: the draft of the bill gave the President such extensive power over the regulatory commissions that Gulick feared it would meet with a storm of criticism.[84] Although the Committee's efforts to clarify its proposals received little encouragement from the White House,[85] Congressional pressure proved effective. Each of the reorganization bills drafted in 1937 to some degree spared the independent regulatory commissions.

Senator Byrd's concern and the Brookings report combined to make the issue of financial control a center of controversy. Gulick insisted that spending money was an executive function, that to blur the distinction between audit and control inevitably destroyed audit, "because the man who is participating in the making of decisions cannot, for psychological reasons, be impartial." Byrd, from a different constitutional stance, argued that the pre-audit must be retained as a check upon spending; he held that "money should not be spent unless the restrictions and regulations placed upon it by Congress are obeyed."[86] The contrast between executive interest in administrative efficiency and legislative concern with administrative accountability emerged clearly in one exchange:

*Sen. O'Mahoney:* . . . Are you not suggesting a plan which amounts to reporting stolen horses, whereas we now have a plan which amounts to at least an attempt to close the door before the horses are stolen?

*Mr. Gulick:* And to keep the horses locked in the barn all the time so you cannot get any plowing done.

*Sen. O'Mahoney:* Of course the analogy does not go quite that far. We will have some plowing done.

*Mr. Gulick:* Not if you want to keep the horses locked in the barn all the time.[87]

From the start, Byrd and Gulick could not agree on the program which together they had put through in Virginia a decade before. After four hundred pages of expert testimony they had come no closer to understanding each other's position. When Byrd asked: "You mean you do not provide any preaudit or precontrol?" Gulick replied wearily: "No, no, no; we provide that under the Executive acting through the fiscal control agencies."[88]

Many congressmen considered control over bureau transfers an

important legislative prerogative. Brownlow's insistence that reorganization was a presidential function, a "continuous process"
that should not be subject to a time-limit, antagonized those who
believed that Congress knew best and that limitations upon executive power were indispensable.[89] Senator Charles McNary of
Oregon, refusing to belittle "the brains that are found somewhere
in the Halls of Congress," stated bluntly: "Well, I think my knowledge is superior to that of the President, or any member of the
commission. I have been a student of that all my life. Is it up to
me to pass my rights to you folks?"[90] A strong undercurrent of
Congressional hostility toward outside meddling could be detected.
Brownlow and Merriam told Charles West, an Administration
trouble-shooter, that "some of the members of this Joint Committee
take the attitude toward [us] of being 'outsiders' trying to promote
something instead of friends trying to explain the measure to
them."[91]

The reluctance of the President's Committee to discuss specific
agency transfers also aroused suspicion. Gulick explained: "We are
not going into those details . . . we are engaged as efficiency
engineers."[92] But congressmen were skeptical. They complained
that the witnesses were "dodging the issue," that their ideas seemed
"very indefinite, very illusory."[93] Congressional devotion to pet
bureaus was apparent. Senator McNary admitted: "Here is the
thing that bothers me: I am tremendously interested in certain
agencies remaining where they are. I want them static." When
Representative Cochran of Missouri put in a word for his favorite
bureau, Gulick replied doggedly: "I think we will have no occasion
to make any suggestion that it should be moved or it should not be
moved."[94]

By June the Joint Committee was ready to draft its version of
a reorganization bill. But a procedural rift between leaders of the
House and Senate arose. Senator Robinson, Chairman of the Joint
Committee, yielded to Byrd's desire to hold public hearings during
the summer; the House members, led by John Cochran, wanted no

part of them. In addition, Senator Robinson resolved upon a single bill, whereas Cochran favored splitting the proposals into four separate measures.[95] Roosevelt seems to have kept hands off the dispute: "That is a matter entirely for them to decide—it is procedural," he told reporters. The two groups went their separate ways, more or less at odds with each other.[96] Senator Robinson proceeded to draft his bill, introducing it as S. 2700 on June 23, 1937.

The Robinson bill indicated the nature of the pressures to which congressmen responded.[97] In certain respects S. 2700 carried out Roosevelt's recommendations: it granted broad reorganizing power, provided six assistants, set up a civil service administrator, created a Department of Public Welfare, and provided for a genuine audit. The variations from the Brownlow report were more striking. The bill omitted salary increases. It said nothing about a Department of Public Works. It exempted nine independent commissions, the Corps of Engineers, and the Mississippi River Commission.[98] It demanded that executive orders lie before Congress sixty days before taking effect.

The most flagrant deviation, however, concerned the civil service. The bill, which exempted policy-determining posts and brought other employees under civil service without regard to existing regulations, represented a genuine retreat from the merit system. Gulick admitted publicly that the civil service provisions were "ambiguous and . . . contradictory."[99] Budget Director Daniel Bell warned the President that the bill would weaken rather than strengthen the civil service. Worse, it "would place the Civil Service System far more definitely in politics than has been the case for years. It would destroy incentive and ambition among employees." Bell concluded that "the extent of the career to which a person might aspire in the Civil Service would . . . be a career as a high class clerk."[100]

The sudden death of Senator Robinson on July 14 altered the prospects for government reorganization. James F. Byrnes of

South Carolina, who took over as chairman of the Senate Committee, informed Roosevelt that he thought it would be best to postpone the measure. On July 26 the President urged Byrnes to go ahead with the bill. He explained that when he first proposed reorganization "it was well understood . . . by Senator Robinson and all of our friends that it would be better to do this at this session of the Congress rather than to have it drag along in the 1938 session."[101] Byrnes therefore dropped S. 2700, called public hearings, and set about drafting a new reorganization bill, which was introduced in mid-August. By then, however, the Senate could not take up the measure before adjournment.

Reorganization made a better showing in the House. On April 26 a Democratic caucus had turned down an omnibus bill; it decided to introduce four separate measures and dispose of them seriatim.[102] Negotiations with Senator Robinson, who rejected this strategy, seem to have cost some time. On May 20 the House leaders assured the President that reorganization was still "very much alive." Roosevelt reported: "They are getting on very well . . . . Probably the legislation will come out fairly soon."[103] But the House Committee frittered away most of June debating the accounting and auditing problem. It had expected to take this up first, but a meeting on June 15 revealed so many conflicting opinions that the bill was pushed back.[104]

The work of the House Committee was given new impetus on June 21 when Clinton M. Hester of the Treasury Department, acting as Administration spokesman, submitted several drafts of bills to "serve as a working basis."[105] For weeks Hester coaxed and cajoled recalcitrant congressmen. When Representative J. W. Robinson of Utah offered several different bills to provide six assistants for the President, Hester chose one "saying he was sure the President would want it and not the others."[106] The effect was apparent. On July 24, 1937, Chairman Cochran assured the President that "we really have been making progress." He expected that Representative Robinson's bill would pass easily:

"Among the Democratic Members there is absolutely no dissension and it appears to me they are in full agreement on this bill."[107]

On July 27 the House began debate on H.R. 7730, to provide six presidential assistants. Congressman John Taber of New York, ranking Republican on the Reorganization Committee, had no serious objection to the bill, but Minority Leader Bert Snell thought his party stood to gain some political mileage in House debate. The debate confirmed Cochran's judgment that "their opposition is purely political."[108] The Republicans attacked Roosevelt's past reliance upon intellectuals. Six new assistants would inevitably be "nonpublicized brain children lacking any practical experience in public affairs." Representative Dewey Short of Missouri predicted that they would be "theoretical, intellectual, professorial nincompoops who could not be elected dog-catcher." Opponents of the measure tried to ruffle legislative pride by pointing out that these "satellites and sycophants" would receive the same salary as congressmen.[109] "Can the gentleman tell me why the President wants six?" inquired Dudley White of Ohio innocently. "He has not that many sons."[110] The Democrats listened impassively. They pointed out the urgent need for presidential assistants and ascribed Republican opposition to "pure, plain cussedness." "Upon my word, it is peanut politics," commented Fred Vinson.[111] The House passed the bill by a vote of 260–88.

Debate on the Warren bill, giving the President power to regroup agencies and creating a Department of Welfare, was conducted on a somewhat higher plane. John Taber's support for the reorganization provisions of the bill blunted the Republican attack and shifted most of the criticism to the proposed Department of Welfare.[112] Republicans, led by Taber, contended that it would burden the taxpayers with an enormous expense and fasten a "permanent relief set-up" on the nation. In addition, it would give free rein to more New Deal innovation carried on by the "experimentalists from Columbia and dear old Harvard."[113] Democrats countered that the bill was bound to bring economy. They asserted that the measure, which exempted many independent regulatory commissions and was limited to two years, fell short of what Congress had given President Hoover.[114] The leadership easily beat down efforts to exempt various agencies, and secured victory by a vote of 283–76.

The House debate saw a putative attempt by certain Republicans to raise the issue of dictatorship. Representative Short linked reorganization with the Supreme Court proposal as part of an insidious scheme to bring "one-man rule—government by executive decree."[115] Representative Hamilton Fish asserted: "This is just a step to concentrate power in the hands of the President and set up a species of fascism or nazi-ism or an American form of dictatorship." Several Republicans attributed dictatorial ambitions to Roosevelt. "No demagogue with personal-power madness must be allowed to assassinate the American Republic," cried one.[116] Democrats scoffed at these charges. Only thirty-seven Democrats voted against either of the bills; only nine voted against both.[117] The support of other groups more than compensated for the few defectors. Eighteen Republicans voted for the Warren bill, seven of the eight Progressives supported it, and not one of the five Farmer-Labor delegates voted against it. Republican efforts to whip up hysteria had failed dismally in the summer of 1937.

Reorganization made no further legislative gains during the year.[118] Although Roosevelt marked reorganization as one goal for the special session of Congress in November and his legislative leaders appeared hopeful, the session proved a failure.[119] Reorganization was one of a string of casualties, as Administration bills were snarled in confusion. In the Senate a filibuster against the antilynching bill thwarted Byrnes's attempt to bring up reorganization.[120] Republican Representative Clifford Hope of Kansas sensed a great deal of "undercover resentment and bad feeling . . . toward the President and his administration among the Democratic members of Congress." "It is a bad situation in a way," he declared, "because it means that we are going to have a session of Congress with very little leadership of any kind. The President has apparently very largely lost his influence and yet the Democrats who oppose him are not agreed upon any program of their own."[121]

While reorganization was stalled in Congress, public opinion appeared gradually to turn against the plan. "Though the plans were greeted with great enthusiasm here in New York in January, I now encounter everywhere an undercurrent of opposition . . . ." wrote Luther Gulick late in September.[122] The disaffection of several discerning journalists was also significant. In a speech at Johns Hopkins, Walter Lippmann declared that the plan would help precipitate a "rapid descent into personal government." In August Arthur Krock lampooned the proposal for six assistants. These "six eremites" were "remindful of a sub-debutante's dream . . . they must labor as does the mole—underground."[123] Bernard DeVoto, in the October *Harpers,* presented a disenchanted New Dealer who viewed with scorn "those glittering bits of happy-dust improvisation, the government reorganization bills." Roosevelt, he complained, seemed "cockily indifferent" to the fact that the program "would destroy all the effective barriers to totalitarianism that exist." The President's attempt to perform the impossible proved that the Administration had "gone millennial . . . lost touch with realities—and . . . doesn't give a damn."[124]

By the end of the year the reorganization program had lost a good deal of its original support. Denounced by Senator Byrd, censured by the Brookings Institution, thwarted in Congress by discord among the Democratic leaders and by legislative inertia, government reorganization was in deep trouble. But Roosevelt persevered and his associates remained hopeful. On January 22, 1938, Frederic A. Delano told his grand-nephew James Roosevelt that despite the opposition to reorganization, "when it comes to *grips* The President might make some concessions and get thro O.K."[125]

PART TWO

# The Sources of Opposition

# CHAPTER III

# The National Committee to Uphold Constitutional Government

ON a Sunday morning in March 1938 a farmer in Muscatine, Iowa, received several special delivery letters. Sent by Frank Gannett's National Committee to Uphold Constitutional Government, they contained broadsides blasting the Reorganization bill as a "colossal snatch . . . for Presidential power," as a scheme to clamp "one man rule" upon a free people. The Senate would vote on the bill the following day. "Get everyone you know who wants personal, religious and economic freedom to protest by telegraph or telephone. There is no time for the mail," urged the letter. The Muscatine resident, a New Deal sympathizer, angrily protested: "The country has been flooded with Gannett communications. I have had my full share." In fact, the Committee had sent out a total of 850,000 mailings attacking the measure. It claimed much of the credit for the deluge of angry letters and telegrams which descended upon Washington. The Gannett Committee rapidly emerged as a powerful force opposing the Reorganization bill.[1]

## 1

Just two days before Roosevelt's second inauguration, Frank Gannett and Amos Pinchot decided to meet informally with some friends who shared their opposition to the New Deal to discuss their political prospects. The recent Democratic triumph at the polls must have made their cause seem hopeless, but suddenly, on

February 5, Roosevelt's proposal to enlarge the Supreme Court jolted the nation and revived his opponents. Telephoning Gannett, who was on vacation at Miami Beach, Pinchot asked if he would underwrite a campaign to arouse public sentiment against the plan. Gannett seemed sympathetic, and the warm response to a trial mailing sent out on Monday, February 8, further encouraged him. Later that week Gannett went to Washington to sound out Senator William E. Borah of Idaho. Borah appealed for a nonpartisan crusade: "Frank, if you don't do this job, it won't be done and we will lose the fight. I think you must do it . . . We can't win on this issue without strong opinion on our side." To marshal the force of public opinion, Gannett organized the National Committee to Uphold Constitutional Government.[2]

A conscious effort was made to secure broad backing for the Committee. Pinchot hoped that the Committee would be "as liberal as we can make it." Gannett later explained: "We were careful not to include any one who had been prominent in party politics, particularly in the Republican camp. We preferred to have the Committee made up of liberals and Democrats, so that we would not be charged with having partisan motives."[3] This strategy proved most effective. The list of sponsors included a neatly balanced group of businessmen, educators, religious leaders, representatives of farm and veteran groups, and public figures. Among the forty-six original members were James Truslow Adams, Charles Coburn, John Haynes Holmes, Dorothy Thompson, S. S. McClure, Mrs. Benjamin Harrison, Louis J. Taber, Frank A. Vanderlip, and Sumner Gerard.[4] But in reality, policies were reached through an informal consensus of Gannett, Pinchot, and Edward A. Rumely.[5]

The three men formed a close-knit team. Frank Gannett furnished an indispensable source of revenue and excellent publicity outlets. Sixty years old in 1937, he owned eighteen newspapers with a circulation of 665,000—the third largest chain in the country. The Gannett Company and its subsidiaries were valued at about $18,000,000. Although he devoted little time to politics in the 1920's, Gannett had always been a Republican. He flirted with Roosevelt for a time in 1933, but rapidly returned to the fold and urged Borah to seek the Republican nomination in 1936. When the Borah boom collapsed, he supported Alfred M. Landon.

Amos Pinchot, then in his mid-sixties, was a wealthy New York lawyer who had in the past been identified with many liberal causes. With his brother Gifford he had been a leading Bull Moose Progressive. But in 1916, disaffected by what he considered the failure of the Progressives to attack monopoly, he broke with Theodore Roosevelt and supported Wilson. Pinchot was known as an anti-militarist, a contributor to *The Masses,* a member of the American Civil Liberties Union, and a friend of organized labor. Although he voted for Roosevelt in 1932, he soon became disenchanted with the New Deal. To the National Committee to Uphold Constitutional Government Pinchot brought many years of experience as a political pamphleteer.

Dr. Edward A. Rumely perfected the organization of the Committee and directed its operations. Raised in Indiana, Rumely received his medical training at Heidelberg and then returned to enter the family business of producing farm equipment. He became for a time a close friend of Henry Ford.[6] In 1907 he founded the Interlaken School in Indiana to promote industrial education. The curriculum emphasized the practical: "The school should prepare the boy for his life's work." Rumely hoped to imbue his charges with a desire "to approach the limits of human efficiency," and, in so doing, help "to establish the Kingdom of God within men here upon earth."[7] His messianic impulse soon found an outlet in the Progressive Party. To a large extent he shared Progressive propensities toward imperialism and racism,[8] but Rumely was drawn to Roosevelt mainly by his assertion of the positive role of national government. Laissez-faire was anathema to Rumely; his goal was a "nationalized United States" in which the government would "bring about a cooperation . . . which will vastly increase the industrial resources of the country and reduce the economic waste to a minimum."[9]

German leadership in social reform, combined with his German ancestry, education, and business associations, shaped Rumely's attitude during World War I. In his prospectus for Interlaken he had praised "the message of Germany, that master modern nation." In 1915 he bought the New York *Evening Mail* and installed S. S. McClure as editor. He explained his pro-German views by stating that the Germans had developed a higher form of societal organization that might serve as a model for the United States.[10] Specifically, their success in scientific agriculture, city planning, and social insurance excited his admiration. In Germany, Rumely believed, the idea of group responsibility for the welfare of the individual had found its fullest expression, and so he favored the German cause.[11] In 1918 Rumely was indicted for failing to report that the German government had financed his purchase of the *Mail*. The trial dragged on until December 1920, when he was sentenced to one year in prison. In 1923 a higher court upheld the conviction. After serving six weeks, Rumely was granted a presidential pardon upon the advice of Attorney-General Harlan Fiske Stone and a deposition by the original jurors who had reconsidered certain evidence.[12] After the trial Rumely faded from public view. He returned to his home town of La Porte, Indiana, where he associated himself with a vitamin-producing company.

Despite individual differences in emphasis, Rumely, Gannett, Pinchot, and their supporters shared many common ideas and interests. From the start they embraced the panacea of monetary devaluation as a cure for the depression. They condemned the New Deal economic program, especially its spending, taxation, and labor policies; they mistrusted executive power and honestly believed that Roosevelt would not hesitate to lead the country into war and totalitarian rule; they had little faith in the alternative provided by a Hoover-type Republican Party. These beliefs molded their response to the New Deal.

Gannett and Rumely were deeply interested in the farm movement, and this brought them into association with George F. Warren, Professor of Farm Management at Cornell University. Warren's monetary theories won their solid support. Warren claimed that, historically, basic commodity prices had varied directly with the price of gold. To end the depression, he argued, the government must raise the price of gold by reducing the gold content of the dollar; this would automatically boost prices.[13] "If the price of gold is raised, then the average price of commodities will rise likewise," asserted Gannett.[14] No radical action was necessary to restore prosperity; a minor adjustment—devaluation of the dollar—would prove a sure remedy. Since the economy suffered from a monetary malady, only a monetary medicine would cure the disease.

To popularize this point of view, Rumely organized the Committee for the Nation late in 1932. The name was inspired by Rumely's desire to "keep alive the idea of the nation or group, as a whole, above all individual interest."[15] Attracting financial support from several important business leaders,[16] the Committee set out to persuade the Administration to adopt a managed currency. Rumely asserted that his group was in reality fighting "to preserve our Constitutional system of free enterprise which can survive only if the monetary mechanism functions."[17] The Committee scored a major victory in October 1933 when Roosevelt accepted its program. Gannett beamed: "We want him to succeed, for his success is our own success and our own welfare."[18] When the President abandoned gold buying after a few months, the Committee worked to regain his support. As late as June 1935 Rumely still believed that Roosevelt could be won over. By 1936, however, New Deal social legislation had decisively alienated Rumely's faction.[19]

As a result, the leaders of the NCUCG came to condemn the "insanity and puerility of New Deal economics." To a large extent they echoed conservative objections to federal regulation of the economy. Pinchot insisted that the government be no more than "a decent, impartial umpire." The country, he affirmed, could not "be blown into prosperity by big bertha laws or executive decrees."[20] Rumely proscribed Roosevelt's adoption of a "centralized planned economy."[21] As the first article of his economic credo, Gannett listed his belief that the government must not try to control everything from Washington.[22] Committee leaders attacked the Administration's progressive taxation policies and denounced deficit spending. They particularly abhorred New Deal support for organized labor. "Roosevelt has promoted class feeling," said Gannett. "He has made labor restive and stirred up labor against employers." Gannett attacked the Wagner Act as a "one-sided arrangement" which tended to "promote strife, prolong disturbances and work havoc with all industry."[23] "However the Court fight comes out," Pinchot told Gannett in April 1937, "we must go on with the fight against managed economy. That is the major consideration."[24]

This hostility to New Deal reforms stemmed in part from a deep suspicion that Roosevelt harbored dictatorial ambitions. Pinchot followed Lord Acton: "There are no good grants in politics or economics. The possession of great power means its abuse."[25] Once he, Rumely, and Gannett had convinced themselves of Roosevelt's bad faith, all Administration proposals became suspect. In 1936 Gannett told a friend that if Roosevelt appointed New Dealers to the Supreme Court "then the America that you and I love will be a thing of the past, and we will be on the road to dictatorship such as they have in Italy and Germany. God save us from this!"[26] Pinchot, too, was genuinely alarmed. "I have been so worried, almost terrified, by what seems to me to be happening in this country that I am simply overcome."[27] Rumely wrote to him: "No dictator in history has held greater power over the lives of a nation than President Roosevelt holds."[28] At times their fears bordered on paranoia; they considered the President to be a "power-mad," "thoroughly unscrupulous" politician, and pointed to the existence of "an international conspiracy, and not a passive one either, to destroy private enterprise and bring about a dictatorship."[29] "Just now we're in a sort of a fascist craze in this country for which Roosevelt is responsible," Pinchot informed Ezra Pound.[30]

They did not doubt that the President would lead the country into war in order to retain his power. In May 1939 Gannett pledged that he would "fight to the last against America becoming involved in any way in any European struggle."[31] His reasons were clear. Should the country be dragged into war, said Gannett, "a dictatorship in America would be virtually certain."[32] Similarly, Pinchot became a leader of the New York chapter of the isolationist organization, America First. He warned that war would "plunge us into a totalitarian regime which will be headed by the rusophile liberals . . . at Washington."[33] The NCUGG, however, was badly divided on foreign policy. Several Committee supporters were outspoken interventionists and even Gannett's isolationist fervor had cooled by 1941. The Committee never served as a vehicle to attack Roosevelt's foreign policy; it could unite only on domestic matters.[34]

Notwithstanding their hostility to the Roosevelt Administration, Gannett's followers did not see in the Republican party an attractive alternative to the New Deal. They had little use for old-guard Republicans who stubbornly refused to accept monetary devaluation as a remedy for the depression. They detested Herbert Hoover: "He is such a fool that he is always misinformed . . . . The man isn't even honest."[35] Pinchot referred pejoratively to Wall Street, "the smug Republican hierarchy and its silly and futile strategists."[36] Republican speeches against the Supreme Court plan, which served to close Democratic ranks, reinforced his estimate of the GOP. "For the Republican machine to butt in at this time is simply unbelievable folly," Pinchot exclaimed. "This is no time for the Republicans . . . to peep."[37] The blame for alienating Democratic support, Pinchot warned, would rest on "the foolish virgins of politics who couldn't wait."[38]

The National Committee to Uphold Constitutional Government,

created to fight the Supreme Court plan, was led by men whose opposition to Roosevelt's program ran deep. Their political and economic convictions conflicted sharply with those of the Administration. The nature of their objections to the New Deal made it unlikely that they would confine their efforts to the Court struggle. Events during 1937 would clarify their aims.

### 2

Before embarking upon any campaign the Committee needed to raise money. Gannett personally advanced $49,000 before the mail brought in any contributions.[39] In little more than a year the Committee collected $320,000. It derived its support largely from persons of modest means; of some 21,000 contributors, 19,500 had given less than $25.[40] In truth, the Committee relied on small contributions out of necessity rather than choice. It failed in its heroic efforts to attract wealthy benefactors. In March 1937 Rumely suggested asking Henry Ford to match every donation under $100 up to a total of $50,000; but there is no evidence that Ford consented.[41] A year later, Rumely hoped to raise $120,000 by appealing to ten thousand affluent people. In addition, he wished to assemble a list of several hundred persons who could each give $250 to $1000, and planned to dun the wealthiest women in the country.[42] Although some businessmen gave generously, the Committee met with much resistance.[43] Gannett lamented that a mailing to "six thousand of the biggest givers in the Republican Party" had fallen flat: "Isn't it sickening the way men with big interests fail to realize how serious is the situation."[44]

In fighting the Supreme Court bill the Committee made the most of the means at its disposal. Freely using Congressional franks, it spent less than $200,000 to distribute fifteen million letters stuffed with speeches and statements condemning the plan.[45] Month after month an average of 100,000 mailings a day flowed from its offices. The Committee aimed its barrage at special groups. Gannett blanketed officials of every farm organization, editors of every agricultural publication, and 23,000 individual farmers. The Committee culled for its lists the names of 161,000 lawyers, 121,000 doctors, 68,000 business leaders, 137,000 clergymen of all faiths, influential women, and numerous politicians.[46] It also supplied two thousand daily newspapers with press releases. "We have sent out tons of literature," Gannett declared. In addition, three hundred radio stations carried talks transcribed by the Committee.[47] At all times the Committee assumed a scrupulously nonpartisan stance and played up Democratic opposition to the bill. On July 15 Democratic Senator Edward R. Burke of Nebraska informed Gannett that the modified Court bill had an eight-vote majority; its fate hinged upon twelve senators who favored the plan but were wavering. Gannett sped more than 30,000 telegrams to the twelve borderline states. A few days later, their offices flooded with protests, eight of the senators capitulated and the President was beaten.[48]

The Committee claimed credit for the victory. "Let me say again that we could not have won this fight if it had not been for you," Gannett told Amos Pinchot.[49] Although the Committee played a vital role in arousing public opinion, defeat of the bill had been made possible by Chief Justice Hughes's artful opposition, Justice Van Devanter's resignation, Senator Robinson's death, and the Court's reversal on New Deal measures. Opponents of the President decried his lack of sincerity in disparaging the age of the justices when he really objected to their ideology. Men like Gannett, Pinchot, and Rumely, however, attacked the plan less out of reverence for constitutional tradition than because they agreed with the Court's viewpoint. Pinchot thought that Roosevelt really wanted "to crack down on business and regiment it from the White House . . . And that is the reason why I, for one, feel so much alarmed."[50] In later years, when the Court championed liberal causes, the Committee's fervor was conspicuously absent.[51]

Having scored one victory, the Committee shifted its attention to the Black-Connery Wages and Hours bill, which came to a vote in the Senate only a week after the Court bill had been laid to rest.

Handicapped by a lack of time, Pinchot and Gannett did their best to portray the measure as a step toward regimentation of economic life. They stated that the vote would determine whether "democracy and private enterprise shall endure or be discarded in favor of a despotic, fascist, personal government."[52] But this effort to whip up hysteria failed; the Senate passed the bill by a large majority. Gannett then threw his energies into persuading Republicans on the House Rules Committee to smother the measure.[53] "I sent long telegrams to every state committeeman and every national committeeman and did a lot of telephoning," he recalled. With the support of Democratic Congressman Eugene Cox of Georgia, the bill was bottled up in committee.[54]

Although Gannett asserted that his personal efforts had blocked the bill, he may have exaggerated. The deciding votes in the Rules Committee were cast by Southern Democrats, not by Republicans. Still, the problems that he encountered in opposing the Black-Connery bill are revealing. Unlike the Supreme Court plan, Wages and Hours was an attractive economic reform upon which liberals stood united. The Committee was unable to manufacture popular opposition where the basis for it did not exist. Also, the large membership of the House made it more difficult to apply pressure than in the Senate, where a few critical votes might be swayed by an intensive campaign. Moreover, the Committee had been formed to save the Supreme Court, and its leaders had not had the opportunity to find out whether they could use it as a vehicle to denounce other New Deal reforms.

But Gannett's followers were already turning to a more grandiose scheme. The "Constitutional Freemen" movement was a natural outgrowth of the nonpartisan nature of the Court fight, the weakening of the New Deal in 1937, and the ambition of the Committee's leaders. Pinchot reasoned that "we are united with both the Republicans and the anti-New Deal Democrats in our opposition to certain administration measures."[55] Why not build a coalition of these forces for action in the 1938 primaries and elections? Why not make a determined effort to sustain friends of "constitutional government" and defeat Administration "rubber-stamps?"

This project captivated Gannett's group as early as October 1937, when it decided upon a drive to mobilize voters in preparation for the coming campaign.[56] The Committee set out to recruit "a bloc of 10,000,000 men and women to exert a deciding influence in the elections of 1938 and 1940." These "Constitutional Freemen" would pledge to support "men who are upholding our constitutional system," but need not change their own party affiliation.[57] Gannett described his goal to those senators who had opposed the Court bill. "When we get a great enrollment of voters . . . we expect to go into your state to help you and into the other states where senators are up for re-election." Pressure would also be brought upon members of the House.[58] Ultimately, Gannett envisioned "the creation of a new party which can have loftier ideals and finer objectives than either of the parties today." The key, of course, was the South; "The Southern Democrats are rebelling against many of Roosevelt's proposals, but will not vote the Republican ticket."[59] A new party would enable Southerners to oppose the New Deal without voting for the party of Lincoln. "I feel that we have hit upon a great idea," said Gannett, "I am rather optimistic about our Constitutional Freemen."[60]

The attempt to create an anti-New Deal political force was related to Rumely's expectation that Gannett could be built up as a presidential candidate. In June 1937 he told Pinchot that Hoover must be prevented from controlling the Republican convention. "You, I, others have helped Mr. Gannett build himself into the pivotal position to take such leadership. I ask myself, has he the willingness to use the powers at his command to solve this situation in the right way?"[61] Later in the year, Rumely advised Gannett to "regard each talk that you make as a major effort. . . Your Constitutional Freemen movement is a challenge to President Roosevelt's course. You must be willing to join issue with him."[62] Rumely planned a mammoth rally in Washington at which prominent senators would praise Gannett and at which he might put forth his program.[63] Gannett himself seems not to have been struck by presidential fever until 1938 or 1939; when he was, Rumely directed his campaign and Pinchot complained wryly that the Committee had developed into an effort to make Gannett president.[64]

In the fall of 1937, however, enrollment of Constitutional Freemen trickled to a halt. Realignment of political parties faced awesome obstacles: ideological lines drawn so sharply over the Court plan blurred on other issues; parties, which reflected state rather than national interests, resisted alteration; and politicians proved reluctant to sacrifice their stake in years of service to a party.[65] Although Gannett retained some hope for an anti-Roosevelt coalition, he admitted encountering "such a deep-seated partisanship that it is discouraging to expect a Republican ever to vote for a Democrat or vice versa."[66] He still wished to bring "under one tent all those who . . . want to defeat the New Deal," but by March 1938 conceded that only "time will help us in solving that problem."[67] The momentum acquired in the Court fight had been lost. If Gannett's conservative coalition was to become a reality, if Rumely's aspirations were to be realized, fresh impetus would be required. It was provided by the Executive Reorganization bill.

### 3

As Franklin Roosevelt listened to the election returns on the evening of November 9, 1932, he placed his arm around Amos Pinchot's shoulder and said: "Pinchot, we're going to have a truly *liberal* administration."[68] Five years later, picturing Roosevelt as a man who had betrayed the liberal ideal in an unending quest for power, Pinchot violently condemned the Reorganization bill. After all, he once told Rumely, Roosevelt had "marked constitutional government for slaughter," and the Committee's task must be "to break down the public's faith in the administration."[69] After some hesitation, the National Committee to Uphold Constitutional Government launched a major campaign to defeat the bill. Once again the fires kindled in the Supreme Court fight burned brightly.

During the spring of 1937 Pinchot hunted zealously for a copy of the bill presented by Louis Brownlow to the Joint Congressional Committee. Tantalized by rumors, he told Gannett on May 12 that they might have an excellent opportunity to link the Court bill with the Reorganization bill, if he could obtain a copy.[70] Several days later, while visiting his brother, Gifford Pinchot, in Pennsylvania, he saw a confidential print which Gifford had managed to obtain. Pinchot redoubled his efforts to acquire a copy, enlisting the aid of his brother and an old friend, Louis Glavis. "Finally," he recalled, "a copy appeared mysteriously, in a manilla envelope, at my house."[71] On May 24 he wrote excitedly: "I've finally got hold of a copy of the executive reorganization bill. It's pretty hot." He called in Lewis Douglas, who had resigned as Budget Director in 1934; together they pored over the text in his office, scribbling criticisms in the margin.[72] Brownlow's bill, Pinchot believed, "provides for the abdication of Congress and the virtual setting up of an American dictatorship." He then decided that the next step should be to brace reorganization with the Court bill.[73]

Although the National Committee explored this line of attack, it made no sustained drive against reorganization during 1937. It considered doing so; on July 22 Gannett informed James Truslow Adams that reorganization was "just as menacing" as the Court bill and should be opposed.[74] Four days later, in an open letter to the President, Pinchot asserted that the Wages and Hours, Court, and Reorganization bills evinced "a clear pattern of dictatorship." Had these measures passed in their original form, he claimed, they would have brought fascism to the United States.[75] After these early gambits, reorganization received little further attention. Letters describing Committee prospects refer vaguely to pending legislation of a dangerous nature, but do not mention the Brownlow plan.[76] In September Gannett still had come to no decision concerning reorganization; a month later he alluded to it only as "another subject of research."[77] The Committee took no action when the House considered the matter during the summer; indeed, its spokesman, Samuel Pettengill of Indiana, voted for the Warren Reorganization bill.

What explains this reluctance to take up the cudgels against reorganization? In part it reflected absorption with the Constitutional Freemen movement during the fall. In part, the failure of the Senate to consider a bill precluded any campaign; in the House, debate lasted only a few hours, and the measures had a clear majority. The hesitation was also produced by a division of opinion among the members of the Committee. Gannett explained that some members "feel that the work we set out to do was accomplished when we won the Supreme Court issue. Others feel that the pending legislation in Washington is just as dangerous."[78] James Truslow Adams, for example, warned Gannett that the Committee might "become a sort of Liberty League or permanent Anti-Roosevelt Association" and lose much of its support.[79] Moreover, the Committee doubted whether it could "arouse any interest on such a dry subject as reorganization." The Supreme Court issue could be grasped easily and had a certain inherent appeal, but reorganization seemed to be a dull, complex subject. Gannett was not certain that the public could become excited about "an abstract measure of this sort."[80]

By 1938, though, reorganization had become the Committee's prime target. Constitutional Freemen had failed to sign up; Congressional debate had riveted the nation's attention on reorganization; and the scruples of the more timorous Committee members were easily overcome.[81] More important, a way had been discovered to bring a drab subject to life. Another open letter from Pinchot to the President, late in January, signaled the nature of the campaign. Passing over the measures actually before Congress, Pinchot declared that the President's original plan of reorganization would have established one-man rule. The imagery of dictatorship pervaded the screed. The proposal, Pinchot argued, would permit Roosevelt to control the government "with an iron hand." Should Congressmen enact it, "they would be like condemned men who, on the eve of execution are required to dig their own graves."[82] The letter was timed to reach the President on the same day it was released to the press, because, as Rumely said, "this is a public document and not a private communication."[83]

The Committee deliberately decided to center its attack upon the "Brownlow bill" since it was most susceptible to criticism. Drafted at Roosevelt's request and submitted during the Congressional hearings in February 1937, the bill represented a hasty attempt to frame Brownlow's recommendations in legislative language. When flaws were exposed, Brownlow had agreed to modify the measure. This came to light when the Joint Committee published its hearings in the summer of 1937.[84] Although the bills before Congress in 1938 differed substantially from the original, Gannett's group focused upon the earlier version.[85] Pinchot justified these tactics by insisting that the Brownlow bill pointed up Roosevelt's real intentions, and might be introduced without warning.[86] Still, by conjuring up an artificial menace, the Committee helped to confuse the issue.

Not only did the Committee concentrate upon a phantom "dictator bill"; it also exploited the discontent bred by the "Roosevelt recession." The sharp economic decline that began late in 1937 had led to increasing dissatisfaction with Administration policy. Early in February 1938 Rumely suggested several slogans which might be used. "We must pick a short, snappy few sentences to project over the whole country as a basis for the people's appeal to their Congressmen," he informed Gannett.[87] "More recovery before more reform," was the battle-cry selected. Although it was never spelled out, the Committee's recovery program seemed to include restoration of business confidence through repeal of radical New Deal legislation and adoption of monetary devaluation. Gannett wired prominent Senators: "The country would be mighty glad if Congress would stop piddling with debatable or unessential reforms and work exclusively for recovery."[88]

An examination of the Committee's literature illustrates its technique. A typical mailing in February included five separate items. First, a mimeographed letter from Henry L. Stoddard, on personal stationery, appealing for funds: "We are not now far from absolute control by one man of government, finance and business." Second, a postcard petition condemning Roosevelt's spending program and pledging a fight against every attempt to give more power to the Chief Executive including *"reorganization of the government now."* The petition demanded that Congress "concentrate on getting the country out of depression by establishing conditions which will permit private enterprise to revive and give employment. RECOVERY NOW—BEFORE MORE EXPERIMENTS OR MORE REFORM!" Third, a letter from Gannett asserting that "Our nation is in its THIRD CRISIS," as a result of the "alarmingly dangerous" Reorganization bill: "Who, in this Third Crisis, will defend our own and our children's liberty if we ourselves do not act?" Fourth, a copy of Amos Pinchot's long letter to the President bristling with charges of dictatorship. Fifth, a statement by Samuel Pettengill glorifying America, calling for election of public-spirited men in 1938, and attacking state control of private enterprise; "Let your slogan be: 'We support no candidate who does not carry the Flag and keep step to the music of the Union.' "[89]

As the Senate approached a vote on the Reorganization bill late in March, the Committee's mailings became more specific, but no less shrill. A mailing sent to citizens in fourteen states whose senators seemed to be vacillating including four items. First, a mimeographed letter: "Your Senator, Guy M. Gillette's vote is one of the six needed next Monday . . . to save your government from . . . one man rule. . . Tell him he MUST NOT vote away your rights." Then, a copy of a telegram by James Truslow Adams that scored the Reorganization bill: "The preservation of liberty is not a party question." Next, a photostat of an article written by former

NRA Administrator Hugh Johnson roaring that "a bad, dangerous bill" was being "strong-armed" and "bums-rushed" through Congress. Last, a reprint of Dorothy Thompson's column affirming that if the bill passed "we shall have gone a long way toward establishing authoritarian government in the United States."[90]

Under Rumely's expert guidance, more than 850,000 such mailings were sent out in less than two months, a rate equal to the deluge during the Supreme Court fight.[91] Once again a series of radio transcriptions and press releases supplemented the mail. The mailing campaign, moreover, revealed more than just the Committee's strategy of emphasizing one-man rule and exploiting the recession; it also revealed Rumely's conception of how public opinion could most effectively be molded.

Rumely believed that bulky, exhaustive mailings proved most successful in generating action and in raising funds. Other members of the Committee were dismayed by these "heavy" mailings. Pinchot complained that the long, boring epistles required "super-natural mental power" to be understood. He urged that they be shorter and to the point, suggesting that Rumely had committed an "error in the psychology of persuasion." Rumely staunchly defended his policy, pointing to past success and his years of experience. The Reorganization bill mailing, he asserted, "was one of the most effective mailings ever done in the United States." For thirty years he had been handling mass mailings and evaluating their results. "It is an old experience that desiring people to do something positive, and particularly, to write a check, necessitates giving very full information and creating the feeling that they know pretty much all about the situation."[92] Despite some criticism Rumely had his way.

Mailings were addressed to a carefully chosen group of people. Rumely had no desire to reach everybody; he aimed at influencing "leadership individuals": doctors, lawyers, clergymen, editors, business executives, farm leaders, educators, members of civic bodies and patriotic organizations, members of women's clubs. He concentrated on these "individuals of great influence" and saw no reason to secure new mailing lists because he was confident that he had covered completely the 700,000 individuals who comprised the country's leadership.[93] Most people, the Committee believed, did not think for themselves. "There are about one million men and women, one for every twenty-five families, who give leadership to this nation's thinking." The inert "unthinking" masses might best be awakened by contagion rather than by infection.[94]

Once it had converted these "leaders of thought," the Committee hoped to win a larger segment of the population. Gannett called for the creation of "a GREAT MIDDLE-CLASS BLOC," composed of "the thrifty, frugal, hardworking, self-respecting and God-fearing men and women who built America."[95] Privately, leaders of the Committee asserted that Roosevelt derived much of his support from "the slackers, the shirkers, the incompetents and the unfortunate," whom he held together by attacking wealth. "What we should do," they thought, "is build our support on the vast middle class. Middle class being not a property division, but to include everyone . . . who believes in and wants to uphold the enterprise system." By "emphasizing the rights of a broadly defined middle class, we shall have before us a majority group to appeal to in building support for the Constitution and the enterprise system."[96]

Attracting such support was largely a problem of mass psychology—finding the right slogan or symbol "that will dramatize and make vivid to the masses who will follow leaders."[97] In 1916 Rumely had written: "There is a psychology in cheers and enthusiasm which catches up in the maelstrom millions of men who are not sufficiently intelligent to analyze their emotions."[98] The Committee, he claimed, invented the term "court-packing"; it had projected the phrase "one-man rule" in fighting reorganization.[99] "Every great movement as it passed from the leadership to the masses had to have a symbol—the cross, the crescent, the sickle and hammer, the swastika," Rumely told Gannett. To appeal to the middle classes the Committee must stress tradition; "I have racked my brain for over a year to get some symbol that would be dignified . . . that would have associations with the founding of the country and . . . would create just the right kind of memories."[100] Despite numerous experiments Rumely never quite discovered a symbol so compelling, but one float borne aloft by Committee members in a veterans' parade read: "Flag of our Fathers—Faith of our Fathers—Constitution of our Fathers— Good Enough For Us."[101]

Rumely's fascination with mass hypnotic appeal suggests a link with, or at least admiration for, the work of Father Charles Coughlin. In fact, Rumely, Pinchot, and Gannett had a high regard for Coughlin,[102] and saw eye to eye with him on the need for monetary devaluation. Pinchot approved of his return to the air in 1937, "for I think that what he has been teaching has been, in the main, sound and useful." Coughlin's *Social Justice* prominently displayed Pinchot's open letter to the President.[103] Although the Committee's leaders regarded the radio priest as an ally in the battle against reorganization, there is no evidence that they coordinated their campaign against the bill with his.

The Committee devoted most of its efforts to securing a Senate majority against the Reorganization bill. By March 1 Gannett reported a bloc of thirty-five senators committed to opposing the measure and hoped to win enough votes to defeat it. During the month of March, while debate dragged on in the Senate, Gannett grew increasingly optimistic. "Word from Washington is encouraging. We can win this fight," he asserted.[104] By March 24 he had secured a list of fourteen doubtful senators, and the history of the Supreme Court fight seemed to be repeating itself. Rumely inundated the fourteen states with letters and telegrams. On March 26 he wrote: "The vote will be close. We may win. If we lose, it will be by only a vote or two." He was not far wrong; the bill went through by a five-vote margin.[105]

Although Gannett imagined that the Senate might defeat the

bill, he viewed the situation in the House with less confidence. The Committee was hampered by its inability to single out a limited number of congressmen as targets for a concerted drive. In addition, significant concessions by the House leadership weakened the opposition. Nevertheless, Gannett threw himself into the struggle, devoting twelve to fourteen hours a day to it.[106] "The protests which were registered in Washington," he recalled, "were little short of amazing."[107] When the House voted to recommit the bill, Gannett believed that he had inflicted a second major defeat on the Roosevelt Administration.

### 4

New Dealers had observed Gannett's activities with increasing resentment. In the midst of his campaign they suddenly struck back. On Thursday afternoon, March 17, 1938, two investigators for the Senate Lobby Investigating Committee appeared at the offices of the NCUCG on East 42nd Street in New York. The Senate Committee, created in 1935 to scrutinize lobbying by private power interests, had lain dormant for years. In 1937 Sherman Minton of Indiana had replaced Hugo Black as Chairman. Now, with Gannett's group conducting a ferocious assault upon the Reorganization bill, Minton revived his Committee. His investigators served subpoenas on Rumely and on office manager Glen Hancock, requiring their presence in Washington the following morning with all files pertaining to their attempt to influence federal legislation.

The chief investigator, Herbert A. Blomquist, then produced a letter from Chairman Minton authorizing him to examine the relevant documents so that only the most important would have to be brought to Washington. Obviously taken by surprise, Hancock agreed: "Well boys, I guess you have a right to look at anything in the office. Where do you want to commence?" He explained the arrangement of the filing system and, after showing Blomquist several folders of correspondence, brought forth the letter files of

Gannett and Sumner Gerard. Hancock cleared a desk in his office and invited the sleuths to take off their coats and make themselves at home. "His courtesies extended to drawing up some chairs for us," reported Blomquist. Selecting the most important letters, the investigators began making a descriptive memorandum. The office staff, Blomquist told Minton, seemed "friendly, non-antagonistic and co-operative."

Meanwhile, as Blomquist happened to overhear, Rumely had returned to his own office to call his lawyer, Elisha P. Hanson, in Washington. Then, while the investigators were excitedly copying the letters, Rumely returned and informed them that his lawyer had advised him not to permit such a search. "Don't you think that we should abide by the advice of our counsel?" he asked. Blomquist replied that failure to produce subpoenaed material could, in his opinion, be construed as contempt of the Senate and might lead to legal action. By this time, however, he sensed "slight antagonism" and departed. The visit had lasted less than an hour.[108]

At ten o'clock the following morning Rumely appeared before Senator Minton's committee in Washington. Responding to general questions about the activities of the NCUCG, he described its role in the Court fight, its campaign against the Reorganization bill, and its financial situation. The first clash occurred when Minton demanded that Rumely turn over the Gannett and Gerard letter files. Rumely refused—although he had the files with him—on the grounds that the subpoena was too vague and that Minton could not describe the specific contents of the letters.[109] Although Rumely seemed to be risking a contempt citation, Amos Pinchot, an observer at the hearings, explained: "Burt Wheeler . . . told me that there was little or no chance of [Rumely] going to jail because the Senate would not sustain the Committee. And he thought that Minton and his crew would not dare to risk the issue. Wheeler's advice was the same as Nye's, who advised us to go right after them and call them precisely what they are."[110]

Then, quite suddenly, Minton launched a venomous attack upon

Rumely's past career and associations. He demanded to know whether Rumely had been connected with the Ku Klux Klan in Indiana. The witness hotly denied the charge, although he admitted visiting D. C. Stephenson, formerly a leader of the Klan, in the penitentiary; "I rather like the fellow," he added. Was it not true, then, that Rumely had been sent to jail after the First World War for failing to report that the German government had financed his newspaper venture? Rumely retorted that his newspaper had been the organ of Theodore Roosevelt, that a majority of jurors had asked for clemency, that President Coolidge had granted a full pardon. Above all, he had been a victim of the times. "The conviction was a war conviction." Minton remarked icily: "It was just like Eugene Debs, was it?"[111]

The Senate Committee hoped that airing the unsavory aspects of Rumely's past would blacken the public image of the NCUCG and destroy its effectiveness. Blomquist explained to Minton that it was necessary to establish the official link between Rumely and the Gannett Committee, since he held no official position. In the case of Rumely, he explained, "We have a convicted felon, aiding and abetting the enemy in time of war, now masquerading as an 'Upholder of Constitutional Government.' A public airing of . . . this . . . would unquestionably result in a different interpretation of the aims and purposes of this honorable Committee to Uphold Constitutional Government." The investigators wished to show that the "whole business reeked with Rumely-ism."[112]

Minton and Rumely also tusseled over the purpose of the NCUCG. The Senator accused the Committee of issuing propaganda to defeat Administration proposals; Rumely replied that it merely wished to "educate public opinion," but was nearly trapped at one point:

*The Chairman:* What is the objective that Mr. Gannett had designated for your Committee now?

*Mr. Rumely:* Why, to defeat—

*The Chairman:* (interposing) Defeat what?

*Mr. Rumely:* To awaken public opinion as to the dangerous aspects in the Executive reorganization bill.

When another senator asked whether the Committee carried on organized propaganda against the bill, the witness countered: "It was not organized propaganda. It was organized education of the country."[113] Clearly, if education is devoted to the transmission of skills and knowledge, and propaganda concerned with the manipulation of collective attitudes by the use of symbols, Rumely was no pedagogue. He was, above all, interested in the development of dispositions to act. Privately, if not publicly, Rumely referred to his mailings as propaganda.[114]

The testimony of Sumner Gerard, late in April, served little purpose. In calling him the investigators wanted to prove that large moneyed interest financed the Gannett Committee or at least to put "in the record the names of such contributors as would appear desirable to publicize." They might even reveal that Gannett used the organization as a front to reimburse his own "personal, political 'slush fund.' "[115] But Gerard testified that he was just a figurehead who had no control of accounts, and refused to disclose the names of any large contributors. He had taken the assignment at the behest of his Yale classmate, Amos Pinchot. Gerard appeared to be ill or tired; he declined to read a statement aloud for the senators, and he proved unable to explain his objections to the Reorganization bill. When the senators sought to force him to admit that mailings had been sent under Congressional franks, he demurred: "I am rotten at figures . . . I can't add up a golf score, even."[116]

The hearings ended in mutual recrimination. Each side impugned the motives of the other. Gannett asserted that " 'Comissar' Minton in his Russian tactics" had hailed Rumely before his committee in order to crush legitimate dissent. He attacked the Senator's "vicious and unlawful activities," and accused him of browbeating citizens.[117] New Dealers, for their part, believed that their opponents were unprincipled reactionaries whose hostility to Roosevelt demonstrated their alliance with malefactors of great wealth.[118] Harold Ickes blasted the "very dishonesty of the attack" upon the Reorganization bill; "Theirs was not to reason why, theirs was to stop Roosevelt or die."[119] "When we have to look to the Gannetts to save us," wrote Sherman Minton, "God save us."[120]

Although the hostility of men like Gannett, Pinchot, and Rumely toward the Reorganization bill may have been wrong-headed, it was not fraudulent. Yet in their zeal to defeat the bill they were prepared to employ means of dubious merit. By purposely centering their attack upon a phantom measure, they prevented a dispassionate consideration of reorganization. The success of their venture depended upon their ability to create an atmosphere in which sober-minded inquiry was not possible. While they denounced Roosevelt as a traitor to democracy, their campaign against reorganization demonstrated a lack of confidence in the ability of an educated citizenry to make thoughtful judgments, which is the essence of the democratic faith.

# CHAPTER IV

# Bureaucracy and the Special Interest Groups

In April 1937 a reporter suggested to President Roosevelt that everyone supported simplification and reduction of government bureaus, "until you get down to individual cases." "Yes," the President replied, "it depends on whose baby gets the measles."[1] The accuracy of this remark was demonstrated three months later when Senator James Byrnes scheduled public hearings on the Reorganization bill. A phalanx of war veterans, labor unions, civil service reformers, doctors, and business organizations opposed the measure. They were joined by spokesmen for various government agencies. For the most part, these groups sympathized with the broader aims of reorganization; they merely wanted exemption for the particular function of special interest to them. Nearly every pressure group in American society took exception to some feature of reorganization. The program commanded no support among organized interests; those that did not actively assail reorganization remained neutral, and their influence counted for little.

## 1

The opposition of pressure groups to reorganization illustrated their attitude toward government and their influence during the New Deal. These groups resisted change because they had welded tight bonds with the federal agencies serving them. Many agencies, while theoretically subject to departmental control, really operated independently. This practical autonomy, in turn, enhanced the influence of interest groups. In general, those groups which brought unremitting pressure for modification triumphed, either through formal amendment or informal agreement. Those which protested less vigorously received short shrift. The Administration gave way before nearly every group whose hostility seemed seriously to jeopardize the program.[2]

Every major serviceman's organization—the American Legion, the Veterans of Foreign Wars, and the Disabled American Veterans —attacked the Reorganization bill. Their influence upon congressmen, especially those who were members of these groups, was formidable. The veterans recalled with indignation the drastic cut in pensions which Roosevelt had pushed through Congress during his first days in office. "We still have a vivid recollection of after March 20, 1933, when broad powers were granted the President and the regulations played havoc with the whole system of veterans' relief," one leader told Senator Bennett Champ Clark of Missouri.[3] Veterans also objected to discarding the Civil Service Commission in favor of a single administrator. Although it was difficult to square this position with their endorsement of the Veterans Administration, also under one man, they continued to criticize the civil service provisions of the Reorganization bill.[4]

What disturbed the veterans was the likelihood that a single administrator might tamper with the time-honored system of veterans' preference in the civil service. "We are unable to ascertain whether such a change would abolish veterans' preference in the governmental service," one legionnaire remarked suspiciously.[5] In fact, Brownlow's group had hoped that, to the extent to which it retarded a career service, such favoritism would be curtailed. Luther Gulick expected that "veteran preference will play a far smaller part in the future than in the past because under the scheme towards which we are working, the government will recruit more young people and plan to bring them forward by promotion instead of recruiting people of all ages up and down the line for all sorts of positions without thought to future promotions."[6]

Above all, ex-servicemen feared that the independence of the

Veterans Administration would be curtailed and their own influence destroyed, if it was brought under the proposed Department of Welfare.[7] "We want protection for the Veterans' Administration," the legislative representative of the Veterans of Foreign Wars asserted bluntly. He would have no quarrel with reorganization if the bureau were exempt.[8] His colleagues argued that an unfamiliar department would delay settlement of claims and muddle their affairs.[9] They presumed that the personnel of the new department, especially its head, rumored to be Harry Hopkins, would not be congenial. Democrat Glenn Griswold of Indiana, upholding the veterans in the House, said that they "might easily find themselves subject to the will and whim of Mr. Hopkins in the newly created welfare department . . . Such a transfer would be almost criminal when the welfare of the veteran is considered." Griswold spoke even more pungently to newsmen: "They don't want to be put there so that Harry Hopkins' social workers could put them on the shelf in a test tube."[10]

Veterans fired a steady salvo of letters to Washington while Congress considered reorganization, and their efforts were quickly rewarded. In the Senate, Bennett Clark introduced an amendment prohibiting transfer of the Veterans Administration which came within an ace of passage. On March 22, the Clark amendment failed by the narrowest possible margin, 41–41. On a second ballot, David I. Walsh, of Massachusetts, an implacable enemy of reorganization, entered the Senate Chamber at the last minute and cast his vote against the amendment, assuring another tie vote. On the other hand, several stalwart New Dealers deserted the Administration. Finally, a motion to reconsider failed by two votes.[11] But in the House the veterans could not be stopped. Forced on the defensive, the President promised not to transfer the Veterans Administration. Sensing victory, Representative William Colmer of Mississippi offered an amendment exempting the Veterans Administration. It passed on April 7 with the uncertain support of the House leadership. The veterans had emerged victorious.[12]

The medical profession objected to creating a Department of

Welfare, but did not do as well as the veterans. Even local medical associations which, in the words of one congresswoman, had been "most loyal to the Administration," insisted that the Public Health Service not be transferred to the new department.[13] To do so, claimed the doctors, would be tragic and illogical. Public health was preventive; welfare was curative and corrective. One administrator could not do justice to both, and the health of the nation would necessarily suffer. The best place for the Public Health Service was where it had always been—in the Treasury Department.[14]

Doctors confessed that the Public Health Service was autonomous under Treasury Secretary Henry Morgenthau. The Medical Society of Virginia argued that the Service, while technically in Treasury, "from a policy and performance standpoint, for all intents and purposes is an organization of its own, subject only to budgetary and other financial control." Dr. Edward H. Cary of the American Medical Association informed Byrnes's Senate Committee: "I agree with you that apparently it has no real reason for being in the Treasury Department. On the other hand, it is left to itself . . . so that it is able to carry on rather independently . . . We are afraid it will, more or less, lose its identity."[15] Besides, in a new department the Service might not be directed by a licensed physician. "We do not feel that laymen or sociologists should direct the scientific programs of the public health of this country," proclaimed one medical society. Dr. Cary feared that public health would become "isolated and simply a department of some social-welfare worker."[16]

But Congress turned a deaf ear. The Senate did not consider special status for the Public Health Service. Dr. Joseph Pfeifer, Democratic Congressman from Brooklyn, tried to stir the House to action: "This would mean regimentation," he cried, "and regimentation means socialization. This is socialization on a large scale. It would eventually mean the socialization of medicine." The House decisively rejected his proposal to exempt the Public Health Service. Even in a Department of Welfare it could safely be assumed that a doctor would be chosen to manage the Service and, as Representative Cochran put it: "Members of Congress practically unanimously agree that if there is one Government Agency that is out of place, it is the Public Health Service in the Treasury Department."[17]

Civil service advocates, who greeted the President's report on reorganization with enthusiasm, soon became disillusioned. They seemed willing to accept a single civil service administrator, provided that he was chosen by a competitive examination administered by an impartial citizens' board. Their support hinged upon proper safeguards in selecting the administrator. One member of the National Civil Service Reform League warned Charles Merriam in March 1937 that if the President controlled the examiners who conducted the test, "the spoils forces have a means of climbing in again."[18] As the Senate began hacking at the civil service provisions, reformers became restive. On July 9 Gulick told the President that "a very extensive and vigorous revolt is threatened on the part of the civic organizations throughout the country in criticism of the civil service provisions of the Robinson Bill . . . They say the Bill has been drawn to look like the real article, but that it is actually a limitation of the scope of Civil Service." These groups, Gulick added, did not want to give ammunition "to irresponsible opponents of the whole program," and would probably "hold their horses," hoping that the bad features of the bill would be corrected. "But they cannot be held in check very much longer without some visible source of hope," he added.[19]

Byrnes's decision to hold hearings in July 1937 may have forced the civil service groups to come to a decision. Mrs. Harris T. Baldwin of the League of Women Voters and H. Eliot Kaplan of the National Civil Service Reform League asserted that the Reorganization bill failed to extend the merit system, opened the door to patronage, and gave no assurance that the administrator would be chosen impartially. The bill set a "dangerous precedent," said Kaplan. "A real career system in the Federal service would hardly be possible under any such plan."[20] By 1938 Byrnes had removed some of the more objectionable features of the bill, and Kaplan endorsed it when it came before Congress. But his organization gave only grudging support, and the League of Women Voters remained neutral; indeed, many local chapters called for defeat of the bill. The civil service forces, which had seemed for a moment to support reorganization, remained immobile and aloof. In fact, their fears seemed well taken; at the last minute the House adopted an amendment that would have ripped the merit system to shreds.[21]

A host of other interest groups lined up against reorganization for varying reasons. The National Association for the Advancement of Colored People opposed a single civil service administrator because it hoped that a Negro might be appointed to a three-member commission.[22] Social workers and women's groups wished to retain the Children's Bureau in the Department of Labor, where it had "come to be a synonym for wise administration."[23] Not only did civil service reformers, women's groups, and Negroes fail to support the bill, but organized labor also deserted the Administration.

The American Federation of Labor bitterly denounced reorganization. Slow to recognize its stake in the dispute, by November 1937 the Federation was demanding that Congress defer consideration, and in March 1938 vigorously attacked the bill. President William Green argued that a civil service administrator would impair public confidence in the merit system; he would constitute a "one-man court" and wield "autocratic dictatorial authority" over government employees. In March Green criticized the measure as a "broad and sweeping delegation of Congressional authority."[24]

Many considerations helped shape Green's attitude toward reorganization. He wished to safeguard the independent status of the Employee's Compensation Commission.[25] He opposed any transfer that would weaken the Department of Labor, such as removing the Employment Service. On one occasion Green told Roosevelt: "We wish that we might have a larger Labor Department. We certainly protest against its curtailment and in any reduction in its standing and influence."[26] Also, the Federation was obliged to support its affiliate among government workers, the American Federation of Government Employees, which opposed any change in the civil service system. It feared that executive authority to make transfers would "keep the Federal service in a state of constant anxiety and turmoil," and that an economy drive might eliminate government jobs.[27] Green warned his state officials that the bill empowered the President to "transfer, abolish or consolidate government agencies or to abolish duties and change wage classifications of employees at will."[28]

In the spring of 1938 Green threw his weight against the bill in both House and Senate. He informed all senators that the AFL was "greatly alarmed" by the "highly objectionable" measure.[29] In addition, he induced many state Federation leaders to light fires under congressmen. On March 21 he notified twenty-three labor leaders in as many states: "Very important you immediately wire your Senators to commit the obnoxious Government Reorganization Bill now pending." A week later he renewed his appeal.[30] Many of his lieutenants responded; the California Federation advised local congressmen that the bill was "dangerous to our well-established system of democracy in American Government."[31] According to Senator Minton, the secretary of the AFL in Indiana told him "that he had never seen the bill, and the only reason he sent the telegram is because Bill Green . . . asked him to do so."[32] On March 28 Green boasted: "The American Federation of Labor is doing everything possible to defeat the Reorganization Bill as it is written."[33]

Opposition within the ranks of labor also came from the railroad unions. The Railway Labor Executives' Association, representing fifteen AFL and non-AFL unions, charged that appointment of the Brownlow Committee was a "political gesture" to ward off Republican criticism, and that none of the "three enthusiastic theorists" had much actual administrative experience.

The Association attacked the proposal to place the ICC in the Commerce Department, which usually responded to business interests.[34] Still, the rail unions sought to disassociate themselves from irresponsible opposition to reorganization: "About 20 or 25 per cent of the opposition is 'on the level.' It includes the American Federation of Labor." They labeled the dictatorship issue "partisan poppycock."[35]

When the Senate took up the bill, the railroad unions demanded protection for the Railroad Retirement Board, the National Mediation Board, and the National Railroad Adjustment Board. The pressure they exerted upon New Dealers is illustrated by the case of Senator William G. McAdoo of California. A number of railroad brotherhoods wired their opposition to the bill, and the Los Angeles Central Labor Council called for its defeat "on behalf of [the] organized labor movement of this city." McAdoo hastily called on Byrnes: "Dear Jim: Here are two telegrams from organizations very friendly to me. I wish you would tell me if the bill holds any threat to the Railroad Retirement Board and all Boards created under the Railroad Labor Act."[36] Recognizing the extent of labor disaffection, Roosevelt capitulated. On March 25 he authorized the Senate leaders to promise that the railroad boards would not be transferred. Byrnes conveyed the President's message to McAdoo, who assured the brotherhoods: "The President stated he had no intention of transferring this Board to any Department or merging it with any other activities of the Government." This, said McAdoo, "is convincing to me that you need not be disturbed about the Bill."[37] The railroad unions were appeased but the American Federation of Labor kept up its opposition.

A few weak labor unions stood by the President. The tiny United Federal Workers of America, a CIO affiliate, endorsed the bill. The National Federation of Federal Employees offered perfunctory support. Nonclassified federal employees, who had no stake in the existing merit system, favored the measure. A representative of the

Association of Federal Mechanics, speaking for "men that work in overalls and work with their hands," told senators that only "white-collared workers" received civil service benefits; he saw little merit in the existing system.[38] But these groups provided no organized support, and the CIO itself showed little interest. During March 1938 *The C.I.O. News* concentrated on wages and hours legislation and the recession. An article by columnist Heywood Broun captured its spirit: "It does not seem to me," he wrote, "that the reorganization bill is one concerning which trade unionists should necessarily get passionate on one side or another."[39]

The attitudes of various interest groups were shaped largely by their relationship with government bureaus. The opposition of businessmen, however, seemed to violate a long-standing interest in government efficiency. In January 1937 businessmen had greeted the President's proposals with reserve, but they were not unfriendly and recognized that many of the recommendations mirrored business practice. The United States Chamber of Commerce endorsed much of the program, noting that the reform of accounting and auditing followed its own suggestion. It warmly approved the proposal for six assistants.[40] The *Magazine of Wall Street* noted that businessmen would benefit from less red tape. *Business Week* hoped Roosevelt could prove that "the biggest business of them all can be run on business principles."[41] Even the ardently anti-Roosevelt *Commercial and Financial Chronicle* accepted the need for improved administration and welcomed the report of the Brownlow Committee. The journal especially favored its civil service proposals. But the plan was on "so vast a scale" that it called for more study. In contrast to the Chamber of Commerce, the editors were noticeably cool to the proposal for six assistants and removal of the Comptroller-General.[42] Business opinion was not monolithic, but it seems to have regarded Roosevelt's plan favorably.

In the spring of 1937 businessmen grew more hostile. Increasingly, business journals and organizations censured reorganization.

One writer claimed that the plan would enable the President to cement his control over the nation's banking and credit structure. Fear that Roosevelt could crush the independent regulatory commissions was also expressed.[43] Then in May the New York Chamber of Commerce issued a vitriolic attack which set the tone for future business criticism. Some of the recommendations of the President's Committee were sound, but full acceptance would give the President "such tremendous control over the economic and social activities of the people of this Nation, that it would be only a short step to a dictatorship, and a form of government similar to that prevailing under the Communist, Facist, or Nazi systems." The New York Chamber opposed placing the independent commissions under "politically appointed Cabinet officers," condemned eliminating the office of Comptroller-General, rejected a single civil service administrator, and berated the failure to promise economy. The Brownlow report, it asserted, "is devoted to an expansion of the powers of the Executive branch of the government"; it creates "the hazard of despotic rule, and the loss of economic and political freedom."[44] For a year thereafter business comment on reorganization echoed this refrain.

When Congress debated reorganization in March 1938, business groups did not rest their case on the charges of executive dictatorship and wasteful spending. They also claimed that ending the recession should take precedence. Reorganization would not aid recovery; on the contrary, it could impair frail business confidence and prevent an upturn. "May I respectfully request information as to just how the present paramount issue, 'The Reorganization Bill,' which is now before Congress, would help in any way to bring us out of this current Depression?" a New York businessman asked the President. Passage of the bill "will tend to affect business adversely" complained the Milwaukee Association of Commerce.[45] Business must be allowed to catch its breath, and frustrating a grab for executive power would provide the needed respite.

Businessmen hailed the defeat of the bill as a popular victory that would help restore confidence. The New York Chamber of Commerce asserted that it had played a leading part in arousing opposition. "Public opinion," declared *Boston Business,* "caused the defeat of the reorganization bill"; a "dramatic upheaval of the people" had taken place.[46] The President's reversal was a good omen. "It is one of the best business signs we have seen in a long time," said one magazine. "Washington is paying more attention to the voice of business than at any time since March, 1933," declared another.[47] "Now, there wasn't much wrong with the reorganization bill," admitted the *Commercial West Weekly* when the dust had cleared. "As a measure of economy in public administration of our affairs it had considerable merit. But the people did not want it administered by one man. The word 'dictator' appalled them. . . And so they arose in their might and defeated the bill."[48]

The opposition to reorganization grew out of a broader political philosophy formulated by businessmen during the 1930's. Faced with what they regarded as a hostile administration, businessmen argued that strong government inevitably bred dictatorship. The process seemed almost to be beyond man's control. "We oppose the growth of centralization which in the end may lead to some form of totalitarian government," said the United States Chamber of Commerce.[49] The distinction between executive "authority" and executive "dictatorship" grew dim. Giving the President control of executive agencies would mean that "a long step has been taken toward the centralization of administrative powers which in turn is a long step toward dictatorship."[50] By 1938, spokesmen for business had concluded that "the centralization of power always ends in tyranny."[51]

## 2

Heartened by the warm reception first accorded reorganization, Luther Gulick told Brownlow that he had found people "surprised to think that anyone could come forward with a program of reorganization without encountering the solid undercover opposition of the whole federal service!"[52] His hopes were soon shattered. Office-holders of all ranks—Cabinet members, White House aides, com-missioners of the regulatory agencies, bureau chiefs, and ordinary federal employees—tried to evade the plan. Although government agencies were not permitted to lobby openly, close personal con-tact with congressmen made them a potent force. Senator Joseph C. O'Mahoney of Wyoming finally concluded that most of the criticism was inspired by Washington bureaucrats who did not desire any change in the established ways of doing things.[53]

Members of the executive branch of the government strongly resented any abridgment of their authority. After extensive inter-views the Brownlow Committee found that few administrators cared deeply about improved administration. Instead, they con-sidered "the immediate and particular interest of a department or a bureau as if it were a satrapy."[54] One official who wanted to bring certain bureaus to his department knew he must sacrifice others. This "would possibly appease or satisfy the heads of other divisions who are naturally jealous in retaining any and all power."[55] Even the President's staff cast a cold eye on reorganization. Marvin McIntyre, Roosevelt's personal secretary, and Steve Early, his press secretary, viewed the proposal for Presidential assistants with apprehension, and Brownlow believed that members of the White House staff attempted to sabotage the program.[56]

Among Cabinet members, Harold Ickes, Henry A. Wallace, and Frances Perkins proved especially eloquent in defending their prerogatives. When Harold D. Smith, Director of the Budget Bureau, informed Miss Perkins of plans to shift bureaus out of her department, "she wanted to know who was proposing to reduce the Department of Labor to zero, and intimated that there would be severe repercussions. She also said that [she considered] the removal of the Employment Service . . . a slap at her and that she wondered how many more such slaps she would be justified in taking." "Madam Perkins lectured me for an hour on the historical and philosophical conception of the Labor Department," Smith continued, "I scarcely got a word in edgewise."[57] Ickes and Wallace, too, had a proprietary attitude toward their departments. For the most part, however, it appears that Cabinet members limited themselves to importuning the President and his advisers rather than attempting to muster Congressioanl opposition to the bill.

Members of the independent regulatory commissions, however, did not hesitate to appeal to congressmen, and many went before the Senate Committee to plead for exemption. J. Warren Madden, Chairman of the National Labor Relations Board, insisted that the Board remain independent. The United States Tariff Commission argued that it should function without the interference of a "political official." The Chairman of the Federal Trade Commission stated that the bill permitted a Chief Executive "to impair or thwart the functions of the Commission—perhaps even to render the Commission helpless." Only a few of the independent commissions failed to register a protest; most contended that fair performance of their duties required absolute freedom from interference or control by Cabinet members.[58]

The Interstate Commerce Commission most actively opposed reorganization, and rallied immense support for its cause. In 1937 the ICC was celebrating its Golden Anniversary. Eight of its eleven members antedated Roosevelt's first term, and its most influential member, Joseph B. Eastman, had been appointed by Woodrow Wilson in 1919. Eastman took the Commission's independence for gospel. Recognizing legislative attachment to the ICC, he declared as early as January 27, 1937: "Congress will be reluctant to make such a change in the administration of the Commission as has been proposed by the President's committee."[59] In a speech before the Boston Chamber of Commerce, Eastman attacked the President's plan of reorganization. The ICC had "kept its skirts clear of politics"; nothing should be done that would impart to it "the slightest political tinge." "My own feelings on this point are very strong indeed," wrote Eastman to an admirer.[60]

In July 1937 Eastman drafted the Commission's letter to Senator

Byrnes which rejected the claim that the regulatory agencies were irresponsible and unaccountable. Appearing before the Senate Committee, he argued that Brownlow's group had made "ill-advised and dangerous recommendations" which threatened the impartiality of the Commission. Any modification of the ICC should be determined by Congress. "We do not think a blank check ought to be given to the President."[61] The special interests surrounding the Commission aided and abetted Eastman's efforts. Carriers, shippers, and practitioners before the Commission stoutly defended it. Should the bill pass, warned the president of a major shippers' organization, "you will find the Commission shot through with politics, and pursuing a policy of political log-rolling, rather than of expert non-partisan administration."[62]

The independence of the ICC had universal approbation. While railroad labor feared that the Commerce Department catered to business, railroad owners feared that a Secretary of Commerce might be too "political."[63] Also, most congressmen sympathized with the Commission's point of view and believed that other regulatory agencies should remain independent. As a result, the Reorganization bills considered by Congress in 1938 exempted, in addition to the Interstate Commerce Commission, the Federal Power Commission, the Federal Communications Commission, Federal Trade Commission, Securities and Exchange Commission, and U.S. Maritime Commission.

Not only regulatory commissions, but government agencies threatened by the proposed reorganization, conspired to block the plan. Both the General Accounting Office and the Civil Service Commission were in jeopardy. The General Accounting Office was not at full strength; McCarl's retirement in 1936 elevated R. N. Elliott to the post of Acting Comptroller, but Roosevelt did not appoint a new Comptroller-General while reorganization hung fire. Elliott and a contingent of officials from the G.A.O. appeared before the Senate Committee to denounce the transfer of any functions to the Treasury Department. "I do not think the G.A.O. should be disturbed," said Elliott, ". . . because the Treasury Department has got enough there now." What public loss would occur, asked Senator O'Mahoney, if auditing were given to Treasury? "Well, now, when you get back to that, where would it benefit the general public to put it over there?" retorted Elliott. O'Mahoney then complained that Elliott had merely stated that he opposed the bill, but had not explained why: "Well, that is about all that anybody can give anyhow on these things," was the reply.[64]

Chairman Harry B. Mitchell and his fellow civil service commissioners also assailed reorganization. Having had no opportunity to discuss Brownlow's recommendations with the President before publication, Mitchell presented Roosevelt with a detailed critique of the plan to replace the Commission with a single administrator. The Commission performed judicial as well as administrative duties, he affirmed, and three members allowed it to escape political favoritism. Indeed, public confidence in the Commission depended on its bipartisan character, for although one man might be impartial, "a decision made by a Commission representing various points of view will meet with readier acceptance." Mitchell added that any inadequacy of the Civil Service Commission could be traced to lack of appropriations and the attitude of Congress.[65] Brownlow drafted Roosevelt's reply, which reiterated his belief that one administrator was necessarily more efficient than a board. In August Mitchell warned Byrnes's Committee that a single administrator would open the door to political influence in government employment.[66]

In September 1937 Roosevelt named Samuel B. Ordway of Massachusetts to the Civil Service Commission, and the new appointee joined in denouncing reorganization. Luther Gulick was acquainted with Ordway and considered him a man of "energy and fearlessness" who ardently desired to revitalize the civil service.[67] But Ordway's views diverged from those of the President's Committee. He felt sure that Congress would emasculate the provisions for civil service in any reorganization bill. To avoid this the President should issue Executive Orders extending the merit system, thereby "performing an act of leadership on an issue in which the public is greatly interested and on his side." Roosevelt must make use of this authority, wrote Ordway; otherwise "the civil service side of the program is going to fall by the wayside in the concentration upon the more outstanding reorganization provisions."[68] Roosevelt seemed inclined to go along if Brownlow, Merriam, and Gulick approved, but they were not willing to detach civil service reform from their reorganization program. Ordway's views did not prevail. In February 1938 Ordway publicly blasted the Reorganization bill, terming it "a definite threat" to the merit system.[69]

Bureau chiefs provided still another source of opposition to reorganization. Washington observers unanimously agreed that the heads of bureaus resisted change in their status with remarkable tenacity.[70] Congressman Cochran lashed out at "the officials of the various Government agencies, who, regardless of the cost to the tax-payers, will desire that their set-ups be left alone." Congressman Lindsay Warren of North Carolina took note of their prevailing attitude: "Every board and every agency down the street here says that they believe in reorganization, but say, 'For the Lord's sake, don't touch us.' "[71]

Bureaucratic lobbying against the bill probably occurred most frequently at informal meetings with congressmen. Everyone was sure that it went on constantly. Charles Merriam informed Ickes that the head of the Children's Bureau was trying hard to prevent its transfer from the Department of Labor. Senator McNary told Ickes that the Chief of the Bureau of Fisheries had solicited his opposition to a Department of Conservation.[72] The head of the Government Printing Office warned that if it were placed in a department it would no longer be able to treat all agencies alike, but would have to give priority to its own department.[73] The head of the Employee's Compensation Commission informed Senator George Norris that his agency performed quasi-judicial functions and deserved special consideration.[74] Senator Byrnes recalled that he "was so bombarded by department lobbyists that I could hardly work in my office."[75]

Ordinary government workers did their utmost to prevent a reshuffling of jobs. One federal employee found "a great deal of uneasiness among the people employed in the different offices in regard to the proposed reorganization bill."[76] Representative Charles L. Gifford of Massachusetts feared that the Reorganization Committee would "be hounded to death by every man in any department who may be fearful lest he lose his job."[77] To Henry Morgenthau the need for secrecy in drawing up plans of reorganization was apparent: "If Mr. Jones and Miss Smith get wind that they are going to be consolidated or transferred, they are immediately going to go and do everything they can to stop it—go to see their Congressmen or anything to keep the thing from happening."[78] Congress did adopt an amendment providing that any employee discharged because of a transfer would, if qualified, be given preference when a job opened in another agency. For government employees fearing dismissal this must have provided cold comfort.

Such perturbation is readily understandable. Senator Byrnes agreed that it was to be expected that federal employees would resist reorganization. At a time when memories of breadlines were sharp and millions of unemployed still relied on government assistance, job security came to mean everything. The ever-present opposition to change was heightened during the 1930's. The heads of bureaus, however, feared loss of a job less than loss of authority and independence. Senator Byrnes mentioned this bureaucratic thirst for power to one official: "We have not heard from anyone who wanted . . . any person . . . to have the slightest discretion to take anything from him, but there has been no objection to giving something to him." "That is right," replied the witness candidly.

Senator O'Mahoney thought that many protests stemmed from "the fear of the loss of identity, the loss of power."[79]

### 3

The drive for independence from executive authority can be traced to several features of administrative life.[80] First, the long tenure of many bureau chiefs caused them to regard Presidents and Cabinet members as transients. Second, many bureaus were staffed with persons of special training or experience who naturally resented control by outsiders. Third, the ethos of bureau life permeated officials who, steeped in the traditions of the bureau, adopted its outlook. One administrator tried to explain this process: "When you work in a certain line of work sometimes you have ideas in your head that are put in there by reason of your contact with that work."[81]

Bureaucratic opposition to reorganization enjoyed wide Congressional support. The individual congressman's attitude was conditioned by the local basis of his electoral support and by the limited nature of his demands upon the administrative system. Not only was he elected by local interests that favored bureau autonomy, but his task was to obtain favors from bureau chiefs for his constituents. The ability to secure such consideration depended upon the congressman's sense of familiarity with administrative agencies, and very often upon his personal relationship with particular officials. Whereas the President wished to hold agencies to a standard of accountability, many congressmen were less interested in this than in preserving administrative good will. Reorganization threatened to sever the intricate web of personal association so vital to a successful legislative career.[82]

A page from the diary of Lawrence Lewis of Colorado, an influential Democrat on the House Rules Committee, illustrates this dependence upon personal familiarity to satisfy local needs. Representative Lewis had a busy day on March 22, 1938. He called on Major-General Julian Schley, Chief of the Army Corps of

Engineers, to inquire about a flood control project for Cherry Creek, Colorado. Schley pledged to notify him as soon as the report arrived and promised that he would try to satisfy him. The Congressman then went to see Charles R. Reynolds, the Surgeon-General, to discuss a $1¼ million appropriation for a hospital building which Lewis hoped to secure. Then he visited General Frank T. Hines, head of the Veterans Administration, to request that Hines withhold funds to be used for the hospital. Hines promised to do his best to leave the money unexpended, but explained that he might have to use it for another project. In some way, reorganization threatened each of these agencies, and, indirectly, Congressman Lewis's ability to satisfy his constituents.[83]

The bond between Congress and government agencies is exemplified by the Army Corps of Engineers. Responsible for planning and supervising flood control projects and river development, the Corps exerted immense influence upon congressmen, particularly upon those from the Mississippi Valley.[84] John Cochran warned Roosevelt that if he disturbed the Engineers, "we could certainly have trouble with the Waterways and Flood Control blocs."[85] For decades the Corps had successfully turned aside all moves to reduce its authority or impair its autonomy. On one occasion, when Roosevelt discovered that it was competing with another bureau for control of an important project, he "gave the Army engineers a considerable lecture and indicated in no uncertain terms that . . . [they] had been playing politics with members of Congress, and that he would blow up unless there was evidence of more cooperation." One witness reported, "There was a promise of cooperation, but some doubt as to whether it would be forthcoming."[86]

The Reorganization bills presented in 1937 and 1938 exempted the Corps from transfer, but provided for the creation of a National Resources Planning Board. The Engineers feared that such an agency coordinating public projects might pre-empt their role and disrupt the network of political influence they had so carefully constructed. Representative Cochran explained: "There is a bloc in the House known as the River and Harbor bloc. . . This bloc is very powerful and I have been advised that the leaders of the bloc are almost unanimous in their opposition to the National Resources Committee."[87] Harold Ickes agreed; he believed that the Army Engineers had been "as busy as hell" lobbying against the bill.[88] Nevertheless, the special dispensation the Corps received seems to have muted its opposition. As late as March 25, 1938, a friend of the National Resources Planning Board informed its chairman that "*if* the Army Engineers' lobby got going against the Reorganization Plan the whole program would be jeopardized."[89] Apparently the Corps did not throw its full weight against the Reorganization bill in 1938.

Nevertheless, many friends of the Army Engineers regarded the National Resources Planning Board as too serious a threat to ignore. Senator John E. Miller, a Democrat from Arkansas, attacked the proposed "super-board." "The Army engineers are in charge of flood control and navigation," he asserted. "If flood control work is to be done, who should plan it? It should be planned by the executing agency." Miller warned that if the NRPB was established on a permanent basis, the Engineers' authority would be usurped by "the professional planners." Although a series of amendments sharply curtailed the Board's activity, many senators continued to believe that a vote against reorganization would strike a blow for the Army Engineers.[90]

Some members of the House agreed. Late in April 1938 the National Rivers and Harbors Congress, an influential pressure group, held an emergency meeting to protest a cut in flood control expenditures. Representative William J. Driver of Arkansas, its president, and other congressmen eulogized the Army Corps of Engineers and called for federal grants for river and harbor improvement. In the midst of the oratory Driver complained that he had been criticized for opposing the Reorganization bill. "I placed that on principle, absolutely, and am prepared to defend my attitude on principle." He went on to explain the principle that motivated him: "In that recommendation for a reorganization I found one suggestion that stopped me absolutely from supporting it, and that was the creation of a . . . Board . . . that would stand on an equal plane with your great organization of Army Engineers. I will not stand for its displacement . . . I am unwilling to supplant [it] with a board of theorists." On April 25 the Chief of Engineers visited Boston, where he was greeted by several hundred partisans of the National Rivers and Harbors Congress. "He was told that New England was unanimously and absolutely opposed to the transfer of the control of rivers and harbors work from the Army Engineers to another branch of the Government service in any plan for reorganization of Federal bureaus."[91]

The social forces and group pressures that stood in the way of Roosevelt's reorganization plan were not new. Special interest groups which feared a loss of influence over pet bureaus, and department officials who feared a reduction of their authority had always resisted administrative alteration. There was no sizable constituency for reorganization. Of those groups which supported New Deal economic reform—labor, ethnic minorities, women, liberal intellectuals—some assailed reorganization and others remained uninterested. As Louis Brownlow once remarked: "No one ever burned a hat over government reorganization."[92]

# CHAPTER V

# The Forest Service Lobby

WHILE the battle over reorganization raged, an agitated Henry Wallace sought the advice of Senator James Byrnes. Wallace had just received a letter from Harold Ickes which questioned his integrity. Byrnes agreed that the letter was insulting but added: "The only suggestion I can make is that you either tear up the letter and pretend you never saw it or, when you next see Ickes, punch him and hope you will be separated before harm is done to either; you certainly cannot win a name-calling contest with Ickes."[1] The enmity between the two Cabinet members arose out of Ickes' desire to snatch the Forest Service from the Department of Agriculture and annex it to Interior; Wallace just as tenaciously refused to give it up. The Reorganization bill became enmeshed in the long-standing controversy over transfer of the Forest Service, and the fate of the bill was profoundly affected.

1

Almost from the moment he entered the Cabinet as Secretary of the Interior, Ickes hankered after the Forest Service which had been lost to Agriculture in 1905. He was motivated by an ambition to increase his power and prestige, by a sincere belief that he could succor the cause of conservation, and by a desire to build up public confidence in his department. Ickes wished to blot out the memory of Richard A. Ballinger, President Taft's Secretary of the Interior, who had been accused of turning over Alaskan coal fields to private interests. Determined to redeem his department,

Ickes hired men like Louis Glavis, who had helped expose Ballinger. Ultimately, obtaining the Forest Service as a step toward
creating a real department of conservation became his chief ambition.[2] But at first Ickes moved cautiously, avoided any overt steps,
and seemed content to fend off the sorties of the Department of
Agriculture, which was itself casting covetous eyes upon various
bureaus in Interior.

In April 1933, disturbed by rumors that Roosevelt might remove the National Park Service from Interior under authority of
the Economy Act, Ickes was willing to give up claim to the Forest
Service if only he could keep the parks. "I think the National
Forests ought to be here but I have not raised my hand to bring
that about," he wrote in his diary on April 20. Ickes reasoned that
Interior would suffer no loss of prestige if it did not obtain Forestry,
but added, "It would be a different matter altogether if National
Parks is to be taken to Agriculture. That would be a reflection upon
this Department that would have the tendency to lower it still
further in public estimation." He believed that Agriculture could
afford to give up the Forest Service, but if an "insuperable obstacle"
prevented its "coming back," then he would not press the issue.[3]
There the matter rested for the remainder of the year.

During 1934 the latent antagonism between Interior and Agriculture was submerged in common support for the Taylor Grazing
Bill. The bill, which passed the House in April and the Senate two
months later, gave the Secretary of the Interior authority to create
grazing districts, grant permits regulating their use, and assess fees.
When a Senate amendment sharply reduced the acreage to which
the law applied, Wallace tried unsuccessfully to get the President
to veto it. Still, Wallace had strongly supported the creation of the
Division of Grazing in Interior as a victory for the principle of
regulation, and his last-minute objections seem not to have offended
Ickes.[4] Indeed, during 1934 the two Secretaries discussed a mutual
agreement to exchange bureaus: Forestry, the Bureau of Roads,
and the Biological Service would go to Interior; the Bureau of

Reclamation, the General Land Office, Erosion Control, and Subsistence Homesteads would go to Agriculture. Ickes planned to make Rexford Tugwell Undersecretary of Conservation in his department. But by December 1934 Wallace had decided to reject the package deal.[5]

Relations between the two men deteriorated during the winter of 1934–1935 when Ickes suspected that Agriculture was plotting to steal control of grazing from him. "It begins to look as if the Department of Agriculture is opening a campaign on this Department," he wrote. Roosevelt's transfer of the Soil Erosion Control Division in March 1935 further angered Ickes, although he knew that the bureau belonged in Agriculture. Partly in retaliation, Ickes turned to a proposal to change the name of his department to the "Department of Conservation," and authorize the President to make the necessary transfers. Roosevelt approved, but declined to make the bill an official Administration measure. Introduced late in April, the measure was immediately branded by newspapers as a play for the Forest Service. "They are not far wrong at that," admitted Ickes.[6]

In May representatives of the Department of Agriculture attacked the bill before a Senate Committee. Ferdinand A. Silcox, Chief of the Forest Service, inquired: "I would like to know from the proponents of the bill what they had in mind. There must be some specific purpose for the introduction of such a bill." Ickes replied that only the President could decide the composition of the new department. In June Ickes clashed with Wallace before a House Committee.[7] Friends of conservation joined with the Forest Service to oppose the measure. Late in July Silcox informed all Regional Foresters that the Congressional situation was critical and urged "immediate, definite, and planned action" to beat down the proposal.[8] In August the House Committee on Expenditures rejected it by a vote of ten to five. Finally, in the spring of 1936 Ickes steered the bill through the Senate, only to see it die in the House Rules Committee. Bitterly complaining that Roosevelt had not lived up to his promise to support the bill, Ickes fumed that he had been " 'sold down the river' by the President."[9]

In 1936 Congressional efforts to extend the Taylor Grazing Act touched off another skirmish between the rival departments. Ickes urged the President to support an amendment to bring the Forest Service to Interior. The Forest Service pushed an amendment to turn grazing over to Agriculture, and submitted a lengthy monograph to justify its position. Ickes asserted that this report was inaccurate, gave credit only to the Forest Service, and constituted "a thinly veiled attack upon a sister department." Wallace replied that Interior had not been consulted in writing the report because an exchange of letters "clearly established differences of philosophy and factual interpretation so irreconcilable as to preclude any probability of mutually satisfactory adjustment." In this case, the two adversaries battled to a standstill.[10]

The feud between Interior and Agriculture rapidly assumed the character of an intergovernmental rivalry. Secret strategy meetings were called, strict security precautions were enforced, and cautious high-level conferences were held. One Interior Department agent describing strategy to another remarked furtively: "Doubtless Agriculture is not innocent of our intentions." Ickes harbored a grandiose scheme to seize some half-a-dozen functions from Wallace.[11] When his efforts proved futile, Ickes grew more and more petulant and on several occasions threatened to resign. It took all of Roosevelt's charm to assuage his wounded aide.[12]

Roosevelt had tried to remain aloof from the controversy. Although he sympathized with Ickes' aspirations and thought Forestry belonged in Interior, he had no desire to antagonize Wallace's supporters.[13] "In his heart I think the President does want it," said Ickes of the Conservation Department, "but apparently he doesn't want it enough to help me get it." Neither side managed to win Roosevelt over. In the spring of 1936 Wallace warned the President that transfer of the Forest Service would cost him votes; Ickes promised that "he would not lose a single farmer's vote in the whole country." But Roosevelt was not convinced: "He kept repeating that he did not want a fight . . ." Ickes reported. As pressure mounted and tempers flared, the President seems to have made conflicting promises in an effort to postpone a final decision.[14]

The Forest Service controversy made enemies of old friends. Ickes and Gifford Pinchot, the former Bull Mooser and first Chief of the Forest Service, had been comrades for twenty-five years. In 1933 Pinchot had complimented Roosevelt on his "splendid" choice of a Secretary of the Interior. Ickes replied, "I am a Gifford Pinchot conservationist. I learned the principles of conservation at your feet, just where T. R. learned his."[15] But Pinchot strenuously opposed transfer of the Forest Service, and their friendship deteriorated as Ickes became more belligerent. When Pinchot, who had served as Republican Governor of Pennsylvania, half-heartedly backed Landon in 1936, their relationship was subjected to a further strain.[16] In the following year, reorganization occasioned another angry quarrel. Pinchot attacked "Hot-Spot Harold" and his ambition for power. Ickes replied: "Pinchot is again astride his old hobby horse, but he is facing the tail."[17] Although a brief reconciliation occurred during the winter of 1938–1939 when the transfer issue died down, it was short-lived. As soon as the Secretary resumed his campaign, Pinchot commented, "Ickes and Hitler seem to have the same method and, I might add, certain very definite resemblances in character." Ickes concluded by whitewashing his predecessor Ballinger, attacking the "Pinchot intrigue" as "one of the dirtiest in American history" and sending his adversary a twenty-eight-page letter packed with sarcasm and abuse. "The man must be out of his mind," thought Pinchot.[18]

Into this maze of departmental sniping, presidential irresolution, and personal vilification came the Executive Reorganization bill. The President's Committee on Administrative Management, much to Ickes' delight, recommended that a Department of Conservation be created. As early as May 1936 Roosevelt told Ickes that Brownlow favored such a department; on November 17 he assured the

Secretary that the proposal would be included. On December 20 Ickes noted in his diary that if reorganization went through he would have his Department of Conservation. "That will prevent overlapping and clashing and jealousies in the future," he added.[19] At a Cabinet meeting on December 22 Henry Wallace listened glumly while Roosevelt explained the recommendations of the Brownlow Committee. Later that day, Wallace warned the President that any plan of reorganization which removed Forestry from Agriculture would "excite the serious opposition of the agricultural, wild life, forest conservation, and other organizations which have been and are now so vitally interested in this question."[20]

## 2

Wallace proved to be prophetic. The project had encountered resistance in the past, but never was the Forest Service lobby so active and well organized as in 1937 and 1938. Mustering support throughout the country, especially in the West, it inspired an avalanche of angry resolutions and letters which brought unremitting pressure upon Congress. From the first the Administration was put on the defensive. Eventually, more than 250 organizations recorded their opposition to the proposed Department of Conservation.

The Forest Service lobby was composed of disparate elements that wanted to preserve the status quo for various, even conflicting, reasons. Five distinct groups united to form the lobby: professional foresters in the Forest Service, the Society of American Foresters, and the Association of State Foresters; lay conservation groups such as the American Forestry Association, the Izaak Walton League, and interested organizations such as the General Federation of Women's Clubs; farm organizations such as the National Grange and the American Farm Bureau Federation; the lumber industry through the National Lumber Manufacturer's Association and the West Coast Lumberman's Association; and the grazing interests through the National Livestock Association and the National Woolgrowers' Association. Diverse aims dictated their action, but these groups stood together against transfer of the Forest Service.[21]

Their position cannot be traced to hostility to Roosevelt or to the New Deal. The President of the Pennsylvania Forestry Association harshly denounced the transfer, but added: "I might say, speaking for myself, that I have been a very strong New Dealer; that I have great admiration for . . . our President."[22] The Society of American Foresters censured those who attacked reorganization for reasons of "political expediency," and condemned the "blind opposition" to the President.[23] Although a few Forest Service adherents attacked the entire Brownlow Report, most applauded its "many admirable recommendations" and confined their criticism to the proposed transfer.[24] Gifford Pinchot supported much of the New Deal's social program. When the President delivered his "one third of a nation" address, Pinchot exclaimed, "That sort of program is right, of course, and deserves to win." In March 1937 Pinchot realized that, in general, "no other administration, since that of Theodore Roosevelt, has done so much for conservation as that of Franklin Roosevelt."[25]

Several common assumptions linked the friends of the Forest Service. They believed that, as a crop, trees logically belonged in the Department of Agriculture. "A forest is a crop, and forestry is uniformly classed as a branch of agriculture," said Pinchot in 1911, and his disciples never deviated from the faith.[26] They argued that all organic resources—things that grew—should be in Agriculture; only inorganic resources—coal, gas, oil, and minerals—should be in Interior. To divide the forests on the basis of ownership, by giving commercial forests to Agriculture and national forests to Interior, would create an "artificial distinction which has no existence in nature," and do untold damage.[27] More pragmatic arguments also were brought forth. The Forest Service seemed to be functioning well. "Why rock the boat?" asked Pinchot.[28] Then, again, reorganization might open the Forest Service to political appointments, and undermine the professional esprit de corps built up by strict adherence to the merit system.[29] Moreover, separating the science of forestry from the technical facilities of the Department of Agriculture would be disastrous. Creating a department of "conservation," contended Henry Wallace, made no more sense than creating a department of "integrity."[30]

These arguments failed to impress Ickes' allies, to whom the claim that the Forest Service functioned well in Agriculture seemed an obvious rationalization. The assertion that the merit system would be weakened hinged upon a tortured interpretation of the bill. Objections to renaming the department seemed presumptuous; surely no name could be less precise than "Interior."[31] The President himself came to dismiss the organic-inorganic division, maintaining that Agriculture should deal with the lands of private citizens and Interior with nationally owned land. Any other system produced "ridiculous interlocking and overlapping of jurisdiction."[32] Actually, much of the opposition to the transfer could not be effectively rebutted because it was based on irrational fear, on narrow self-interest, or on serious disagreement about federal land policy.

The antagonism of those conservationists who backed the Forest Service stemmed in part from a nearly pathological distrust of the Interior Department. The memory of Richard Ballinger still lingered, and they recalled all too clearly Albert Fall's pursuit of the Forest Service under President Harding. A California conservationist implored Roosevelt to reject the transfer, "recalling the frightful deal we had in the Cunningham coal claims in Alaska in the Interior Department; the oil proposition under Fall." The Chief Forester assured Pinchot in 1933: "It is the old, old fight, but in an entirely different setting and with a different judge."[33] Conservationists conceded that Ickes was sincere, but asserted that he might be succeeded by another spoilsman. Besides, it was not merely a matter of personalities. The Interior Department, complained Pinchot, "is organized not to manage natural resources, but to dispose of them; and the spirit which has been built up during generations of this policy cannot be changed in a moment." Even Ickes could not overcome the "alien" spirit which permeated Interior.[34]

So long as Ickes avoided scandal the charge seemed flimsy. Therefore, conservationists eagerly seized upon Interior's steward-ship of the Oregon and California lands to buttress their case. In 1916 some 2.5 million acres in the Willamette Valley, granted con-ditionally to the Oregon and California Railroad fifty years earlier, were revested in the federal government. These tracts, covered with valuable Douglas fir, comprised portions of the original grant which the company had forfeited by violating its charter.[35] In April 1936 Ovid Butler published an article in *American Forests* assailing Ickes' management of these lands, charging that the Secretary had "failed to raise his voice publicly against a federal policy that makes his own department a party to land devastation as destructive as can be found in the country." Although Ickes was authorized to prescribe regulations for cutting and removing timber, Butler claimed that the Secretary had failed to do so, thereby permitting operators to "wreck" the land. Over 120,000 acres had been sold under a system which would lead to the "destruction and dissipa-tion" of the forest resources.[36] Congress later accepted Ickes' program to protect the area, but the issue provided a useful pretext; in May 1937 Pinchot asserted that Ickes' handling of the O and C lands "makes it perfectly clear that the Departmental leopard has not changed his spots."[37]

Professional foresters also vigorously attempted to thwart the transfer. In part, their opposition represented normal bureaucratic resistance to change. Senator O'Mahoney ascribed their inflexibility to "small inter-departmental jealousy." Other critics asserted that "the present anti-transfer fight smacks too much of bureaucratic self interest."[38] Foresters had established close bonds with their associates in Agriculture. Rugged, rough-hewn men of the forest felt comfortable with rustic, ascetic Henry Wallace; the Interior Department, under the "Chicago lawyer" Ickes, seemed citified and effete. Gifford Pinchot believed that he remembered how Interior

Department foresters had behaved; one, "a tenderfoot of tenderfeet, utterly ignorant of the West, wore a white tie and shawl, and was afraid to go farther into the Forest he had charge of than the end of the stage line."[39] Some intensely disliked Ickes. One West Coast forester wanted "to be in on the kill if . . . our friend Ickes has exposed the right part of his anatomy for punishment."[40] The Forest Service feared that its traditional autonomy would be lost in Interior. Pinchot believed that Interior "is the most centralized Department in the Government, and Ickes is the worst centralizer among all the Secretaries of the Interior in the last forty years."[41] It seemed unlikely that Ickes would sanction the independence to which foresters had been accustomed since 1905.

Furthermore, the Forest Service and Interior held conflicting philosophies of land management; the former stressed use and renewal, the latter stressed enjoyment and removal. Pinchot and his disciples believed in cutting trees scientifically, so that new trees would, in time, replace them. To them, conservation meant rational planning to promote the use and development of natural resources. They did not want to withdraw resources from use, but to ensure that they were used wisely.[42] The Interior Department, as administrator of the national parks, leaned to the view that forests should be preserved for aesthetic enjoyment and recreation. Ickes' department did not, of course, reject the use of natural resources; but it was much more reluctant to cut down trees hundreds of years old to obtain timber than was the Forest Service. Visiting the site of a proposed national park, Ickes hoped to maintain it as a wilderness area: "It is truly a wonderland of nature and it is more than I can understand how people who pretend to be interested in conservation could be opposed to its creation into a national park."[43] The conflict between Interior and Agriculture was only one phase of a struggle between aesthetic and utilitarian conservationists which had existed since the time of Theodore Roosevelt.

H. H. Chapman, head of the Society of American Foresters, explained the significance of this clash for reorganization. He wrote Roosevelt in February 1937: "The sentiment 'trees should not be cut,' has its proper application to areas to be devoted solely to park use, but if generally applied, it would produce an economic blight."[44] He developed this theme three months later in the *Journal of Forestry*. The "urban ideal" of conservation, he argued, was based not on economic reality but on emotion. Its driving impulse was satisfaction of the "recreational urge"; its program was "absolute prohibition of all utility whatever." This policy conflicted with the ideals of professional foresters, who championed wide use and renewal of organic resources. Foresters wanted parks, Chapman agreed, "but the good of the whole Nation means more to foresters than the unlimited and unregulated extension of the single urban objective of recreational monopoly and nonuse." Chapman considered it unfortunate that the President, "coming from a state where the urban ideal of nonuse and exclusive recreational monopoly has been paramount for 40 years," had proposed putting Forestry into a Department "whose most conspicuous claim to conservation is its service to urban desires."[45]

The arguments against transfer appear to be shot through with contradictions. Many conservationists, with an eye to the past, objected to giving the national forests to Interior because they feared renewed spoliation; yet the foresters opposed the transfer precisely because Interior might carve out more national parks and restrict economic utilization. Indeed, the line between the two groups sometimes seemed indistinct, and men like Pinchot employed both arguments. Still, the controversy helps to account for the support tendered the Forest Service by the lumbering and grazing interests.

Over the years, lumber operators had developed a high regard for the Forest Service. Once initial suspicion vanished, the industry recognized that foresters were not inimical, but sympathetic. William B. Greeley, a former Chief of the Forest Service who became head of the West Coast Lumberman's Association, recalled:

"The industry men lost their resentment . . . They welcomed men from the Forest Service, talked and worked with them freely and, incidentally, took many foresters and wood technicians of government training into their own employ."[46] Progressive lumbermen saw eye to eye with the foresters' view of resource utilization. Both resisted the extension of national parks. One official of a Pacific lumber concern feared that transfer of Forestry would lead to "the including of large areas of merchantable timber within the Olympic National Forest inside the proposed Olympic National Park."[47] Also, the decentralization of the Forest Service proved conducive to good relations. Foresters tended to be men of long acquaintance, who identified themselves with local interests and were subject to local pressures.[48] The lumber industry knew where it stood with the Forest Service.

Similar bonds united the Forest Service with the grazing interests. One stockman described the prevailing sentiment to Senator Joseph O'Mahoney of Wyoming in December 1937: "The Live Stock and Wool Growing Industry of these western states . . . must know exactly where they stand with reference to their grazing permits. . . Many of us hold ten year grazing permits on which our business is based. Should any change or reorganization involving the Forest Service take place, it would undoubtedly affect the present permit system."[49] Fear that Interior would introduce a sweeping program of resource withdrawal also obsessed the grazing industry. The position of the National Woolgrowers' Association reflected this apprehension: "Mining, grazing, and sportsmen interests alike are fearful of the proposed transfer of the National Forests because they know that such a move would remove once and for all the main barriers to unlimited extension of the National Parks, which in turn would automatically eliminate future use of national-forest lands for prospecting, grazing use, and hunting." The industry opposed reorganization because it suspected that "an immediate extension of National Parks would result from the transfer of the Forest Service to the Interior Department."[50]

The partiality of lumbermen and stockmen toward the Forest Service naturally gave rise to charges of collusion. "The exploiters of our forests," snorted Ickes, "want to choose the policemen to protect the forests."[51] But to picture the Forest Service as toadying to these interests would be erroneous. Ferdinand A. Silcox, appointed Chief of the Forest Service in 1933, supported use rather than removal, but antagonized the industry by advocating strict federal control of timber-cutting. Silcox endorsed a proposal to have the government cut timber in the national forests rather than permit private contractors to do it on a stumpage basis.[52] So at the same time that the lumber industry fought transfer of the Forest Service, it accused Silcox of discouraging private enterprise and charged that his social theories were too radical.[53]

Professional foresters, the timber and grazing industries, and many conservationists opposed transfer of the Forest Service for a variety of reasons. The opposition of farm groups is more difficult to explain. Their stance may have reflected the interlocking leadership of farm and forestry associations; it may have represented a natural loyalty to the Department of Agriculture.[54] Moreover, the practical autonomy enjoyed by the Forest Service tended to enhance the influence of special interest groups, such as the National Grange. Still, the position of farm groups seemed puzzling. "Just why the American Farm Bureau Federation should take such an interest in the matter of the reorganization of the Government is a mystery to me," wrote Senator Josiah Bailey of North Carolina. He suggested to the president of the Federation that it might "be much better for the cause you represent if you would concentrate upon farm legislation."[55]

### 3

The Forest Service lobby was organized to perform a dual function: to coordinate the activities of the various factions opposing the transfer, and to chart their general strategy.[56] The lobby differed from Frank Gannett's National Committee to Uphold

Constitutional Government in several ways. It aimed at spurring local organized bodies to action, while Gannett attempted to arouse influential individuals. It concentrated largely on eleven Western states with large national forests; Gannett sowed his literature over the entire nation, focusing upon any state whose senators seemed persuadable. Also, the Forest Service lobby launched its attack upon reorganization much earlier than did Gannett. In March 1937 Ickes learned that "the friends of the Forestry Service were getting ready for a finish fight . . ."[57]

Some sporadic efforts against the transfer were made early in 1937. On January 26 Ovid Butler of the American Forestry Association called for "unified action" to defeat the proposal, and suggested "an early conference" to map out strategy.[58] None was held. During the spring, however, Gifford Pinchot appeared before conservation groups in Chicago, New York, and Cincinnati, "ripping Ickes up the back."[59] Late in May, Pinchot met with Butler, G. H. Collingwood, and James McClure of the American Forestry Association to discuss ways to beat the transfer. They agreed that Collingwood should be "in charge of stirring up action by agricultural representatives on members of House and Senate."[60] On June 11 Butler and Collingwood called a meeting of the interested groups in Washington. Attending the meeting were Henry Clepper of the Society of American Foresters, John Woods of the National Lumber Manufacturer's Association, Fred Brenckman of the Grange, Chester Gray of the American Farm Bureau Federation, and Robin Hood of the National Cooperative Council. They met with Senators Harry Byrd and Charles McNary, who promised to support their cause.[61]

In addition, McNary showed them a confidential committee print of the proposed Reorganization bill, which specifically exempted the Forest Service from transfer to the Department of Conservation. Surprised by this apparent victory, the group hesitantly decided to continue its efforts to ensure that other functions of the Department of Agriculture would not be disturbed. Collingwood appeared almost relieved when the measure, as introduced on June 23, did not exempt the Forest Service; this left the issue clear and easier to fight.[62] Most of the same conservation leaders met on the following day. They decided to attack only those features of the bill that affected Forestry and agreed that each organization would write to all congressmen, issue press releases, and purchase radio time.[63] Early in August half-a-dozen forestry leaders testified against the bill before Senator Byrnes's Select Committee.

Even more portentous was the arrival in the Capital at this time of Charles G. Dunwoody. A lobbyist for the California Chamber of Commerce, Dunwoody had come to Washington originally to press for repeal of certain New Deal tax legislation and developed an interest in the transfer fight. He returned to California early in 1937 and spent the next few months raising money and establishing contacts with "a group of key men in each of the eleven western states who will develop strong opposition each in his district." He planned to set up a central office to rally opponents of the transfer. "Through the key contacts in the states we can contact every worthwhile organization," he informed Pinchot.[64] On July 10, at Pinchot's urging, the Chamber sent him back to Washington, where he rented an office for $125 a month. For several weeks Dunwoody ran his propaganda mill, but by mid-August, when it became clear that the Senate would not take up reorganization before adjournment, he returned to the Coast. Soon afterward Pinchot wrote to him: "The more I think of the work you have been doing the more grateful I am to you and to the Chamber for it."[65]

The Forest Service lobby prepared for a major effort when the special session of Congress convened on November 15, 1937. Late in October leaders of the American Forestry Association met with representatives of five farm and forestry groups to review past achievements and plan for the future. Ovid Butler, at a cost of only $750, had sent letters to every member of the A.F.A., to fifty organizations opposing the transfer, to all state conservation commissioners, and to "picked" individuals—"key people" who might move local groups to join the effort. In addition, he had mailed five thousand pamphlets explaining the transfer issue. The "Washington group" then arranged to place its facilities at the disposal of Dunwoody, who arrived on November 2. For the next six months Dunwoody remained in Washington to coordinate the work of the lobby.[66]

Lack of money no longer appeared to be a serious hindrance. Between April 1937 and March 1938 contributions to the "Reorganization Fund" of the California Chamber of Commerce amounted to about $11,000. Several individuals and concerns gave generously, but four contributors accounted for $8,500 of the total.[67] Besides salaries, the largest single expense was $250 a month for Dunwoody's office. Outlays for travel, postage, telephone calls, and office supplies were nominal. Dunwoody did not require large sums to operate efficiently. He spent little on entertainment; the total cost for nine affairs, mostly dinner parties, was a meager $120, and the largest bill was $21.75.[68] "We are getting excellent publicity, which so far has cost us nothing more than a couple of cocktail parties for a group of the editorial writers," he reported.[69]

Beginning in November 1937 Dunwoody sent a steady stream of letters to groups and individuals opposing the transfer. He provided information on the legislative situation, outlined strategy and exhorted them to action. Calling on his supporters to write to their congressmen, he urged them to inform him of "anyone who will come to Washington on call who can and will help."[70] He worked from a master list of 250 prominent individuals, nearly three fourths of whom lived west of Chicago; in addition, he prepared a special telegraph list of forty-nine key persons for prompt action.[71] By December 3 Dunwoody could report "very satisfactory progress," but he insisted that "there be no let-down in the steady flow of messages . . . from back home. The flow should rather be increased. This will aid in selling them and in keeping them sold."[72]

The response was so overwhelming that Dunwoody grew certain of success. By the end of November he was sure that "we are going to win," and assured Pinchot that at least sixty-six senators opposed the transfer. On November 23 he reported that "Vice-President Garner has joined Senator Pittman in playing our game on Reorganization. . . Talked to Senator Byrnes . . . and he indicated to me that he had practically given up the idea of consideration of the bill this special session."[73] Indeed, Dunwoody now hoped the bill would come to a quick vote and was somewhat disappointed when it was postponed until the regular session met in January 1938. Dunwoody remained sanguine, expecting that "in view of the tremendous opposition we have built up," Byrnes might recall the bill to committee for amendments "that will be entirely satisfactory to our group."[74]

Dunwoody received the fervid support of the General Federation of Women's Clubs. Counting two million members, the Federation was a potent weapon. Over the years it had advocated censorship of books and movies, civil service reform, betterment of education, prison reform, child labor legislation, regulation of wages and hours for women, entry into the World Court, and conservation.[75] Emily G. Bogert, its conservation chairman, backed the Forest Service to the hilt and brought the clubs into line ("heavens knows why, except that their western members liked those nice foresters," said one New Dealer churlishly).[76] But Miss Bogert was handicapped by a scanty budget of $80 a year. In mid-October she asked Pinchot and Dunwoody for help: "I believe that this reorganization would work disastrous havoc . . . and I wish I had . . . the means to direct a vigorous campaign against it. I could do it if I had the funds." Dunwoody gallantly sped $150 to her.[77] By November 10 Miss Bogert reported that she had "the force of the General Federation of Women's Clubs lined up, instructed and informed. . . I love to fight a cause when it is such a worthy one as this is."[78] "LET US THROW THE TREMENDOUS FORCE OF OUR ORGANIZATION AGAINST THE ENACTMENT OF THE REORGANIZATION

BILL," she cried. "WOMEN—THIS SITUATION CONSTITUTES AN IM-
MEDIATE CRISIS IN THE FORWARD CAUSE OF CONSERVATION. YOU
CAN MEET THE CRISIS BY SENDING YOUR LETTERS AND TELEGRAMS
AT ONCE." By 1938 she announced that her colleagues were "all
on the job."[79]

Gifford Pinchot also swung into action. His reputation gave him
access to many legislators, and he used it to full advantage. During
November and December he conducted a buttonholing campaign
in Washington. First he saw Vice-President Garner, who said:
"The transfer will not be made if Congress has anything to say
about it." Garner, wrote Pinchot, "said definitely that he himself
was against the transfer of the Forest Service. It was a highly satisfactory interview." Cotton Ed Smith of South Carolina "actually
with tears in his eyes declaimed how he had been marked for
slaughter politically because he would not follow the New Deal.
He is red hot with us against the transfer to Ickes."[80] Although
not all the senators he saw proved so sympathetic, Pinchot grew
increasingly optimistic. "Franklin is getting into more and more
trouble on the Hill, and pretty much all the Senators from the
Western States, which have National Forests, are against Huffy
Harold and his buccaneering plans," he wrote. He believed that the
chances of victory were "excellent, thanks to Dunwoody."[81]

Pinchot, Dunwoody, and the Women's Clubs were joined by the
Department of Agriculture itself. Wallace's department, as part of
the executive branch, could not openly attack the Chief Executive's
program. Torn between duty and desire, it followed a checkered
course. In January 1937 the Department cautioned all employees
not to contribute "to outside agitation" concerning the Brownlow
Report.[82] After speaking to Wallace in February, Pinchot was
certain that the Secretary would not fight to hold Forestry.[83] All
letters to the Department of Agriculture protesting reorganization
were answered: "It is the attitude of this department that we go
along with it."[84] By the fall, however, Wallace had become more
aggressive. "Henry Wallace has at last turned loose and is on the

war path," wrote Pinchot on November 17, "and that is the very best thing that could have happened." Department replies to inquiries took on a new tone: "Secretary Wallace asked me to tell you that in his opinion forestry is an essential part of agriculture and that the Forest Service should remain in this Department."[85] Last-minute concessions brought Wallace back into line but, even so, a shrewd Washington lobbyist observed in February 1938: "Many of the opponents of the present bills are either friends of Henry Wallace or enemies of Ickes."[86]

All this opposition brought to life the minority of conservationists who endorsed reorganization. On November 4, 1937, Richard Lieber, President of the National Conference of State Parks, confided: "I am at this time engaged in a quiet manner to win over a number of my editor friends and strengthen the attitude of others respecting the Reorganization bill."[87] Two weeks later, Lieber, Tom Wallace, editor of the *Louisville Times* and a past honorary Vice-President of the American Forestry Association, Irving Brant, editorial writer for the St. Louis *Star-Times,* and Horace Albright, Director of the National Park Service from 1929 to 1933, addressed a joint letter to President Roosevelt. They wished to combat the propaganda issued by the Forest Service lobby. "We feel that their campaign may seriously jeopardize the approval of your program by Congress unless steps are taken to counteract their activities." More specifically, they hoped "to set up an effective organization" to promote a Department of Conservation. They conferred with the President in December and then set about publicizing their view. But their efforts did not convince many.[88]

Midway between this group and Pinchot's adherents stood the National Association of Audubon Societies. These devoted ornithologists, whose motto was "a bird in the bush is worth two in the hand," were dismayed by the violence of the transfer controversy. The Association offered a compromise bill creating a Department of Conservation but retaining the Department of Interior, and specifying those agencies, including the Forest Ser-

vice, which would go to the new department. This solution satisfied
neither side. Pinchot would take no chances, and Ickes saw no
point in retaining a Department of the Interior stripped of many
important functions. The effort at adjustment failed, and the
campaign against the Reorganization bill remained at fever pitch.[89]

The effectiveness of the Forest Service lobby could be measured
in the mailrooms of the House and Senate office buildings. Congressmen from the South and West were bombarded.[90] Those who
were loyal to Ickes uneasily requested material with which to
answer their constituents. Representative James Scrugham of Nevada declared: "My office has been flooded with protests. . .
Chambers of Commerce and farm bureaus all over the country have
taken up the cry."[91] Even a dedicated New Dealer like Congressman Jerry Voorhis, who supported reorganization, informed Roosevelt that "a great deal of sentiment in Southern California" opposed the transfer. "And I am writing now," he continued, "to add
my word of appeal to those which I am sure you have already
received on this matter."[92] Lindsay Warren, a sponsor of reorganization in the House, washed his hands of the Department of
Conservation.[93] Representative Bernard J. Gehrmann of Wisconsin
was subjected to more direct pressure; the director of the Wisconsin
Farm union supplied Dunwoody with a letter of introduction to
Gehrmann so that he might be able to "bring additional effort to
have G[ehrmann] perform."[94]

When Congress returned in January 1938, Dunwoody stepped
up his activity. He asked that volunteers come to Washington to
help influence congressmen, and warned his supporters to "be
prepared to meet any *surprise move* for the Department of Conservation plan."[95] On February 12 the surprise move was made:
the Senate Reorganization Committee voted to strike out the Department of Conservation. Rather than hailing this as a victory,
the forestry lobby chose to go on with the struggle. "We have won
an important battle, but what we must now prevent at all costs
is a let-down in the campaign, on the mistaken assumption that

we have won the war," Dunwoody affirmed. Since the bill still empowered the President to transfer Forestry to Interior, a clear-cut defeat was required.[96] When the Senate took up reorganization in March, the groups cooperating with Dunwoody pulled out all stops. The National Grange asked the master of every state Grange to write to his senators. Ovid Butler called for a "Final and Determined Drive" to defeat the bill.[97] As the Senate moved toward a vote, Dunwoody remained confident: "We are heading into the last round-up and things look exceedingly good."[98]

Dunwoody's euphoria was soon shattered. On March 22 the Senate rejected an amendment designed to exempt the Forest Service from transfer by a vote of 50–33. Even worse, only ten senators from the eleven Western states supported the amendment; ten voted against it, and two were absent. What had gone wrong? The elimination of the Department of Conservation had undermined the lobbyists in two ways. First, it allowed the Administration to make verbal promises not to transfer Forestry, which satisfied many senators. "There is no danger of any such transfer," said James Pope of Idaho, "I have received assurances which are entirely satisfactory."[99] Second, it permitted Henry Wallace to come out for the bill, since no transfer was necessarily implied. Wallace seemed willing to take his chances if the bill passed without a Department of Conservation. "I would be pleased to have your advice as to modifications which will best help the cause," he wrote to Senator Byrnes when drafting his public statement.[100] Department of Agriculture letters no longer even hinted that the bill was dangerous.[101] Moreover, Dunwoody seems to have mistaken friendly statements for firm commitments. For example, on March 7 he commented that Senator Alfred E. Reames of Oregon was supporting the anti-transfer forces. But Reames voted against exempting the Forest Service, voted against recommittal, and voted for the bill.[102]

When the House defeated the bill on April 8, Dunwoody claimed credit for the victory. He asserted that nineteen Western congressmen had voted to recommit solely because they opposed transfer of the Forest Service, but this was undoubtedly an exaggeration.[103] Western Republicans would have voted against the measure in any event. Of the Democrats from Western states, twenty-five voted for the bill and only nine voted against it. Still, the Forest Service lobby had played a crucial role in the conflict over reorganization. Given the closeness of the vote, Dunwoody could have determined the outcome by swinging only four doubtful votes. Also, the lobby had been instrumental in killing the Department of Conservation, which had been an integral part of Roosevelt's plan of reorganization. Moreover, the Administration's promise not to transfer the Forest Service meant that the lobby had been successful.

The transfer fight blazed anew in the years that followed, but Dunwoody took little part. In the summer of 1939 he lost his job with the California Chamber of Commerce; "I can get along for a month or so but *need a job badly*," he told Pinchot. He dreamed of leading a Western Forestry Association, to be "eternally on the job" to ward off a transfer, but even with the aid of Pinchot he could not raise adequate funds. He sold his house, hunted desperately for a job, and finally, in March 1940, was hired by the Food Stamp Division of the Federal Surplus Commodity Corporation.[104] But he yearned to return to the old fight. In 1940 he traveled through the West seeking to stir up opposition: "It is a godsend to me to be able to again get back into the harness even if it is only for a few weeks," he wrote. Although his reputation made it unwise for him to return to Washington, he never forgot the happy days when, in the thick of battle, he had commanded the anti-transfer forces.[105]

During the 1930's few observers managed to view the transfer issue in proper perspective. Conservation societies devoted so much effort to denouncing the Reorganization bill that they often lost sight of—or took for granted—the Administration's numerous contributions to their cause. Moreover, in their zeal to protect the position of one administrative agency, the groups which comprised the Forest Service lobby blocked the creation of an executive department which, in the long run, could have provided leadership and coherence for the conservation movement. Roosevelt's encouragement of rivalry among his subordinates often proved conducive to good administration; carried too far, as in the case of the Forest Service, it bred suspicion and distrust. It was ironic, but perhaps unavoidable, that the President's far-reaching plan for administrative improvement should have fostered that bureaucratic jealousy which was so disruptive of good administration.

# The Conflict

# CHAPTER VI

# The Senate Approves

On February 14, 1938, Harold Ickes and James Byrnes met informally with North Carolina's Senator Josiah W. Bailey. Bailey seemed "offish" at first, "but he warmed up after he had had a drink of whiskey, in which I joined him," reported Ickes. When Bailey conceded that Ickes had done a great favor in constructing a parkway for his state, Byrnes seized upon the senator's affability to solicit his support for reorganization. "While Bailey didn't commit himself, I rather think that he may go along with us on this bill," wrote Ickes. Just two weeks later, however, when the measure came up for consideration, Bailey took a leading role in opposition, and Byrnes remarked caustically: "I know that if I talked from now until Doomsday I would never convince the Senator from North Carolina."[1] The episodes in Byrnes's office and on the Senate floor were revealing. By the time the Senate took up reorganization, many had come to regard the bill as a symbol of New Deal reform. As a result, lines were tightly drawn.

1

The Reorganization bill which came before the Senate in March 1938 faced danger from several sources. First, it ran up against a cabal of conservative Democrats who had battled the Supreme Court proposal and resisted such reforms as wages and hours legislation. They believed that the President had deserted democratic ideals. Josiah Bailey voiced their concern; he wrote that Roosevelt's Court bill and Reorganization bill "would have given him all the powers of a dictator."[2] Virginia's venerable Carter

Glass asserted that Roosevelt had conspired with the "C.I.O. social desperadoes" to foment class hatred. Certain that the New Deal presented a "socialistic threat," Glass promised to maintain an "implacable antagonism to the dangerous and fool things that are being done in Washington."[3] Other Democrats—Edward Burke of Nebraska, Millard Tydings of Maryland, Royal Copeland of New York, Harry Byrd of Virginia, Bennett Clark of Missouri, Frederick Van Nuys of Indiana, Augustine Lonergan of Connecticut, Rush Holt of West Virginia—also belonged to this bloc. With the aid of the Republicans, anti-New Deal Democrats constituted a hard core of opposition to Rooseveltian reform. In all, they controlled about thirty-five votes.

In addition, reorganization drew the fire of many Democrats who could not be classified as anti-Administration. Many New Dealers deserted President Roosevelt to support amendments diluting the bill; several even voted for recommittal. Some senators, like Joseph O'Mahoney of Wyoming and Robert Wagner of New York, were reluctant to replace the bipartisan Civil Service Commission with a single administrator. Others, such as Key Pittman of Nevada and Elmer Thomas of Oklahoma, were unwilling to place pet bureaus at the mercy of the President. But it was the desire to retain Congressional prerogatives which united most factions against the measure.

Senatorial resentment toward increased executive authority ran deep. Banking on this, the conservative coalition hammered at one theme: Congress should not turn over still more power to the President. Senator Burke affirmed: "I am not willing, in the search for efficient management, to establish one-man rule in this country." Congress, cried Hiram Johnson of California, must not permit the bill to be "rammed down" its throat. "It is certainly up to a self-respecting Congress to see to it that this last vestige of congressional control is not taken away from us," protested Senator Hale of Maine. Bailey, rejecting the bill as a vast surrender of power, added sternly, "I shall make no confession of my incompetence."[4]

This jealous regard for Congressional prerogatives, combined with a general distrust of intellectuals, produced strong hostility toward the President's Committee on Administrative Management. Senator Clark sneered that Brownlow, Merriam, and Gulick were "not sufficiently familiar with the processes of government" to make wise recommendations. Even worse, "no member of that committee had any real belief in Congress or any real use for the legislative department of government." The difficulty with Brownlow's group, according to Senator Hiram Johnson, "was that they wrote a thesis from a schoolman's standpoint." One Republican hinted darkly that Brownlow was inspired by "special admiration for the British form of government." This would not be strange, he continued, since "this has been closely studied for many years at Harvard University and the University of Chicago."[5] Byrnes tried to assure his colleagues that the bill bore no academic stigma, but was not wholly successful.[6]

Critics of reorganization also asserted that the spread of German fascism should heighten Congressional determination not to permit an erosion of its privileges. Although a fear of totalitarianism may have influenced some senators, others merely used exaggerated claims for their rhetorical value and as a way to cloak more substantive objections. In addition, several senators argued that European dictatorship had caused the American people to be suspicious of executive authority. In the words of Senator Wheeler of Montana, it would be most unwise "for the Congress to make a further delegation of power at this particular time, when a certain form of hysteria is sweeping over the United States."[7]

For the most part, senatorial attitudes toward the Reorganization bill closely corresponded to confidence in President Roosevelt or suspicion of his motives. One senator stated: "It is a question of whether or not . . . we believe reorganization is of sufficient importance to delegate the authority to effect it to the President; and whether or not, in delegating that authority, we have confidence that the President will not abuse the power. I have such confidence."[8] George Norris pointed out that every assignment of power carried with it some danger of abuse but that government could not function unless such grants were made.[9] Opponents of reorganization, however, did not share this confidence in the President. They proceeded from the assumption that any grant of power would be abused unless hedged about with insuperable restrictions. At bottom, the issue was one of trust in the President.

## 2

Debate began on the Byrnes Reorganization bill on February 28. For two weeks, the Senate discussed general aspects of the measure, but lost several days on other matters. Finally, on March 8, Majority Leader Alben Barkley suggested taking up the noncontroversial Committee amendments. Byrd protested that only eight days had gone by and hoped that the Kentuckian would not insist upon an immediate vote. Barkley beat a rapid retreat. Two days later Byrnes clamped down upon digressions and even threatened to hold evening sessions. One Senator admitted: "It is perfectly obvious we have not been making any progress with the Reorganization bill." On March 11 opponents disclaimed any intent to filibuster, and Barkley managed to extract a pledge to vote upon the routine Committee amendments.[10] Events moved more swiftly during the week of Monday, March 14, as Committee revisions and two key amendments offered by the opposition were debated and voted upon. On March 18 the Senate leaders secured an agreement to limit debate.[11] The week of March 21 was devoted to several other important amendments; a final vote was scheduled for Monday, March 28.

The first challenge to the Reorganization bill was offered by David I. Walsh of Massachusetts, who submitted an amendment to retain the Civil Service Commission. His colleagues argued that the single administrator proposed in the bill would invite a "legalized expansion of spoilsmanship"; a bipartisan commission prevented bias and ensured public confidence. Die-hard opponents of the bill denounced the proposed change in more extreme language. Senator Clark foresaw "an absolute dictatorship" over government personnel, and Senator Borah remarked that "Mayor Hague might be appointed to fill this position."[12] The Civil Service Commission also commanded wide support among normally pro-Administration senators. Joseph O'Mahoney of Wyoming remained loyal on every other vote, but bolted to support the Walsh amendment. Even Senator Byrnes, who performed yeoman service in upholding the bill, let slip: ". . . I may say to the Senator, as I have already indicated, that my present preference is for the retention of the Civil Service Commission."[13]

Friends of the bill saw little reason to fear a civil service administrator. The work of the Commission, they claimed, was largely of a routine administrative nature and could best be performed by one man. Senator Robert La Follette pointed out that since the tenure of commissioners had averaged only four and one-half years, they tended in any case to reflect the President's views. Party labels were often illusory, he asserted, and the fifteen-year term for the proposed administrator would make his dismissal without good cause unlikely.[14] On March 15, when the Walsh amendment came up for a vote, it was defeated 50–38. The vote, however, was not a true test of strength. Some pro-Administration senators supported the amendment, and others voted against it who would soon throw off the traces. Senator Alva Adams of Colorado, for example, admitted that he had voted "rather contrary to my own inclinations. I did so because I wished to follow the wishes of the administration."[15]

Burton K. Wheeler of Montana then introduced an amendment designed to preserve Congressional authority. The Byrnes bill permitted the President to issue reorganization orders that would become effective within sixty calendar days unless both houses disapproved. Should they disapprove, the President might still veto their joint resolution, and only a two-thirds majority of both houses could override his veto. The Wheeler amendment allowed the President to submit orders, but they would not become effective until a majority of House and Senate approved. Each house would have just ten days in which to act. Whereas Byrnes wanted the order to take effect unless two thirds of both houses disapproved, Wheeler did not want the order to take effect until a majority of both houses approved.

Wheeler's reaffirmation of legislative prerogatives revealed both suspicion of Washington bureaucrats and disdain for Eastern intellectuals. The President would not decide each transfer, said Wheeler:

So who is going to do it? Some professor or some clerk in the department is going to do it. They are going to be the boys who will do the work, and they are going to say to my people in Montana, "We are going to abolish the Bureau of Indian Affairs" . . . Although they have never set foot on an Indian reservation in their lives, and have never seen an Indian, except in a moving picture in New York City, they are going to sit down in some office in Washington, prepare reports and tell the Members of the Senate and of the House what ought to be done . . .

Senators will have to "go down to the department with their hats in their hands and say . . . 'Please, Mr. Bureaucrat, don't do anything to hurt our people.' " Wheeler refused to concede that "some professor from Columbia University or from Harvard University" was more competent than Congress. To the Montanan the issue was one of moral rectitude; he would never admit that Congress lacked the "moral character," the "moral stamina," the "courage," to fulfill its role.[16]

Supporters of the Administration endeavored to refute Wheeler's arguments. They held that 531 Congressmen could not carry out reorganization because of conflicting pressures. It was less a matter of principle than of past performance; Congress had failed to do the job, and the President must be allowed to try. Besides, the bill did not alter governmental policies; it concerned the "purely executive matter" of improving "housekeeping facilities."[17] Roosevelt had not abused the power from 1933 to 1935; why assume he would do so now? Byrnes dismissed talk about the moral fiber of Congressmen: "We can make Fourth of July speeches about the matter, but the history of Congress shows that Congress just cannot make these changes."[18] Friends of the bill believed that making reorganization dependent upon affirmative legislative action would spell its doom.[19]

Although the Senate was prepared to vote on Wheeler's proposal on Wednesday, March 16, a hasty poll convinced Byrnes that he lacked two or three votes. He summoned supporters to run out the clock while he regrouped his forces. George Norris emerged from the cloakroom to assist, "his hair disheveled from a nap and his voice still heavy from sleep." Feverishly, Administration sides buttonholed Senators. Borah commented: "Certain things are being promised on and off the floor which amount to a reorganization of the Government before the bill is passed." Barkley then tried to set a definite time for voting on Thursday, but Wheeler refused since some of his partisans would be addressing St. Patrick's Day crowds.[20] By Thursday evening Wheeler recognized that Administration pressure had taken its toll: "I'm afraid we lose now by a few votes," he told reporters.[21] The vote on the amendment took place on Friday, March 18, after a bitter personal debate; the Administration scraped home by a tiny margin, 43–39.[22]

Every ounce of pressure had proved necessary to defeat Wheeler. The amendment failed partly because wavering senators like Cotton Ed Smith of South Carolina and Hattie Caraway of Arkansas held fast, and partly because four pro-Wheeler senators who were present agreed to pair their votes with four absentees; Bennett Clark ascribed the defeat to "four 'dead' pairs."[23] But the crucial votes were cast by Farmer-Laborite Ernest Lundeen of Minnesota and Tom Connally of Texas. They were the only senators to vote against the Wheeler amendment and, ten days later, against the Reorganization bill.[24] Ickes described how their votes were gained. Jesse Jones talked to his fellow-Texan Tom Connally and told Ickes: "Well, I think he is going to be all right, but don't say anything about it." Tom Corcoran concentrated on Lundeen, making several telephone calls from Ickes' office—to Governor Elmer Benson of Minnesota, to Lundeen's campaign manager, and to an influential judge, "all of whom brought pressure to bear upon Lundeen. It had been felt that Lundeen was lost to the cause, but he came through in the end." Having helped defeat Wheeler, Lundeen promptly turned around and voted against the Administration on nearly every other ballot.[25]

With the Wheeler amendment beaten, the economy bloc in the Senate, guided by Byrd, Bailey, and Burke, moved to cripple the bill. Byrd insisted that savings be a prime objective of reorganization and introduced several amendments to that effect. His followers had accepted reorganization in 1933 because the President promised economy, but now "we have been repeatedly informed that there is no intention and no hope of reducing the expenditures of the government."[26] Burke explained to an admirer: "If the Bill offered even a little efficiency or a little economy . . . I would be wholeheartedly supporting it, but the proponents of the Bill refuse to allow us to insert a clause demanding as little as five per cent reduction in governmental expenses."[27] Byrd fought hard to have his principle adopted, but Byrnes insisted that only a reduction of governmental functions, not a plan to transfer agencies, could save large sums of money. This failed to appease Byrd, who argued that Roosevelt had embarked upon "the most reckless spending orgy" in history. Still, his call for specific economies failed by a large margin.[28]

Byrd's attempt to preserve the power of the Comptroller-General—also inspired by his fiscal orthodoxy—found more support. The Senate debate on the accounting features of the bill rehashed familiar arguments. Byrd still insisted that the Comptroller prevented illegal expenditures and served as a legislative check upon wasteful spending; "He has been like a policeman patrolling up and down the streets."[29] Byrnes restated the case for separation of audit and control.[30] The two sides were hopelessly divided. When Byrnes affirmed that officials of the General Accounting Office had testified that they could only make a pre-audit when requested to do so by a department, Byrd retorted: "The General Accounting officers did not tell the Senator from Virginia that."[31] On March 24 Byrd's amendment protecting the Comptroller-General was beaten 47–36.

In Byrd's view, not only did the bill fail to insure economy and destroy an important check upon spending, but it proposed to create a Department of Welfare which, he believed, would saddle the nation with vast expenditures. Byrd asserted that the measure "blasts the last hope that the Federal Government can balance its budget." Above all, creating such a department would recognize the continuing responsibility of the federal government to care for the needy. The bill would make welfare appropriations a permanent feature of American life. "It ought not to be considered permanent," protested Bailey. "Our present objective ought to be to get rid of Federal relief, not to make of it a permanent national policy."[32] In effect, opponents claimed, creating a Department of Welfare would institutionalize the relief features of the New Deal.

Reorganization also had to overcome the enmity of those senators whose loyalty to special bureaus knew no bounds. Even the steadfast Elmer Thomas of Oklahoma voted for exclusion of the Veterans Administration. Key Pittman opposed the bill because he feared that the Forest Service might be given to his arch-foe, Harold Ickes. Pittman lambasted Ickes on the Senate floor as "stubborn" and "hard-headed." "We know there is nothing on earth he does not want to meddle in." Pittman's estimation of Eastern city-folk was not unlike that of Senator Wheeler: "I care not how great a lawyer a man may be or how great a progressive he may be; if he was born and raised in the Loop of Chicago I doubt his wisdom with regard to subjects having to do with the problems of the West."[33]

The Administration played fast and loose to ward off these incursions. Its spokesmen claimed that any exemption would destroy the principle of reorganization and, to clinch their case, gave private assurances that pet bureaus would be spared.[34] One senator informed worried veterans: "I was assured personally by James Roosevelt . . . that there was no plan to interfere with the Veterans' Administration."[35] Senator Pope of Idaho received "absolute and complete assurance" that the Forest Service would not be disturbed.[36] This expedient gained the votes needed to prevent bureau exemptions, but created what Barkley termed a "delicate situation." Said Wheeler: "If we are going to have private conversations with somebody in high authority in which we will be assured that a certain thing will not be done in order to get our votes, then we certainly have come down to a pretty low state in Congress." "I do not think the word 'assurances' is a happy word," confessed Barkley.[37]

Debate on the creation of a permanent National Resources Planning Board revealed many of the causes underlying the resistance to reorganization: Western distrust of Easterners, especially intellectuals; resistance to economic innovation; resentment at Executive usurpation of legislative privileges; and deep devotion to pet bureaus. Senator John Miller of Arkansas hoped that Americans would not let their lives be laid out by a group of "academic planners." Western senators wrote in a provision that two of the five members of the Board be chosen from west of the Mississippi River. The Senate instructed the Board to report to Congress as well as to the President, and Borah remarked, "I am glad that the existence of Congress has been recognized." The Board could study "natural," but not "human" resources, because the latter term "covers the entire sociological world, from birth control up . . . In the South it could go into the entire question of tenancy, sharecropping, and the effect of tenancy upon human nature." Partisans of the Army Corps of Engineers saw to it that the Board could only recommend, not initiate, river development projects.[38] The truncated National Resources Planning Board that emerged bore little resemblance to the planning agency envisioned by the Brownlow Committee.[39]

### 3

The Senate concluded debate on the Reorganization bill on Thursday, March 24. Fearful that the measure could not be beaten on Friday, opponents decided to defer a vote in the hope that they might attract more support over the week-end. Barkley, threatened with a filibuster, consented to hold the vote on Monday. He wished to take up other business on Friday, and the brief respite might allow him to solidify his forces. Both sides made the most of the temporary truce to try to gain the votes of those senators who appeared to be uncommitted.

The Administration exerted every possible pressure in an effort to put across the bill. On Friday, Senator Burke thought that the bill might be beaten only "if the Administration will assume a hands-off policy. The vote, however, will be close and we are not underestimating the power of the Administration to pick up three or four votes at a time like this."[40] James Farley appealed to senators to stand by the President, and recalled later that "many of them did so." Tom Corcoran helped out, too. On Sunday he called Ickes to assure him that the bill would go through. James Roosevelt impressed upon wandering senators the "imperative necessity" of returning by Monday.[41] "I have observed under different administrations the pressure which an administration can bring to bear," commented Senator Borah, "but I think this instance exceeded all others in the amount of pressure applied."[42]

Opponents of the bill, however, were not entirely without hope. Senator Burke counted 43 votes on each side, with the rest undecided. Frank Gannett believed one or two votes would turn the scale.[43] On Sunday, Gannett's National Committee to Uphold Constitutional Government inundated fourteen states whose Senators seemed doubtful with special-delivery appeals. In addition, Father Coughlin fulminated over the radio in a last-ditch effort to provoke popular protests. The result was staggering. At 8:00 o'clock Sunday night, Western Union had a backlog of 4,000 telegrams in New York, 2,000 in Detroit, 1,000 in Chicago, and 2,500 in Philadelphia. By Monday morning an avalanche of nearly 100,000 telegrams had hit Washington, and wire services had to set aside all other commercial business.[44] Later it was discovered that some telegrams had been forged, but the majority were authentic.[45]

The uncertainty of the vote added to the excitement of Monday's debate. Republicans, who had permitted Democrats to lead the attack on the bill so far, now demanded their due. Arthur Vandenberg of Michigan set the tone. Roosevelt envisioned a "potential dictatorship," said Vandenberg; it would come about "just a little easier after this bill transfers a few more key prerogatives from Capitol Hill to 1600 Pennsylvania Avenue." Arthur Capper of Kansas termed it a "vicious bill" which would "make one man virtually dictator of the Government of the United States for nearly 2 years." Some Democrats, like David I. Walsh of Massachusetts, joined in the attack.[46]

Many Democrats vigorously defended Roosevelt and reorganization. William McAdoo of California considered the President "sufficiently patriotic and sufficiently intelligent" to be trusted with authority. Senator Theodore Green of Rhode Island argued that personal interest and pressure from constituents made it impossible for Congress to carry out reorganization. He pointed out that cries of one-man rule clouded the issue; dictatorship arose from inefficient, not from well-run, government. Robert La Follette, Jr., cut through the tangle of rhetoric when he said: "I think among those who shout cries of alarm there is little realization that they are doing a disservice to the democratic process in crying 'Wolf!' 'Wolf!' and in raising an alarm over measures which do not justify

such conclusions." The retreat of democracies, La Follette suggested, stemmed from their failure to solve the problems of modern
industrialism.[47]

Other senators, who claimed to harbor no ill-will toward Roosevelt, still viewed reorganization with serious misgivings. "In the
main, it is not a bad bill," conceded Millard Tydings of Maryland,
"on the whole it is a good bill, it is a needed bill." Fears that
Roosevelt wanted to create a dictatorship were "unwarranted and
exaggerated." But Tydings thought that in the "present atmosphere
of world fear, at a time when people are looking for stability . . .
when civilization is in retreat, when democracies are going back-
ward step by step," Congress must reassert its role.[48] Senator
Prentiss M. Brown of Michigan agreed; he would stand against
Congressional abdication even though he considered Roosevelt
"the greatest liberal of this generation." Senator Copeland of New
York announced his opposition, adding sorrowfully: "The League
of Nations question did not divide the American people as this
reorganization plan has done."[49]

As the hour of voting approached, all the sentiments of party
regularity and personal loyalty were played upon by the Democrats. Senator Pat Harrison of Mississippi arose to affirm his faith
in the President. Alben Barkley asserted that recommittal would
kill reorganization "for a long time to come." He had done his
best as a member of the Senate Reorganization Committee; if the
bill were rejected he would resign from the Committee, with "no
hope that any bill we might write would be approved." Senator
Byrnes said he could not believe that Democrats would murder the
bill; he too would be obliged to step down from the Committee if
they did.[50] Several last-minute amendments were disposed of, and
the roll call began.

The Senate galleries were packed. The President's daughter-in-
law, Mrs. James Roosevelt, had to sit on a stairway. The diplomatic
galleries hung "Standing Room Only" signs. For a time the recommittal forces led by a slim margin. But the Administration slowly

closed the gap. Key Pittman's vote restored a one-vote lead to opponents of the measure, but then their hopes died. The next eight votes were against recommittal, and the bill was safe. The remaining Senators voted about as expected; the motion to recommit was defeated 48–43. The biggest surprise was Senator Wagner's sudden decision to renounce his pair for the bill and vote for recommittal. The bill then passed by a vote of 49–42 when Robert Bulkley of Ohio joined the majority. "The Administration fought desperately and took three or four votes away from the opposition," wrote Josiah Bailey sadly the next day.[51]

A bipartisan group of senators had voted against reorganization. Counting pairs, 46 Senators opposed the bill—15 Republicans, 2 Farmer-Laborites, and 29 Democrats. Many of the Democrats were disaffected conservatives or members of the Byrd-Bailey-Burke economy bloc. Observers pointed out that the bill was resisted by the same group of "anti-Rooseveltian Democrats who helped defeat the Court plan."[52] But significant exceptions should be noted: both Joseph O'Mahoney of Wyoming and Guy Gillette of Iowa fought Court-packing but supported reorganization. Senator Charles Andrews of Florida voted against the bill for obscure reasons. Months later, after talking to Andrews, Marvin McIntyre reported to Roosevelt: "The Senator says he was and is in favor of the Reorganization Bill including two new cabinet officers. He says that 'as you know I was caught last time in a jam.' "[53]

Of greater interest was the defection of several liberal New Dealers, notably Wagner, Pittman, Bulkley, and Homer Bone of Washington. They were not inspired by personal dislike for the President. But Pittman detested Harold Ickes and would not vote for any bill which might extend Ickes' authority or permit him to seize Forestry.[54] Robert Bulkley, whom Roosevelt backed for re-election later in the year, seemed especially resentful of the National Resources Planning Board. By switching on the final vote he showed his discomfort at opposing the President.[55] Homer Bone, following Burton Wheeler's lead, revealed Western resentment at

centralized authority and at the role of the Washington bureaucracy. When Bone won re-election in 1938 Amos Pinchot told him:
"I now feel justified by events for whatever part I played in urging
you to spit in the eye of the reorganization bill."[56]

But of all these defections, Robert Wagner's hurt the Administration most. Even dour Harold Ickes had to concede that Wagner
was a "genuine liberal." His vote had seemed sure. Although
Wagner supported the Walsh civil service amendment, he consistently sided with the Administration in beating back other modifications. Certainly opponents of the bill did not see in Wagner a
potential ally. When Wagner asked Senator Clark to explain why
he favored exemption for the Bureau of Animal Industry, Clark
responded: "I do not know whether it would be possible to explain
to the Senator . . . what the Bureau of Animal Industry is. Living
in New York, the chances are he has never seen an animal."
Wagner replied acidly: "After the explanation, I am sure I will
vote against the amendment."[57]

To be sure, as the final vote approached, some newspapers
reported Wagner wavering. The Senator was subjected to several
kinds of pressure: he was the target of thousands of telegrams; he
was made forcibly aware of the opposition of the American Federation of Labor; and, according to some, he was influenced by the
Catholic Church, which feared a transfer of the Office of Education.
"Wagner was undecided until the last few days," commented one
Washington observer, "and found the pressure against the reorganization bill too strong to resist." "Wagner was scared in by labor
and the Catholic Church," Ben Cohen informed Ickes.[58]

But Wagner was not a man to be bullied into voting against the
dictates of conscience. In an unusual gesture he released a statement explaining his decision. He strongly favored a Department of
Welfare, he said, and voted as he did "with considerable regret and
only after long deliberation." He gave two reasons for his action.
First, he wished to retain the bipartisan Civil Service Commission.
Second, he believed that Congress "should not shirk its essential

legislative duties." Though he did not go as far as Wheeler, he thought Congress should reserve the right to stop presidential orders by a simple majority rather than by a two-thirds vote: "An amendment to this effect [had] been prepared by several Senators and on Monday morning I strongly urged acceptance of it by the leaders . . . without success. I am sure its adoption would have removed the greater part of the opposition to the measure."[59] Although he did not so state, Wagner may also have seen in reorganization a threat to the independent status of the NLRB, which Frances Perkins ardently desired to annex to the Labor Department, and to the Housing Administration, which Harold Ickes thought belonged in Interior. Wagner's success in thwarting their ambitions had caused ill-will in the past; he apparently felt that administrative location intimately affected the policy and program of the agencies he had fathered.[60]

The bill passed because it found favor with a bloc of pro-Roosevelt New Dealers and a number of disinterested men to whom reorganization seemed urgent. William McAdoo of California explained simply: "No one had offered me any patronage to vote for this bill . . . I think the best interests of the country demand that something be done to effect a more efficient and economic administration of the government."[61] Rhode Island's Theodore F. Green agreed. When Gifford Pinchot tried to persuade him to vote against the bill in order to protect the Forest Service, Green was unmoved. "He rejects emphatically all arguments based on Ickes and the Department of the Interior—and wants to know only what is good administration," reported Pinchot ruefully.[62]

Moreover, if some New Dealers deserted the President, conservatives provided the margin of victory. Influential Southerners like Pat Harrison, Cotton Ed Smith, Richard Russell, and Allen Ellender stood firm, as did several other conservatives.[63] Byrnes also managed to hold three crucial votes: George Berry of Tennessee, Guy Gillette of Iowa, and Fred Brown of New Hampshire supported the bill even though they thought that it delegated too much authority to the President.[64] The Administration applied whatever pressure it could; columnists openly speculated that Hattie Caraway's interest in a $40,000,000 flood control project for Arkansas dictated her vote. Finally, Administration assurances regarding pet agencies gained some votes.[65]

George Norris of Nebraska, who supported reorganization, illustrates the reluctance with which many senators sided with the Administration. Norris voted for the bill as hesitantly as Wagner voted against it. Similar pressures operated upon each. Norris received dozens of letters from constituents asking him to oppose the measure. A few were crank letters, but most were complimentary and came from men and women who had voted for him in the past. A lady in Kearney wrote: " 'You can't beat Norris' has been a Nebraska slogan for many years but if you vote *yes* on this government reorganization bill coming up next week your name will be mentioned hereafter with anything but the respect in which you have been held. It is incredible the way you have lost your grip and play 'follow the leader.' "[66] Most of the mail called for an assertion of Congressional independence. While Norris voted against the Wheeler amendment, he admitted grudgingly that it had some attractive features.[67]

In addition, Norris strongly opposed any change in the location of the Forest Service or in the status of the TVA.[68] On March 16 he was reminded that, if reorganization passed, the TVA might be put under a department. "If that be true," he replied, "then the bill should be amended by including the Tennessee Valley Authority and, perhaps, some others in the exemption."[69] His unhappiness was evident when, a few days later, he announced he would vote against all exemptions "because I have reached the conclusion— although I am not at all enthusiastic about it—that we ought to pass the reorganization bill. When an amendment with respect to the TVA is offered, I shall vote against it. At least, I shall be consistent." Before debate began, he said, he had expected to offer an amendment exempting the Forest Service; now he realized that those who were offering such amendments really wanted to defeat the purposes of the bill. "Perhaps they will perform a good service if they do," he added gloomily.[70]

But Norris's reservations gave way before his knowledge of the need for reorganization, his confidence in Roosevelt's good will, and his aversion to reactionary opponents of the bill. He had "faith," he told the Senate, that the President "will not do a foolish, senseless thing" such as curtailing the independence of the TVA.[71] And who opposed the President? Norris saw the sinister hand of the private power interests: "I am at a loss to know why some . . . interests fought this bill. There was nothing in it that I know of to have induced private power companies to fight it, and yet they did fight it bitterly. I can see no motive in such a course, except that they thought they saw in the defeat of the Reorganization bill an opportunity to destroy the influence of the President in the carrying out of his program in other fields."[72] Norris's private secretary believed that the House liberals who voted against the bill "chose to follow the leadership of those representing the Republican conservatives and Tammany Hall in preference to that of President Roosevelt."[73] Norris probably agreed, and could not bring himself to do the same. Still, when the subject of transfer of the TVA arose at a later time, Norris told Roosevelt: "I would never have supported the Reorganization bill, if I had had any idea or belief that the TVA was going to be modified in any way."[74]

Senatorial opponents of reorganization took heart in the modifications they had won. Senator Bailey wrote: "The Reorganization Bill passed, but we had amended it thirty-two times, not to mention the changes made in the Committee. It is not a good bill. It will be further changed in the House and in the last analysis I hope it will not be really harmful."[75] In final form the Byrnes bill departed in several ways from the recommendations of the President's Committee. It limited to two years the President's authority to make transfers, and excluded the independent regulatory commissions and the Army Engineers. It extended the merit system, but not to cover positions filled by the President with the advice and consent of the Senate; higher salaries were eliminated; the civil service administrator was to be appointed without an examination. The bill created an independent Auditor-General; it eliminated the office of Comptroller-General and transferred its functions to the Bureau of the Budget rather than to the Secretary of the Treasury. The bill set up a Department of Welfare, but made no provision for a Department of Conservation or a Department of Public Works.

But the greatest victory for opponents of reorganization was having the Senate bill sent to the House of Representatives. No one had expected that this would occur. It was assumed that just before the final vote the Senate leadership would move to substitute one of the bills passed by the House in the summer of 1937, strike out everything but the enacting clause, and substitute the text of the Senate bill. In this way the bill could go directly to conference. Each house would then vote on the conference report and, as one Congressman said, "the odds are about one hundred to one" that it would be accepted.[76] The failure of this plan may be ascribed to parliamentary miscues and the hostility of the men presiding over the Senate.

On Thursday, March 24, the Senate had set the rules to govern debate on the following Monday, when the motion to recommit would be considered. Majority Leader Alben Barkley suggested that time be equally divided and that a vote be taken no later than 3:00 P.M. Walter George of Georgia arose indignantly. He pointed out that if a senator offered the antilynching bill as an amendment at 2:45, only fifteen minutes would remain to discuss it. Barkley, seeking a way to avert this, asked unanimous consent that no amendment relating to the antilynching bill be considered in order. The Senate agreed. He then asked that the Senate vote at three o'clock on all pending amendments and on the motion to recommit. The vote on passage might be held up to two hours later.[77]

On Monday, after the motion to recommit had failed, but before the final vote, Barkley moved to take up one of the House bills, retain only the enacting clause, and substitute the text of the Senate bill. Vice-President Garner, in the Chair, replied that this would violate the unanimous-consent agreement which forbade introducing any amendment after three o'clock. Barkley protested that he was offering a motion to consider a bill on the calendar, not an amendment. Garner disagreed, claiming that the resolution forced the Senate to vote on recommittal at three o'clock and on passage by five o'clock. "If the House bill should be substituted for Senate bill 3331, the Senate could not possibly vote on Senate bill 3331. The Chair holds that under that agreement no amendment is in order, and no substitute is in order." No appeal could be made, and the Senate proceeded to vote on the bill immediately. Garner left the Chamber.[78]

When the vote was announced, Byrnes, in a second effort to have the bill sent directly to conference, again moved to consider the House bill. In desperation, Clark called a quorum—92 senators answered. Byrnes again moved to take up the House bill. Clark asked if the motion was debatable; the Chair ruled that it was. The Senate was in an uproar. La Follette shouted: "I make the point of order that the Senate is not in order." With senators clamoring for recognition, Senator Burke obtained the floor.[79] Perhaps Burke was called on because someone tugged at Byrnes's jacket and distracted him.[80] Perhaps the Chair was predisposed to recognize Burke. Occupying it in Garner's absence was the President *pro tem,* a man high in Democratic ranks, a member of the Senate for twenty-five years—Key Pittman of Nevada.[81]

Burke now held the floor and although Byrnes tried several parliamentary maneuvers he could not regain command. Opposition leaders then apparently threatened to launch an all-out filibuster if Byrnes insisted on bypassing the House. Faced with this choice, while Burke droned on, Byrnes sent emissaries to the House to find out if the bill would have to hurdle the Rules Committee. When he was assured that it held privileged status and would avoid Rules,

Byrnes capitulated.[82] The motion to consider the House bill was withdrawn. At the last minute, victory had eluded the Administration. Opponents of reorganization had received a second chance, and, as Senator Bailey said on the day after the Senate voted, "the opposition is continuing to gain strength."[83]

# CHAPTER VII

# Roosevelt, Reorganization, and the Public

By the spring of 1938 Roosevelt's popularity had plunged to the lowest point since he first took office. Alarmed by the advance of dictatorship abroad and angered by the recession at home, Americans grew more and more critical of the President. Confronted with evidence of widespread dissatisfaction, Roosevelt tried to reassure the public; instead, he generated more hostility. The Reorganization bill, which came before Congress just when popular discontent reached its height, became the vehicle through which Americans expressed their displeasure with Roosevelt's leadership.

1

The President's decline in popularity was strikingly illustrated by public opinion polls. In winning re-election in 1936, Roosevelt received slightly over 60 per cent of the popular vote. Nearly a year later, 62.8 per cent of those polled asserted that they would vote for the President; in mid-January 1938, 61.2 per cent still favored him. But the next three months saw an abrupt reversal in popular sentiment. Roosevelt lost support rapidly; by April 13, 1938, only 54.4 per cent declared that they backed the President. Indeed, most people thought that Roosevelt was less popular than he really was. James M. Burns has pointed out that "during the first term Roosevelt always gave the *impression* of popularity, while in 1938 that impression no longer existed."[1]

Many observers agreed that the President's hold upon the people was weaker in April 1938 than ever before. On April 7 a Western mine owner described the prevailing mood to Roosevelt: "I do business with fifty-three firms in Arizona and California . . . A year ago, many of them were mildly New Dealish. Today, they were without exception, panic stricken opponents of all we stand for . . . Particularly was I shocked at the attitude of our Superintendents, foremen and minor executives. They were all friendly to you a year ago. They are all bitter in their attacks on you now."[2] In March a New York minister found evidence of "a steady change of public opinion from pro-Roosevelt to anti-Roosevelt."[3] A lawyer in Wisconsin sensed a "growing tide of resentment against the administration."[4] "I am much impressed by the change from six weeks ago," wrote a Minnesotan early in April: "Persons who would not question a thing the President did then are either beginning to wonder or are against him."[5] On April 1 a New Dealer informed the President sadly: "In recent weeks I have heard many expressions of pity and ridicule where formerly there was only praise . . . The drift seems to be definitely against you . . ."[6]

Despite rising opposition, Roosevelt continued to command the support of a majority of the people. His personal charm seemed undiminished; more than 80 per cent of those surveyed liked his "personality."[7] Many who expressed dissatisfaction with aspects of the President's program were not prepared to embrace the Republicans. "I have never been a Roosevelt enthusiast and am not now," wrote John Dewey on March 11. But he recognized that most people believed in the President and feared "the other crowd." Dewey thought that the President would hold his position "until there is some alternative group with a policy that makes some constructive appeal."[8]

Although Roosevelt retained wide support, his Reorganization bill did not. Polls taken in March 1938 showed 20 per cent in favor of reorganization, 35 per cent opposed, and 45 per cent undecided.[9] Nor can it be argued that those who expressed disapproval were all Republicans. Reorganization had less support among Roosevelt's admirers than any other New Deal measure. Sampling only those who supported the President, Elmo Roper reported in July that 67 per cent also approved of his Wages and Hours bill, 61 per cent approved of his international policy, 57 per cent approved of his attitude toward business and labor, but that only 36 per cent approved of the Reorganization bill.[10] Although the polls showed sharp differences in class response, opposition was not confined to any one segment of the population: 45 per cent of the factory workers, 61 per cent of the farmers, 64 per cent of the small businessmen, and 70 per cent of the white-collar workers condemned the measure.[11] Had a popular referendum on reorganization been held in April 1938, the bill would have been defeated.

The opposition to the Reorganization bill reflected a deep yearning for stability on the part of many Americans. Faced with the dazzling triumph of European dictators, Americans resisted any increase in presidential power. Trapped by the disaster of a sharp recession, Americans rapidly lost confidence in New Deal innovations. The Reorganization bill, symbolizing change and presidential authority, encountered a widespread longing for stability. A woman in Philadelphia captured this sentiment in explaining why she opposed the Reorganization bill: "We are just confused with so many changes and theories, and want to stop until we get on our feet again."[12]

Events in Europe during the month of March 1938 produced horror and dismay in the United States. Newspaper headlines on three successive days trumpeted German conquests: "Nazis Seize Austria After Hitler Ultimatum . . . Hitler Enters Austria in Triumphal Parade . . . Austria Absorbed into German Reich."[13] In the days that followed, Hitler victimized Jews and Catholics and consolidated his control over Austria. In Spain Loyalist resistance to Franco was near collapse. In Russia the purge trials culminated in death sentences for eighteen former Communist leaders. Democracy seemed feeble in the face of totalitarian triumph. Within the space of six weeks, Anthony Eden stepped down as Foreign Minister to protest Britain's policy of appeasement, and Leon Blum, attempting to revitalize France, was replaced by Daladier.

Hitler's triumph heightened American suspicion of executive power. In the spring of 1938 few citizens thought that President Roosevelt should have more authority; many were convinced that increased authority paved the way for dictatorship. "We have just witnessed, in Europe, what happens when one man is permitted too much power—Hitler in Austria," protested one citizen.[14] "Events of the past few days in the final collapse of every vestige of freedom in Austria, resulting from the transfer of too much power by the people to their leaders, should be a lesson," admonished another.[15] A friendly businessman informed the President that his employees had been taught by newspapers "to unconsciously group four names, Hitler, Stalin, Mussolini and Roosevelt."[16] By linking the Reorganization bill with "dictatorship" and "one-man rule," Roosevelt's opponents played upon all the fears and anxieties produced by European dictatorship.

The slump which began in the fall of 1937 and reached rock bottom in April 1938 also strengthened opponents of reorganization. Within ten months, industrial production declined by 33 per cent, and industrial stock prices by 50 per cent. Nearly four million people lost their jobs, boosting total unemployment to eleven and one-half million. National income shrunk by $9 billion, a drop of 12 per cent.[17] "Maybe this depression hasn't hit you folks yet," wrote an irate citizen to his congressman, "but believe me it is on its way to becoming the worst we have ever had. And, whether we like it or not, we can't help its being called the 'Roosevelt Depression' because he has now been president for over five years."[18]

The recession affected reorganization in several ways. Some, who held the Administration responsible for their personal distress, snatched at any opportunity to rebuke the President. Others, who believed that concessions were needed to restore business confidence, hoped that defeat of the bill would appease businessmen and encourage investment. Moreover, the recession bred resentment at the rapid pace of change since 1933. New Dealers had conducted endless experiments, yet once again the nation faced misery. The economic slump, by pointing up the failure of New Deal innovation, aroused hostility to all further innovation. People opposed the Reorganization bill because it was a symbol of change.

Roosevelt's failure to cure the recession turned many people against the Reorganization bill. Deprivation caused anger and dismay; the bill became a target for resentment. One appeal to Roosevelt from a midwestern doctor revealed the frustration bred by distress: "We are absolutely suffering from this depression. My clients are unemployed, underfed, nervous, harassed. Although working day and night I cannot pay my bills, we can only stand so much persecution, then desperation sets in. We had confidence in you but that confidence is fading. Why not use your splendid ability in restoring confidence, in putting aside this pernicious Reorganization bill."[19] Letters to members of Congress sounded the same note. "Times are terrible out here," one citizen reported: "The home folk are . . . distrustful, dissatisfied and unhappy."[20] "There is so much resentment, anger and confusion in the minds of the people," explained another, "that they are likely to wipe the slate clean."[21] A substantial majority of those hardest hit by the recession, the unemployed, opposed the Reorganization bill.[22] "The country is in a bad mood to receive such a bill under present economic conditions," noted one observer.[23]

Those who held the Administration responsible for the recession called for concessions to renew business confidence. The idea that government hostility to private enterprise caused the slump gained broad acceptance. Since businessmen feared reorganization, the bill must be sacrificed. It was not the bill's effect upon the economy, but its effect upon business psychology that mattered. "Everyone is scared to death, even if they are working yet," reported a Kansan: "What this country needs is a good dose of confidence."[24] One constituent informed Representative Hull of Wisconsin that "something must be done quickly to help restore business confidence instead of still further destroying it as the Reorganization bill is doing. . . DON'T LET US DOWN! ! !"[25] An Oklahoma oil producer asked his congressman: "Why don't you folks wake up to the fact that we are facing a very serious depression; that the President is making no efforts to stop the business decline, but rather is continuing to give business a kick in the pants at every opportunity, and certainly the Reorganization bill will only aggravate the situation."[26] A New England lawyer expressed a common belief when he asserted: "The total defeat of the Reorganization bill would . . . add more than any one event to the general public confidence."[27]

The recession also helped produce a national mood hostile to experimentation of any kind. Success, measured by rising indices, had justified New Deal innovations in the realm of spending, taxation, and government control; the new downturn brought an inevitable reaction—revulsion at further change. "What is the use of giving the President any more power than he already has? Things are just as bad as they were in 1932," commented a woman in New York. A resident of Minneapolis asserted that "Congress cannot afford to waste time on NEW DEAL schemes and plans to bring about Utopia, but must get down to brass tacks to do something constructive to save business and industry,—they are facing disaster!"[28] For many the Reorganization bill represented another radical break with tradition. One citizen complained bitterly that "things are mighty tough and seem to be getting worse every day." All of his neighbors, he continued, "feel that for the time being we have had enough new schemes that are intended to work miracles, but instead make things worse, so for God's sake don't let us down now. KILL THIS REORGANIZATION BILL."[29]

Outspoken enemies of the New Deal thought that this popular dissatisfaction heralded a return to conservatism. Frank Gannett crowed: "The common man is beginning to realize that he has been bunkoed with the Roosevelt program. Once he loses faith in Roosevelt's magic, there will be a great over-turning in politics."[30] But the nation was not rejecting what Roosevelt had already done; it was affirming that enough had been done. Most Americans did not wish to undo the New Deal, but neither did they wish to renew it. A shrewd Washington politician caught this sentiment when he advised Speaker William Bankhead to postpone reorganization: "We have been feeding the people too fast; they have not had time to digest the reform legislation of the last five years . . . I sense a feeling that the country wants us to stop breaking the speed laws in Congress."[31]

The anxiety spawned by depression and dictatorship helps explain a unique episode in the reorganization controversy: the journey of the "Paul Reveres." The Reveres were inspired by Father Coughlin's radio sermon on Sunday, April 3, 1938. Although Coughlin had called for a mass telegram campaign to defeat reorganization in the Senate, he now admitted that modifications had improved the bill. Nevertheless, the "original spirit" of the bill—"the spirit of centralization of power, the spirit of perpetuating a needless emergency, the spirit of defeatism"—remained noxious. Moreover, should the bill go to conference, a "hand picked group" of New Dealers could wait until the popular clamor subsided and, "with lightning rapidity," submit the original bill. "At that time my broadcast season will have terminated," he added modestly.[32]

To ensure defeat of the Reorganization bill Coughlin devised a bold plan. Advocates of the measure, he knew, expected him to call for a renewed telegram campaign. "That would be unsound strategy at this moment," he explained. "This is not the time for sending more telegrams. It is inopportune." Written messages had already exerted their influence upon Congress; now, more direct protests were needed. Accordingly, Coughlin advocated that small committees of "intelligent, educated, judicial" citizens act as "modern Paul Reveres whose business will be to ride to Washington and rouse from slumber their respective Representative and Senator within the next 2 weeks."[33] Coughlin did not envision a mass march upon Washington but stressed instead the desirability of small groups from widely dispersed areas.

Recruitment of Paul Reveres got under way on Monday, April 4. Coughlin's radio audience was large. "Right now," wrote one listener, "I came from down town, the pool halls, hotels, restaurants, and taverns, too, seems everyone is listening in on the air, and commenting on what Father Coughlin . . . gave out."[34] The Hearst newspapers swung into the campaign, providing front-page publicity and information concerning ticket-buying and times of departure. The demonstration was sponsored by a cluster of ultra-right-wing organizations which included the National Defenders, the Friends of Social Justice, the American Guardian Society, the American Coalition, the Society for Money Reforms, and the Junior Order of United American Mechanics. A few business groups, such as the New York Board of Trade, and local veterans' organizations, joined the drive.[35] Two New Yorkers, Hugh O'Connell and James O'Kelly, actually directed the operation. O'Kelly, describing himself as a salesman, said "business was bad and he had nothing to sell."[36]

On Tuesday evening, twenty-five hundred people packed the Hippodrome in New York City to rally Reveres to the cause. They heard several speakers blast the Reorganization bill. Representative Arthur Lamneck of Ohio cried that it would give Roosevelt immense power "without the Congress having a damn thing to say about it." One newsman observed: "The audience was obviously composed of solid citizens, unaccustomed to attend mass meetings. They filed in quietly. They joined in the singing of patriotic songs. They stood reverently and sang 'Onward Christian Soldiers.' " Late Wednesday night, fourteen hundred New Yorkers boarded a chartered train for Washington; a round-trip ticket cost $4.50.[37]

They arrived in the Capital for breakfast on Thursday morning and greeted smaller delegations from Philadelphia, Boston, and

Baltimore. A reporter described the marchers as members of the "inarticulate middle classes." About half of the demonstrators were women; Paul Revere's great-great-granddaughter led the Boston contingent. One man donned the garb of the midnight rider and bore a sign reading, "KILL THE BILL." Another asserted: "I see no reason why Congress should give the President powers of a Julius Caesar." A Philadelphian told the marchers: "You must impress upon the Congress that unless they vote against the bill they will not return here next fall."[38] More than one hundred New Yorkers demanded that their congressmen leave the House floor to meet them. The congressmen obeyed. Representatives Matthew Merritt and William B. Barry promised that "the vote on final disposition will please you all." Representatives Donald O'Toole, John Boylan, and Eugene Keogh were evasive. "We have a right to know where you stand," insisted one citizen. "The record will show that," Keogh parried.[39] The petitioners returned home that same evening, and within a few days a leader announced: "The Paul Revere headquarters will remain open as a permanent institution to watch legislation in the future."[40]

The ride of the Reveres was an exaggerated expression of the discontent which existed in the spring of 1938. The rapid expansion of German Fascism and the failure of American democracy to provide prosperity had produced widespread anxiety. This malaise was exploited by frenzied opponents of the Reorganization bill, who succeeded in duping many Americans. Few clearly understood the provisions of the bill. Nevertheless, the measure had come to symbolize executive power and radical change at a time when men, above all else, sought security.

## 2

On March 2, 1938, Harold Ickes wrote in his diary: "It looks to me as if all the courage has oozed out of the President." With mounting despair, Ickes repeated his complaint in the weeks that

followed. Roosevelt, he said, acted like a "beaten man." Others
close to the President agreed: Tom Corcoran admitted that he was
"thoroughly disgusted" with Roosevelt's "lack of aggressive leadership." One Washington columnist, Raymond Clapper, believed that
"the whole country is feeling Roosevelt's indecision and flounder-
ing."[41] As the recession worsened and attacks upon the Reorganization bill grew more vicious, Roosevelt appeared unable to provide direction for the country or for Congress.

In part, Roosevelt's helplessness stemmed from the kind of
criticism leveled at the Reorganization bill. The charges were
often so unfair that they defied effective refutation. Bewildered by
conflicting claims, many citizens hoped for clarification. "From such
information as I have been able to gather from Radio addresses
and the Press," a man from Rochester wrote the President, it
seemed that the bill would make the President a dictator. "If this
is true, will you kindly instruct someone to advise me in *simple,*
*understandable* terms 'Why such drastic action is necessary?' " he
asked.[42] Indeed, Roosevelt considered it beneath the dignity of his
office to respond to wild, irresponsible charges. When, early in
April, several friends suggested that he explain the bill in a fireside
chat, Roosevelt declined: ". . . the President of the United States
cannot engage in a radio debate with the Boake Carters and Father
Coughlins of life!"[43]

Roosevelt's irresolution also reflected his anxiety over the recession. The President was not prepared to abandon his drive for a
balanced budget. He told Ickes that deficit spending was justified
"when the water had reached the bottom of the well," but not
when it was "within twenty-five or thirty per cent of the top."[44]
Henry Morgenthau's advice and the pressure of the business community reinforced Roosevelt's fiscal orthodoxy. The President refused to embark upon renewed spending until economic conditions
were so bad that no other alternative remained. To the public,
therefore, Roosevelt appeared indecisive and inept. According to

one congressman, people were wondering if the recession "has President Roosevelt licked, and if he has no more program than Hoover had six years ago."[45]

Roosevelt's actions late in March illustrate the extent to which he had—for the moment—lost his political touch. His involvement in the internal affairs of the Tennessee Valley Authority, his statement to the press when the Senate passed the Reorganization bill, and his public disavowal of dictatorial ambitions tended to increase popular suspicion. Each of these three events enhanced the fear that Roosevelt sought unreasonable power. In each case the press played a crucial role in magnifying minor lapses into issues of national importance.

For some time, Dr. Arthur E. Morgan, Chairman of the TVA, had carried on a running feud with his fellow Board members, Harcourt A. Morgan and David Lilienthal. Harcourt Morgan and Lilienthal considered Arthur Morgan's emphasis upon central planning to be dangerous and impractical. The Chairman feared that Lilienthal's bellicosity toward the power companies would jeopardize the effectiveness of the Authority.[46] The dispute flared into the open in December 1937 when Dr. Morgan accused his colleagues of showing bad faith in settling a claim brought against the TVA by Major George Berry of Tennessee. Harcourt Morgan and Lilienthal, in turn, charged that the Chairman pursued a "rule or ruin" policy and suggested that he resign. The controversy simmered until early in March 1938 when Arthur Morgan publicly assailed his colleagues, calling Lilienthal a man of "evasion, intrigue, and sharp strategy" who made "Machiavelli seem open and candid." Branding the Berry claims an "effort at a deliberate, barefaced steal," he posed as protector of the public interest, fighting to preserve "honesty, openness, decency, and fairness in government."[47]

With charges of chicanery filling the air, Roosevelt had no choice but to intervene. At a White House conference on March 11 he asked Arthur Morgan to substantiate his charges by producing specific evidence of dishonesty. Morgan refused to answer, but instead called for a Congressional investigation. The President adjourned the hearing for a week, but Morgan remained adamant. He would produce no evidence, would answer no questions, and would not submit to any presidential inquiry. Condemning his "reckless and astounding conduct," Roosevelt insisted that Morgan either withdraw his charges or resign. Morgan replied that the President did not have the power either to remove or suspend him. On March 23 the President proceeded to remove Morgan from the Board of the TVA.[48]

Although a Congressional investigation later failed to uncover any scandal, Arthur Morgan gained a good deal of public sympathy in March 1938. Newspapers portrayed him as a champion of the little man, unjustly persecuted by a power-hungry President. Senator Styles Bridges of New Hampshire predicted that Morgan would be remembered as another Dreyfus. Roosevelt had "convicted an innocent man without a trial," Bridges claimed; this was "typical of the acts of a dictator."[49] On March 20 the noted historian Allan Nevins wrote: "From being on the whole an admirer of Roosevelt, I have swung now into active dislike of the man. He has made one blunder after another since his reelection; some of them beyond all forgiveness. The Supreme Court proposal was bad . . . and now he seems capping the climax in the way he is handling the T.V.A. The man lacks principle."[50] The Morgan case became enmeshed with economic discontent and hostility toward the Reorganization bill. One angry citizen wrote the President: "So you promise 'I don't want to be a dictator.' Why, in Hell, did you fire Dr. Morgan then? This Reorganization Bill *Shall not pass*. I wish you had my job of trying to sell lumber to dealers whose sheds are full and see no customers. Why don't you do something?"[51] Roosevelt's high-handed dismissal of Morgan, asserted a North Carolinian, proved that he could not be trusted with broad power.[52]

On Tuesday, March 29, while Roosevelt was vacationing at Warm Springs, reporters crowded about his car for an impromptu

press conference. When asked to comment upon Senate passage of
the Reorganization bill, Roosevelt, who rarely permitted direct
quotation, responded: "It proves that the Senate cannot be purchased by organized telegrams based on direct misrepresentation."
His use of the word "purchased" caused an immediate uproar.
Senators rushed to defend their honor. Hiram Johnson snapped
that the remark was "unjust and outrageous and should never have
been made by a President of the United States."[53] Lawrence Lewis,
of Colorado, a prominent Democrat, believed that the statement
had "produced a very bad reaction."[54] The President's remark offended congressmen and their constituents who had expressed reservations about the bill. Representative Clifford Hope of Kansas
said: "The President didn't help his bill any by his remarks about
the Senate not having been bought. That really did stir the animals
up."[55]

What led Roosevelt, master of the apt phrase, to commit such a
blunder? The text of the press conference indicates that his remark
was made not in a moment of anger, but in bantering with reporters.
A steady stream of jokes had marked the interview. Then a reporter asked: "How about the Senate fight on the passage of the
Reorganization Bill?"

*The President:* I would love to give you a direct quote on that.
*Question:* We would take it in a minute. [Laughter]
*The President:* Mac says, 'No.' Didn't he? [Laughter]
*Question:* I would love to get something on that bill.
*The President:* Well, I will tell you, I will take a shot at it: It proves
     that the Senate cannot be purchased by organized telegrams based
     on direct misrepresentation.
*Mr. McIntyre:* Do you want to use that word, 'purchased'?
*The President:* Yes, it is all right.
*Question:* Can we put this in direct quotes?
*The President:* Yes it is all right. Is that all right?
*Question:* Yes.
*Mr. McIntyre:* Fred [Mr. Storm] can remember the time that that
     would be embarrassing to him. [Laughter]
*The President:* That was in his other life. [Laughter]

*Question:* How many has he now? [Laughter]
*The President:* He was in a coma for a few months. [Laughter][56]

Egged on by the newsmen, Roosevelt had, in effect, taken a dare. Having used the unfortunate phrase—which probably expressed his honest opinion—he refused to retract it. As one reporter said, "any tyro in politics" could have foreseen the angry reaction.[57]

Two days later, on March 31, newspapers throughout the nation again ran banner headlines. Roosevelt had roused reporters at one o'clock in the morning to release a letter denying that he wanted to become a dictator:

As you well know I am as much opposed to American Dictatorship as you are, for three simple reasons:
A. I have no inclination to be a dictator.
B. I have none of the qualifications which would make me a success-ful dictator.
C. I have too much historical background and too much knowledge of existing dictatorships to make me desire any form of dictatorship for a democracy like the United States of America.

Roosevelt strongly defended the Reorganization bill, asserting that "a carefully manufactured partisan and political opposition . . . has created a political issue—created it deliberately out of whole cloth." The President dismissed rumors regarding the transfer of the Forest Service and Veterans Administration as "silly night-mares," inspired by "those who would restore the government to those who owned it between 1921 and 1933, or [by] those who for one reason or another seek deliberately to wreck the present administration . . ."[58]

This letter to an "anonymous friend" caused much apprehension. Strangely, the fact that Roosevelt thought it necessary to disavow dictatorial ambitions only lent credence to the accusation. "Think of it," sputtered one congressman, "needing to assure the country about it—that he did not want to be a dictator. In Heaven's name, why did he mention it."[59] Opponents also seized upon the odd way in which the letter was released. Republicans asserted that the

President had summoned newsmen in the dead of night for an "eerie midnight performance." "Was he dreaming?" asked Senator John Townsend of Delaware, "did they wake him up from a dream?"[60] Representative Lawrence Lewis wrote in his diary: "To me it seems most unwise for him to have issued such a statement and at such an ungodly hour."[61] In one cartoon, Roosevelt preened before a mirror in a hat store wearing a crown labeled "Dictatorship." The caption read: "I Don't Look Good in it—I Don't Want It—It's Terrible—Wrap it up!"[62]

Not until several days later did the true story concerning the letter become known. The letter had been written Wednesday afternoon, March 30.[63] At about 10:30 P.M. McIntyre notified the reporters at Warm Springs that he would have an important story shortly. Some of the newsmen were playing cards; others were at a nearby carnival. Within twenty minutes they had gathered together. "There was nobody in bed. There was nobody with a nightshirt on," recalled one scribe. At 12:40 A.M. McIntyre finally returned with the President's letter, indicating that it should be held for the afternoon edition. But a reporter for a morning paper complained that he had waited for two hours and deserved the story. After some argument, McIntyre telephoned Roosevelt, who had gone to bed, and received permission to release the letter at once. The limited clerical facilities at Warm Springs had been responsible for the various delays. Since the real story was not nearly as sensational as the original, it received little publicity.[64]

Roosevelt's attempt to refute the charge of dictatorship reveals his deep anxiety at the end of March 1938. Just three weeks earlier, when reporters referred to the charge, Roosevelt had replied: "Well, I don't think that it needs discussion with any of you people who have come into this room."[65] The President, who recognized the many obstacles to administrative reorganization, was unprepared for the vicious assault upon his intentions.[66] He seemed bewildered by the hysteria whipped up over the bill. "I don't want the powers, God knows," he told a group of editors. He would be glad to see

Congress undertake reorganization, but Congress faced too many conflicting pressures. "As far as powers go, I figured out the other day that there is not a single power I have that Hoover and Coolidge did not have," he asserted. Roosevelt was convinced that the charge of dictatorship was inspired by political partisanship. In self-defense, the President tried to play down the importance of the bill. "It is nothing in my life," he said. "If the thing does not go through, I will rock along all right."[67]

The President's nonchalance betrayed his apprehension. When the House took up reorganization early in April, his prestige was at a low point. At a critical moment his political skill appeared to have deserted him. The President, recognizing that democracy must provide economic security in order to combat totalitarianism, was deeply troubled by the recession.[68] Moreover, the viciousness and unreasonableness of the attacks upon reorganization seemed to raise real dangers to representative government. "Demagoguery and stupidity," Roosevelt wrote on April 12, "are the natural and perennial enemies of democracy."[69]

# CHAPTER VIII

# Defeat in the House

SHORTLY after the Senate passed the Reorganization bill, James Farley spoke to Roosevelt on the telephone. "That was too close a vote," he told the President. "If this thing doesn't go through the House you are going to lose control of your party." Farley suggested that Roosevelt take a more active part in lining up Congressional support: "The thing to do is call in some of these people and sit down with them—not put yourself in a shell and just let lightning strike where it will." Roosevelt appears to have given a noncommittal reply. Indeed, when the House debated the measure during the first week in April 1938, Democratic disunity became more pronounced. "This is the bitterest fight that has occurred in the House of Representatives in the last fifty years," reported a veteran Democrat.[1]

## 1

When the House took up the Reorganization bill, the third session of the Seventy-fifth Congress was nearly three months old. The session had proved listless. The President had offered no program to combat the recession, and the opposition was weak and divided. The Wages and Hours bill and a regional planning bill lingered in committee. On January 10 the House came within a dozen votes of defying the Administration to bring the Ludlow war referendum to the floor. There were a few positive accomplishments. In February the members granted an emergency relief appropriation. In March the House passed a revenue bill and authorized a $1 billion naval expansion program. As the spring primaries approached, many congressmen hoped for an early adjournment.

Legislative lethargy snapped when the Senate sent the Byrnes Reorganization bill to the House. The bill, which had privileged status, went directly to the Select Committee on Government Organization under Congressman John Cochran of Missouri. On March 30 the Committee decided to report an amendment to the Byrnes bill striking out everything after the enacting clause and substituting the four House bills drawn up in 1937.[2] The House version therefore differed from the Senate bill in several respects: it did not create a National Resources Planning Board; it provided for a Civil Service administrator but also set up a citizens' advisory board to watch over the merit system; and it left fiscal control in the hands of the Comptroller-General, who was made responsible to the President.[3] Roosevelt's legislative chieftains insisted upon these modifications. "I am bitterly opposed to the bill passed by the Senate and that is also the attitude of the House," said Lindsay Warren of North Carolina.[4]

Most Washington observers predicted that the House would pass the Reorganization bill. The Democratic majority of two hundred and twenty-five votes in the lower chamber seemed ample enough to sustain the President. On March 29 Representative John Dempsey of New Mexico assured Harold Ickes that the bill would go through. Foes of reorganization had little hope. Gifford Pinchot admitted: "There doesn't seem to be much chance to stop it in the house." Representative Clifford Hope believed that the Administration was "making the effort of its life to pass this bill. It will be a miracle if we are able to beat it in the house."[5]

On Thursday, March 31, the House took up the measure in a wild session "punctuated by boos, laughter and sarcastic comment." The debate rarely attained a high level. When Republicans insisted that the entire Senate bill be read, one Democrat asked whether it should be "reprinted in words of one syllable so that the Republicans can understand it?" Numerous quorum calls were demanded. "They are coming in over there, Mr. Speaker," cried a congressman as one count proceeded; "They are going out on the other side," shouted another. When the issue of presidential responsibility arose, Representative Dewey Short of Missouri bellowed: "Assurances are not worth a continental when they come from men who care no more for their word than a tomcat cares for a marriage license in a back alley on a dark night."[6] Dispassionate discussion was the exception, not the rule.

At the outset, House leaders hoped to wind up debate in six hours.[7] On Friday, April 1, when unanimous consent could not be obtained, the House discussed the bill in Committee of the Whole. After five hours of wrangling, Representative Cochran moved to close debate. "This sudden move without warning . . . threw the House into an uproar," reported one congressman.[8] Rank-and-file Democrats, chafing at this arbitrary procedure, deserted the leadership. Such New Dealers as Herman Eberharter of Pennsylvania and Lawrence Connery of Massachusetts helped defeat the motion by a vote of 149–191. Opponents of the bill were jubilant. "You are evidently making a great fight in the House," wrote Senator Josiah Bailey to a leader of the opposition.[9]

Thwarted in its drive to cut off debate, the Administration abruptly changed tactics. Its spokesmen no longer pressed for an early vote. Indeed, Representative Hull of Wisconsin believed that the administration was postponing action on the bill until it was able to get its congressmen into line. By Wednesday, April 6, when debate had dragged on for more than twenty hours, both sides wearily agreed to call a halt. On Thursday a motion to strike out the enacting clause was defeated by a vote of 169–191. The Administration then beat back several crippling amendments. After a week of exhaustive debate, one reporter noticed "highly strung nerves and anxiety over large blocs of votes which were not committed to either side."[10]

Representative John O'Connor of New York, Chairman of the

Rules Committee, led the Democratic opposition to reorganization. O'Connor, whose mail ran overwhelmingly against the measure, asserted that the bill was a " 'brain child' . . . of the 'professors' who have been poured into the Federal service." He was
distressed, however, by the reluctance of some Democrats to break
with the President. On February 15 he reported: "I am doing all
I can but not getting much assistance." And just before the House
took up the bill he told Father Coughlin, "I am the only fellow
here who is standing up. . . It is a question of hanging on to coat
tails with most of the fellows."[11] But O'Connor was convinced that
reorganization enjoyed little popular support, and when a New
York politician asked if he could not "soften up" his opposition
to the bill "without sacrificing principles too much," O'Connor
replied: "I am positive I am not wrong this time, taking into
account what it will mean to our party."[12]

Although some of the ninety Republicans in the House joined in
the attack on reorganization, others saw the wisdom of permitting
Democrats to lead the fight. "I think probably the fewer speeches
that come from the minority the better off will be our cause,"
remarked one Republican. Clifford Hope of Kansas explained his
party's tactics on April 4: "It seems to me the best strategy has
been to let the Democrats take the lead in opposing the measure . . .
The chief danger in having the Republicans take too active a part
in the matter is that it gives the Democratic leaders the opportunity to raise the partisan issue which they cannot do if the
leadership in the fight comes from their side of the aisle."[13]

The vote on recommittal was set for Friday, April 8. "It is the
biggest issue I have ever seen in my life," said Representative
O'Connor, who had served in the House for fifteen years. Just
before the vote, Speaker Bankhead and Majority Leader Sam
Rayburn begged Democrats not to desert the President. The roll
call began after six o'clock, and when it was concluded many
members shouted for a recapitulation. Bankhead refused. He then
announced that the bill had been recommitted by a vote of 204–

196.[14] Representative Michael Stack of Pennsylvania raced across the floor and raised O'Connor's arm, shouting: "Here's our leader! Here's our leader!" But O'Connor slipped quietly out of the chamber: "There was no hint of elation in his face," observed one reporter.[15] After six weeks of furious debate in the Senate and House, the Reorganization bill was dead. "A tense, hushed and dramatic final hour," wrote Lawrence Lewis that night.[16]

### 2

Why did the House defeat the Reorganization bill?[17] Most congressmen believed that a vote against the measure would reaffirm Congressional independence. Others responded to pressure exerted by their constituents and by other interested groups. Republicans and conservative Democrats took advantage of the opportunity to damage President Roosevelt's prestige. Even so, the bill might have passed if it were not for strategic blunders committed by the President and his legislative leaders.

The history of the New Deal had been, in part, the history of the enlargement of presidential power. The Reorganization bill, which implied a new attempt to whittle down Congressional prerogatives, became a target for smoldering Congressional resentment. "Let us tell the world that the Congress is not impotent," declared Representative Andrew J. May of Kentucky. Democrat Arthur Lamneck of Ohio asserted that the House must stop delegating authority. "If it does not do that pretty soon, there will not be any use for Congress. Members . . . might just as well stay at home and endorse Executive desires by mail."[18] Looking back at the years 1937–1938, Representative Eugene Keogh of Brooklyn proudly recalled that "it was President Roosevelt's inability to dominate and dictate to the House" which prevented his having absolute control of the government. Nor were assertions of Congressional importance meant merely for public consumption. Representative Lawrence Lewis wrote in his diary: "I am opposed to Congress abdicating its prerogatives or delegating any more power to the Executive."[19]

Hostility to specific provisions of the bill reflected, in part, Congressional attitudes toward executive authority. Many who opposed the creation of a Civil Service administrator believed that the existing bipartisan three-member commission curbed presidential influence. Other congressmen, following Senator Byrd, insisted that a Comptroller-General responsible to the legislature provided a necessary check upon spending. Those who wished to prevent the transfer of the Forest Service and other pet agencies balked at placing these bureaus at the mercy of the President. For example, Representative Robert Crosser of Ohio, an Administration Democrat who was a partisan of railway labor, voted to recommit the bill when he failed to obtain formal exemption for the Railroad Retirement Board and the Railroad Mediation Board.[20]

Congressmen who were reluctant to delegate additional authority to the President were even less willing to yield to New Deal administrators. The proposed Department of Welfare drew the fire of those who envisioned a permanent relief program divorced from Congressional control. Harry Hopkins, slated to head the new department, was seen as the bureaucrat incarnate—arrogant, aggressive, and cockily indifferent to Congressional pride.[21] Representative Malcolm Tarver of Georgia asserted that the "one thing" that dictated his vote was the specter of Hopkins as Secretary of Public Welfare.[22] Clifton Woodrum of Virginia, a consistent supporter of the Administration, accepted every feature of the bill except creation of the new department with increased relief expenditures.[23] Representative Lyle Boren of Oklahoma explained that his "strongest opposition" was to the proposed department, which, he argued, "would throw our government into a permanent relief business."[24] According to Harold Ickes, Speaker Bankhead had been told that twenty-five votes would be gained for the bill by eliminating the Welfare Department.[25]

The Department of Welfare proposal also stirred the suspicion of some Catholics who feared that transfer of the Bureau of Education to the new department would jeopardize parochial schools.[26] Father Coughlin made this the central issue in his early attacks upon the measure. Representative Charles Eaton of New Jersey termed the department "a serious menace to parochial schools and other religious educational systems." A Pennsylvania Democrat read a statement denouncing the bill by Dr. Edmund A. Walsh, S.J., Vice-President of Georgetown: "I am sure [that] the gentlemen . . . will get the significance of the letters 'S.J.,' " he added.[27]

The President found it hard to take such charges seriously. He pointed out that the location of the Bureau of Education would not have the slightest effect on Catholic schools. He denounced the charge that he was attempting to subvert the independence of parochial schools as an "utter absurdity."[28] The National Catholic Welfare Conference, led by Archbishop Edward Mooney of Detroit, refused to attack the bill. More positive support came from George Cardinal Mundelein of Chicago who stated: "I cannot find that the welfare or freedom of the Catholic church is in any way menaced by the pending reorganization bill."[29] Nevertheless, enough Catholics were alienated to trouble proponents of the measure.

In an effort to allay fears of executive usurpation, the Administration granted key concessions. On April 2 the President authorized the House leaders to exempt from transfer both the Veterans Administration and the Bureau of Education. In addition, an important limitation upon presidential authority was accepted. On April 7 Frank Kniffin of Ohio submitted an amendment providing that a simple majority in both houses might override a presidential transfer by concurrent resolution. This was designed as a compromise between the original bill, which required a two-thirds majority in each house to overrule the President, and the Wheeler amendment, which required the approval of a majority in each house before an order could take effect. Roosevelt and his advisers, who had held that veto by concurrent resolution was unconstitutional, put aside their scruples under the stress of the emergency. The Kniffin amendment, which made the President a legislative agent and directed him to prepare plans of reorganization, gave Congress the right to determine whether or not the plans conformed to the standards laid down in the delegation of power. With acceptance of the Kniffin amendment, friends of the bill could claim that ultimate control remained with Congress.[30]

As a result of the compromises made in the House, the Reorganization bill was badly watered down. One Senator thought that a real question existed as to whether "more than a remnant of the legislation" could be salvaged. Representative John Kerr of North Carolina admitted that the measure "had been stripped of almost everything except its nightshirt . . ."[31] President Roosevelt himself told James Farley: "This bill doesn't really mean very much. You and I know it. The teeth have been taken out and there really isn't very much to it except the principle of the thing."[32]

Why did these concessions fail to muster a majority for the bill? Some congressmen argued that the Kniffin amendment was a decoy of doubtful constitutionality.[33] Others believed that the concessions would be deleted when the bill reached conference. Lindsay Warren denied that the House conferees would accept the Senate version,[34] but opponents refused to take the risk. "I do not care how white a document it may be when it leaves this chamber," said John McClellan of Arkansas, "when it goes into conference and lies down with the Senate bill it is going to come back here contaminated." Clifford Hope of Kansas assumed that the objectionable features "will likely all be back in again when the conference report is made." A Wisconsin Progressive expected that "the bill will go to conference and be fixed up to suit the senators, if the usual custom is followed."[35]

The concessions had also proved ineffective because Roosevelt's enemies recognized that recommittal would be interpreted as a personal defeat for the President. Many conservatives who opposed reorganization did not care greatly about the provisions of the bill; they wanted to impair Roosevelt's prestige and hinder the New Deal. The charge that Roosevelt aspired to dictatorship was, as a prominent Republican later admitted, "partisan exaggeration."[36] Many congressmen agreed that the opposition was "purely political." A Farmer-Laborite from Minnesota asserted that a majority of those who voted to recommit "did so because of their dislike for the President and for the political effect this defeat might have upon the future political fortunes of Franklin D. Roosevelt."[37] Lindsay Warren claimed that "the whole fight is being waged by Republicans . . . and those Democrats who hate Roosevelt."[38] John Cochran rebuked Amos Pinchot: "It is clearly evident to me, that you are not so much opposed to the legislation as you are to the President."[39] The opposition, concluded Louis Brownlow, was "just anti-Roosevelt."[40]

Not all Democrats who voted to recommit, of course, were inspired by animosity toward the President. Representative Lyle Boren of Oklahoma told a close friend, "Ross, this bill was one of the most difficult to decide. I am certain . . . you can appreciate the fact that it was not a question of voting administration or anti-administration, but a question of the merits of the bill."[41] Lawrence Lewis of Colorado contended that it was "pure nonsense" to construe a vote against the bill as hostility toward the President. Lewis told Majority Whip Pat Boland that his vote "would be no indication whatsoever of my loyalty as a party man to the party or to the head of our party . . . my decision would be based on whether I conclude this is a good bill for the country."[42] Because Roosevelt's prestige had become bound up with the fate of the bill, even those Democrats whose opposition was sincere were put in the position of voting against the President.

Democrats inclined to vote against the measure because of devotion to Congressional prerogatives or disillusionment with the Administration were encouraged by a flood of letters and telegrams attacking reorganization. Representative Alfred F. Beiter of New York ascribed his vote to a desire to please his constituents.[43] Mail ran overwhelmingly against the measure and threatened reprisals at the polls for those who ignored the public will. "You can count on my voting 'No' at the time of your re-election if you vote 'Yes' for the Reorganization bill," wrote a woman in Shawnee, Oklahoma, to her congressman.[44] To go against public opinion in an election year seemed to be inviting disaster at the polls. An old friend advised Merlin Hull of Wisconsin: "I have always felt very close to you, Merlin, and I believe that you will make friends with a 'No' vote on this measure. Needless to say, with the large amount of opposition showing itself in this district, you will lose many friends if you support this bill. Folks here are dropping party lines and falling in against this bill as it creates a larger issue."[45] Amos Pinchot recognized the lack of popular support for reorganization: "No Congressman can gain votes at home by voting for this bill, but can lose plenty of them."[46]

New Dealers charged that congressmen who yielded to such pressure had been hoodwinked. They asserted that most telegrams were at best inspired, and at worst falsified. One congressman from Oklahoma was told to discount a batch of letters, which were "born in the brain of the Republican boss of this city and Bill Skelly of Tulsa . . . two of the blackest Republicans one ever finds."[47] Representative Teigan of Minnesota, who received more telegrams against reorganization than against any other measure since his election, was not perturbed: "The brevity of both letters and telegrams indicates that those who are signing them don't know what the hell they are talking about." Some evidence substantiates these charges. A woman in Kentucky received a reply from her representative to a telegram she had not sent. Several congressmen found that letters they mailed to opponents of the bill were not deliverable.[48] Lindsay Warren claimed to have received "hundreds of letters from N. Y. and Chicago—many of them anonymous, names taken from graveyards."[49] But most of the mail received by members of the House did not fall into this category. The barrage of letters, stimulated in part by Frank Gannett and other opponents of reorganization, helped persuade some congressmen to vote against the bill.

### 3

Considering the extensive opposition to reorganization, it was significant that so many congressmen voted for the measure. "That the bill received 196 votes in spite of the obstacles placed in its way and the tremendous barrage laid down against it seems to me a real tribute to the good sense of the Congress," said Jerry Voorhis of California.[50] Nearly two thirds of the Democrats in the House stood by the President. Some supported the bill purely on its merits; others did so out of loyalty to the President. In addition, the concessions offered by the Administration and the pressure it exerted gained some votes.

Many congressmen voted for the bill because they believed that reorganization was greatly needed. Robert Lee Doughton of North Carolina stated he supported the measure "not because Mr. Roosevelt is insisting upon it, but because my knowledge of the matter formed upon a basis of twenty-seven years' service in Washington convinced me that it is the right and proper thing to do."[51] One Democrat considered the bill so perfect that to oppose it "would be very much like arguing against the Ten Commandments."[52] Fred Vinson, Lindsay Warren, James Mead, and many others were convinced that reorganization was an executive responsibility. Some Southerners who were disturbed because the bill did not reduce expenditures supported it none the less. "The President must be authorized by Congress to abolish useless Agencies," asserted John H. Kerr of North Carolina, "for the reason that the President is the head of the Executive Departments of the Government and the Congress must, under the Constitution, carry out its wishes through the President." And he concluded, "Most of the propaganda being distributed against it is much to do about nothing."[53]

Some Democrats supported reorganization out of devotion to Roosevelt and the New Deal. That the President's leadership was at stake seemed reason enough to back the bill. "As a Roosevelt Democrat, believing in the New Deal, I have no hesitation in voting for this bill," stated Representative Thomas F. Ford of California. "I emphatically declare that I am with the President of the United States in his major objectives, and I stand for the policies of the New Deal," said Knute Hill of Washington in explaining his vote.[54] Representative John Flannagan, the only Virginia Democrat to support reorganization, affirmed his loyalty in a letter to the President: "To fall out of the ranks is bad enough; but to fall out during the thickest of the battle, and at a time and under circumstances that can only be construed as deserting your Captain, and go over and supply the enemy with fresh recruits when the fighting is the hottest is a political sin that no man, in my opinion, can live down. I would hate to leave that record behind for my enemies to gloat over and my descendants to view with shame."[55]

The substantial concessions granted by the Administration swung a number of votes for the bill. On April 8 Representative Ira Drew of Pennsylvania announced that the amendments satisfied him, even though he had consistently opposed the bill "on the ground that the Congress should no longer abrogate its constitutional rights." Joe Starnes of Alabama stated that he could accept the bill as modified. Herman Eberharter of Pennsylvania, who had attacked reorganization in a radio address on March 30, came to support the measure when the House leadership adopted a more conciliatory attitude.[56] Not only did the concessions dispel some Congressional doubts; more important, they permitted those who had publicly denounced the bill to switch sides gracefully.

The Administration also tried to crack the patronage whip to line up support for the bill. "It is impossible to exaggerate the desperate efforts which the administration made to pass this bill and the pressures which they brought on Democratic members of Congress," said one opponent.[57] James Farley was on the telephone until the last minute trying to round up votes. Charles West, Under Secretary of the Interior, also pressed recalcitrant Democrats.[58] The distinction between proper persuasion and improper pressure could easily become blurred. John M. Coffee of Washington, who strongly opposed transfer of the Forest Service, had to back down on a promise to insert a speech by Gifford Pinchot into the *Congressional Record*. Coffee needed Ickes' approval for key projects in his district and feared he would be jeopardizing his political career if he offended the Secretary. In April 1938 Ickes recalled that when another congressman, Abe Murdock of Utah, had voted to exclude Forestry, "I signed an order separating his nephew from our payroll."[59]

Promises, pressure, and appeals to party loyalty might have saved the bill had the President and his legislative lieutenants not committed certain tactical blunders. Roosevelt's dismissal of the Chairman of the TVA and public disavowal of dictatorial ambition did not help his cause.[60] Moreover, the President's statement implying that opponents of the bill in the Senate had been "purchased" antagonized members of the House. As Senator Thomas of Utah stated: "The President undoubtedly . . . considered it more or less of a personal fight on him, and showed that in some of the remarks he made. This, I think, as it always does, proved fatal." Republican Usher Burdick of North Dakota asserted: "I have supported the President more regularly than 90 per cent of the Democrats in this House . . . and I resent the statement that the President made and the use of the word 'purchased.' "[61] Finally, a speech by Roosevelt at Gainesville, Georgia, on March 23, which implied that those southern congressmen who opposed economic reform favored "feudalism," may have hurt the bill. Representative Thomas Amlie of Wisconsin reported that Southerners were seething: "The southern Congressmen feel that the president made the speech solely to insult them." Vice-President Garner told James Farley that the speech "had made a solid bloc that would vote against almost anything the President might propose."[62]

Mismanagement by the House leaders on Friday, April 8, spelled defeat for the Reorganization bill. Confident of victory, the leaders lost count of the vote during the roll call.[63] As a result, some congressmen who might have supported the bill if their votes were required were never called upon. According to Ickes, Farley explained to the President how the bill was defeated:

> He said that he had had as many as twenty-five Democratic Congressmen, all of whom were willing to support this bill . . . if their votes were needed. However, they did not want to vote for it unless their votes were needed. At the end the leadership seemed to become panicky. At any rate, it didn't have an accurate count of noses. It didn't know who were for and who were against. No wonder we lost when no opportunity was given those Congressmen to change, whose votes the other way would have reversed the result.[64]

The epitaph for the Reorganization bill was inscribed by Democratic Whip Pat Boland: "Eight members who personally assured me they were for the bill voted to recommit it."[65]

The demise of the Reorganization bill was brought about, then, by a combination of forces. Congressmen who wished to restrict the Executive authority, protect pet bureaus, or inflict a defeat upon the President united against the measure. They were encouraged by powerful interest groups and ordinary citizens whose fear of dictatorship and resentment at the recession were exploited by opponents of the bill. The countervailing forces—Roosevelt's political skill, his influence over New Deal Democrats, the need for reorganization—were offset by lapses in political strategy. Even in a diluted form, reorganization could not overcome these obstacles.

4

"History will probably mark the crisis of President Roosevelt's political career by yesterday's defeat of the Reorganization bill," remarked the New York *World-Telegram* on April 9, 1938. Seasoned political observers agreed. "It may be the turning point in our history," chirped Frank Gannett.[66] The defeat assumed such significance because it was a shattering blow to Roosevelt's prestige. The vote indicated that the President had lost control of Congress. Opponents of the Reorganization bill had apparently forged the "first successful anti-Roosevelt coalition in Congress."[67] The very magnitude of the Democratic majority in the House had tended to serve as a source of disunity; no menacing opposition existed to unite it, and not enough favors existed to satisfy it.

This "lack of party cohesion"[68] caused Republicans to view their own prospects with new enthusiasm. "The country appears to think we did a very good job in the fight on the Reorganization Bill. . . I believe it has also strengthened the party tremendously," said Representative Joe Martin.[69] More important, the vote on reorganization pointed up the defection of many groups that had in the past actively supported reform legislation: Northwestern Progressives, big-city Democrats, and several staunch New Dealers.

Seven Wisconsin Progressives served in the House; six voted to recommit the Reorganization bill. Since their votes provided the margin for defeat, most liberals angrily denounced their action. "The disgrace of it is that the Farmer-Laborites and Wisconsin Progressives could have saved the day for the President," commented Representative Teigan bitterly.[70] Just three weeks later, when Governor Philip La Follette launched a new party—the National Progressives of America—the vote on the Reorganization bill took on new meaning. La Follette justified his call for a third party on the grounds that disunity made the Democratic party a futile vehicle for reform.[71] Many assumed, therefore, that La Follette had thrown his influence against reorganization in order to discredit the President and give added force to his argument. The Governor "meant the House vote to be the opening gun in a 1940 struggle," reasoned Arthur Krock of the *New York Times*.[72]

The Progressive vote against reorganization, however, may be explained in other ways. The Wisconsin representatives abhorred further delegation of power to the Executive. Merlin Hull termed the Reorganization bill "the most astounding grab for power that has ever been made here." He feared that the bill would place control of governmental operations "in the hands of bureaucrats who are constantly seeking to become more and more independent of legislative control."[73] When the House rejected Gerald Boileau's amendment providing for affirmative action by Congress before reorganization orders took effect, Progressive opposition to the bill was assured.[74] Indeed, Progressive hostility to presidential authority, especially in the field of foreign affairs, had become increasingly apparent early in 1938. The Progressives favored the Ludlow war referendum, they opposed the big Navy bill, and they denounced the May bill which would have given the government broad powers in time of war.[75] The emerging conflict between Roosevelt's liberal internationalism and midwestern Progressive isolationism rendered suspect every effort to expand executive authority.

By 1938 the Democratic party no longer seemed responsive to the vital interests of Wisconsin Progressives. The Progressives received no patronage. Replying to an old acquaintance who needed a job, Merlin Hull said: "As you probably know, Senator F. Ryan Duffy is in charge of all so-called patronage here for our state and our progressive Congressmen have not been considered in connection with it."[76] In addition, the Works Progress Administration seemed to discriminate against Wisconsin. When the Senate passed a special relief appropriation in February, La Follette inserted a provision that WPA labor be used in his state's limestone crushing industry. Officials of WPA, who assured Wisconsin's congressmen that they favored the project, then appeared before the conference committee and sanctioned its elimination. Representative Bernard J. Gehrmann snapped: "It proved how heads of different departments pretend to be definitely in favor of certain things when individual members approach them, simply to gain the members' favor but behind our backs they do just the opposite."[77] Moreover, the Administration seemed peculiarly insensitive to the plight of Wisconsin's dairy farmers. Progressives fought the Farm bill, which failed to satisfy the dairy interests. The Administration's drive for Canadian reciprocity antagonized those who feared that tariffs would be reduced on goods which competed with Wisconsin products. "It does seem to me the dairymen have suffered enough under this administration without that added burden being imposed upon us," Hull grumbled. The rift between Progressives and Democrats had become so pronounced by March 1938 that Lawrence Lewis of Colorado referred to the Progressives as "allies" of the Republicans.[78]

Democratic congressmen from New York City also cast decisive votes against the Reorganization bill. Their behavior sharply contrasted with that of Chicago Democrats who, coaxed by Boss Ed Kelly, stood by the President. With Illinois primaries only four days away, Kelly personally urged his delegation to remain in Washington for the final vote, and promised that "in the meantime the organization will protect your political interests at home." Lindsay Warren thought that the "loyal and unselfish" Chicagoans deserved high praise. "In every battle and in every fight you and your colleagues have gone down the line . . . We never have to ask where you stand," he told Representative Raymond McKeough.[79] In New York, however, the situation was reversed. Although most Democrats from Brooklyn and the Bronx supported reorganization, Tammany Hall did not. Led by Tammany chieftain Christy Sullivan, six of the nine Manhattan Democrats voted to recommit the measure.[80]

Ill-concealed hostility had always marked Roosevelt's relationship with Tammany Hall. With the exception of Ed Flynn of the Bronx, Tammany sachems had stubbornly supported Al Smith's candidacy at the 1932 convention. Roosevelt cooperated with Tammany during his first term because he wanted to keep New York City under Democratic control in order to aid Herbert Lehman's gubernatorial campaign and his own prospects for re-election. By 1937, however, Tammany leadership was so fatuous that Roosevelt backed Fiorello La Guardia for Mayor.[81] In April 1938 Tammany Democrats found other reasons to vote against the Reorganization bill aside from their desire to reassert Congressional independence and satisfy aroused constituents.[82] They felt strong resentment toward Harold Ickes and Harry Hopkins. Representative Joseph Gavagan recalled: "I never cared much for Harry Hopkins . . . My observation of Hopkins . . . led me to the belief that he was a very spiteful person . . . I never had much use for him and would avoid him whenever the occasion would present itself."[83] Moreover, Frank Gannett believed that those New York Democrats who opposed reorganization had been influenced by Senator Wagner's vote.[84]

Many liberal Democrats who normally supported New Deal measures helped to recommit the Reorganization bill. The defection of such liberals as Robert Ramspeck of Georgia, Robert G. Allen of Pennsylvania, and Norman Hamilton of Virginia proved costly.[85] Other Democrats—among them Vincent Harrington of Iowa and Herbert S. Bigelow of Illinois—voted against the measure partly in protest against Roosevelt's failure to halt the recession. Bigelow thought recovery should take precedence: "Do we want to go back home—how will we feel going back home facing these millions out of work? How will they feel and how will we feel when we have to say to them, 'No; we did not get you jobs, but here is a nice reorganization bill.' "[86] A Washington reporter for the *New Republic* said of the vote on reorganization, "The wounds it has created in the liberal bloc cannot be easily healed."[87]

Some liberals deserted the President not only because he offered no program to meet the recession, but because he seldom offered to meet with them. Presidential liaison with the House was largely confined to legislative leaders—Rayburn, Bankhead, and committee chairmen. In April 1938 Representative Kent Keller of Illinois told Roosevelt: "There is a group of aggressive progressive Democrats who have stuck by you through thick and thin, about seventy-five in number, as well as a number of other progressives not classed as Democrats, and I do not believe that you have ever called in a single one of this group in consultation as to administration policies."[88] The case of Congressman Frank Fries of Illinois is instructive. On April 5 he sent the President editorials favoring reorganization which he had inserted in the *Congressional Record.* "In the past some of my communications to the President apparently have not reached him," Fries wrote to Marvin McIntyre: "I feel this is a courtesy due members of the Legislative branch of our Government." No reply was made until April 11; Fries had already abstained when the House voted on reorganization.[89] Perhaps remoteness from rank-and-file members of the House was the price Roosevelt paid for the support of its leaders. In voting on the Reorganization bill, however, many leaders lined up with the opposition. Observing that Speaker Bankhead had declined to vote for the bill himself, Merlin Hull added: "Twenty Democratic committee chairmen voted against the bill, including some of the President's most intimate advisors."[90]

The defeat of the Reorganization bill seemed to herald the end of Rooseveltian reform. The President's name had lost its magic. "Congress found that it could defy Roosevelt without being hit by lightning," recalled one New Dealer.[91] Senator Elmer Thomas reported that the defeat had thrown the Democratic organization into disarray: "We do not know just what legislation may be brought up for consideration before we adjourn."[92] It appeared likely that all reform would be postponed. Even while the fight over reorganization raged, a group of Democrats who backed the measure implored the President, "For God sakes, don't send us any more controversial legislation."[93] After the defeat, the Wages and Hours bill appeared to be doomed. Representative Mary Norton of New Jersey, chairman of the Committee on Labor, commented: "Up to last night I had every reason to think that the committee was very anxious to report a wage-hour bill . . . but now it is difficult to tell."[94] On April 8, 1938, Roosevelt was at a low point in his Presidential career.[95]

# CHAPTER IX

# The Reorganization Act of 1939

ON July 5, 1938, Louis Brownlow, Charles Merriam, and Luther Gulick met with President Roosevelt. More than two years had elapsed since they had been asked to draw up a program of governmental reorganization. Now their plan lay in ruins. Even worse, it had been used by the President's enemies to discredit his leadership. "The campaign against you," Brownlow told the President, "in which the Reorganization Bill was merely a pawn, was of such a despicable character that I would like to express to you as a citizen a renewed assurance of my loyalty to the cause of which you in all the world today are the outstanding representative."[1] Roosevelt, however, was unwilling to concede final defeat. He believed that reorganization had fallen down on a matter of "detail." Most congressmen, he explained, "were in favor of the principle and in favor of ninety per cent of the details but did not like ten per cent."[2] To Brownlow and his colleagues, the President made clear his desire to pass a Reorganization bill at the next session of Congress.[3]

## 1

The President had recovered swiftly from his defeat in April 1938. Having decided to resume pump-priming to combat the recession, Roosevelt, on April 14, submitted a $3 billion spending program to Congress. Defending his policy in a fireside chat, the President once again sounded confident and vigorous.[4] Then, on April 29, he asked Congress to undertake a study of the concentration of economic power in the United States. Both measures passed by large majorities. Indeed, by granting large relief appropriations without earmarking expenditures, Congress may have given the President more power than it withheld in the Reorganization bill. Public opinion polls began to show a marked increase in Roosevelt's popularity. On April 15 Frank Gannett remarked in despair: "The President doesn't give up easily, does he? Some one has referred to him as 'resilient' and I think that's a good word for him, for he certainly does bound back."[5]

Congressmen carefully gauged the extent of the swing toward Roosevelt. Not only was the spending program enacted, but in May the Wages and Hours bill was discharged from the Rules Committee and passed. Public opinion even seemed more favorable toward reorganization. Worried congressmen began to receive letters condemning them for deserting the President.[6] By April 20 John Cochran informed Roosevelt that "those who are now suffering with headaches are the Democrats who voted to re-commit the Bill."[7] On May 14 Governor Landon described the turn of events: "Immediately after the Reorganization Bill was defeated and the Wage and Hour Bill seemed to be side-tracked, it looked as if Roosevelt's control over his own party was weakening more rapidly than anyone expected . . . But now the pendulum is swinging back . . . Roosevelt is regaining control."[8] As Congress neared adjournment in June, one columnist declared that the independence demonstrated during the fight on reorganization was "in a state of collapse."[9]

In fact, many New Dealers urged President Roosevelt to use the vote on reorganization as a test of loyalty to the Administration. On April 9 Roosevelt had made public a letter to Sam Rayburn stating that the vote offered "no occasion for personal recrimination."[10] Still, several friends of the Administration suggested that patronage be cut off from those who had betrayed the bill. Representative Adolph Sabath of Illinois wrote: "I am bitter and I feel that many of the members, who for selfish motives or imaginable grievances voted against us, are not entitled in the future to any consideration. I feel, Mr. President, that some consideration should be given to those who at all times stood by you . . ."[11] On June 22 Senator Josh Lee advised the President to punish his opponents. "What would you think about bearing down on those who voted against your program, who are now patting you on the back in their campaigns, feeling for a soft place to stick a knife after elections? The vote on the Reorganization Bill might be a good one to use as an example or test of loyalty."[12]

Two days later Roosevelt announced his intention to purge the Democratic party of conservatives. The defeat of the Reorganization bill influenced this decision, but Roosevelt chose his targets in pragmatic fashion. He supported some congressmen who had opposed reorganization and proscribed others who had voted for it.[13] Roosevelt was interested in whether "really, in his heart, deep down in his heart," a candidate believed in the broad objectives of the New Deal. The vote on the Reorganization bill could not, in every case, serve as a valid test of Congressional "liberalism."[14]

The shift in popular sentiment in April and May convinced many that Roosevelt should renew the fight for reorganization at once. Harold Ickes advised: "Mr. President, if I were you I would call a special meeting of my Cabinet. I would say to them: 'God damn you, I am not going to be satisfied with lip service with respect to this bill. I want every one of you to get out and line up every vote you can.'" On April 19 Morris Cooke urged Roosevelt to reintroduce the bill as soon as possible.[15] On May 5 a loyal congressman told the President that many Democrats who had voted against the bill were sorry: "I believe that a vote today on the reorganization bill, with no changes in its provisions, would result in its passage." A few weeks later Ickes learned that Congressman John Dempsey had induced fifteen Democrats who voted to recommit to change their position.[16] On May 27 Luther Gulick was informed that although many congressmen had pledged to support a new Reorganization bill, no final decision had as yet been made.[17]

Although the temptation to follow the advice of optimists was great, Roosevelt and his Congressional leaders decided, on May 31, to postpone the measure.[18] This decision was based on several considerations. The President wished to allow the furor to subside. "The most important thing is to let passions die down and wait until the American public . . . recovers its calmer second thought judgment," one sympathizer told James Roosevelt.[19] Moreover, the prospect of another bitter fight repelled the President. Such a dispute might wreck the recovery program before Congress just when elections were drawing near. Roosevelt had been misled in the past by overly optimistic reports. "He wants to be sure that the votes are there to be counted if an attempt is to be made," reported Ickes.[20] Opponents of reorganization seemed as determined as ever. "We'll be here until the snow flies if the reorganization fight starts again," threatened Senator Burke.[21] The possible risk of a second defeat outweighed the advantages of a probable victory. Also, Roosevelt found it possible to accomplish certain objectives without legislation. On June 24 he issued an Executive Order bringing 81,000 government employees under the merit system and providing for more effective administration of the civil service.[22] Having resolved to go ahead with a new Reorganization bill, Roosevelt was reconciled to waiting until Congress reconvened.

## 2

The Reorganization bill introduced in 1939 stood in sharp contrast to the measure defeated by the House the previous year. It was extremely mild, omitting nearly every controversial feature of its predecessor. It was drawn up by legislative leaders who paid little heed to the recommendations of the Brownlow Committee. It sparked no storm of controversy; public fear was absent and pressure groups were quiescent. And although the Republicans picked up eighty seats in the House and seven in the Senate in November 1938, the Reorganization bill of 1939 passed with little difficulty.

Plans to bring reorganization before the Seventy-sixth Congress were made late in 1938. On November 11 Lindsay Warren of North Carolina learned that the President still had "some sort of reorganization in his mind."[23] Warren urged the President to proceed cautiously. Pointing out that fifty-eight Democrats who had voted for the measure in 1938 were no longer in Congress, whereas only thirty-four who had voted to recommit were not, Warren suggested that the bill be "drastically curtailed." The Senate bill, he held, was "impossible," and even the House bill should be modified so as to protect the Comptroller-General and the Civil Service Commission. "The practical situation calls for a dropping of some phases of it and a revamping of others," explained Warren.[24]

On December 8, 1938, the President discussed legislative strategy with Luther Gulick, Charles Merriam, and James Byrnes. They decided to detach the civil service and accounting features from the Reorganization bill, to accept the principle that Congress might overrule a presidential plan by a majority vote, and to permit the exemption of many bureaus.[25] Byrnes insisted that the measure be taken up first by the House, where debate could be limited: "I think it useless to again waste thirty days of the time of the Senate if the House is not willing to pass this legislation."[26] On December 20 Representatives Cochran and Warren conferred with the President. Describing the "serious situation" in Congress, they pressed for further modification. Lindsay Warren drafted the revised bill early in 1939; the President's Committee was not consulted.[27]

Nothing better illustrates the erosion of the New Deal than the contrast between Roosevelt's bold proposals of 1937 and the bland Reorganization bill offered in 1939. The Warren bill was shorn of most controversial features. It authorized the President to suggest plans of reorganization subject to a veto by a majority of both houses, and appoint six administrative assistants. The modernization of the civil service system, the renovation of accounting procedures, the creation of new departments of government—all were dropped. "I think the bill is so greatly modified that most of the objections have been removed," chortled Harry Byrd. "I am sure you realize we had to make a lot of concessions," Cochran informed Gulick: "I regret this very much, but it was a case of get what we could."[28]

The modest nature of the measure helps account for the lack of opposition to it. For a brief time Frank Gannett's National Committee to Uphold Constitutional Government seemed ready to launch a new campaign. Early in December the Committee's Washington representative suggested that "we should do all we can to revive this issue." He hoped to "utilize opposition to the word 'Reorganization Bill.'" In January the Committee warned that "many of the obnoxious provisions of the Reorganization Bill . . . will be reintroduced."[29] But while Gannett and Pinchot mistrusted Roosevelt's motives, they found little in the bill to criticize. It seemed unlikely that the public could be aroused on such an issue. Pinchot advised Gannett, "I don't think we ought to go to the bat and try to make a big issue of it." Although he favored some modification, Pinchot admitted grudgingly, "I think the bill is probably O.K."[30]

The House passed the Reorganization bill on March 8, after three days of debate. The critical vote occurred on an amendment offered by Hatton Sumners of Texas. Going one step beyond the Kniffin amendment, but not so far as the Wheeler amendment, Sumners proposed that either house be permitted to veto reorganization plans by a majority vote. The amendment was narrowly defeated.[31] Democratic ranks held fast; the motion to recommit failed by 236 to 163. When the bill passed, Lindsay Warren beamed: "It received the largest Democratic vote [of] any measure in the last eight years, only five being against us." Indeed, on the final vote, several liberal Republicans joined the majority. Clifford Hope explained that "all the objectionable features" of the bill had been eliminated. The sole motive for opposition, commented the Kansas Republican, was "just pure politics."[32]

The Senate, too, acted swiftly. On March 20 it accepted without dissent a Byrd amendment making economy in government one of the purposes of the bill. On the next day Wheeler's proposal requiring affirmative action by both houses before an order could take effect was approved by a vote of 45–44. A motion was then made to reconsider the vote; the proposal to table this motion lost 44–44 when Senator Borah, who never voted to cut off debate, abstained. On the next day the Senate reversed its decision, turning back the Wheeler amendment by a vote of 46–44. Overnight the Administration had won over Dennis Chavez of New Mexico; in addition, Harry Truman arrived from Missouri to bolster Byrnes's forces. The measure then passed with a large majority. House and Senate conferees speedily reached agreement, and on April 3, 1939, President Roosevelt signed the Reorganization Act.[33]

Although administrative experts had little to do with drafting the act, they were largely responsible for its implementation. On March 20 Roosevelt asked Brownlow, Merriam, and Gulick to "come right down" to Washington when the bill passed so that reorganization plans could be presented at least sixty days before Congress adjourned.[34] Gulick thought that the President should bring forth an extensive and sweeping program, but Brownlow hoped Roosevelt would not be "too optimistic about what can be done" in the short time available. On March 31 Brownlow's group drew up a timetable for reorganization: the first step would be to consolidate agencies into existing departments and into a new Social Security Administration and Public Works Administration; then, interdepartmental agency transfers and intradepartmental changes could be made.[35]

In the weeks that followed, Brownlow and his associates worked with Budget Director Harold D. Smith and a few other officials in drafting plans of reorganization. On April 23, after several conversations with the President, they presented their proposals.[36] "On the whole he appeared to be pleased with the manner in which the orders were drafted," Smith noted. Roosevelt, whose "knowledge of the details of the Federal establishment" impressed Smith "as being nothing short of amazing," gave individual consideration to each agency transfer.[37] Plan I, which was sent to Congress on April 25, created a Federal Security Agency, a Federal Works Agency, and a Federal Loan Agency, and placed related bureaus under them. Moreover, the plan established the Executive Office of the President, and brought the White House Office, the Bureau of the Budget, and the National Resources Planning Board into it.[38]

Although the speed with which it had been drawn up took many by surprise, and the scope of its provisions caused some bureaucratic dismay—Harold Ickes considered himself a "heavy loser"— Plan I received Congressional sanction with less trouble than had been anticipated.[39] On May 3, after a short debate, the House upheld the President by better than a two-to-one margin. "Brownlow is well pleased as I am with the reception which the reorganization orders are receiving," Smith wrote in his diary. "There is apparently little or no opposition." Smith came to believe that even bolder changes could have been proposed, but admitted that everyone "seemed to have had the jitters as a result of previous experience with the reorganization proposals."[40]

Plan II, confined to interdepartmental transfers of a noncontroversial sort, was presented on May 9. It, too, encountered little resistance in Congress. In fact, Representative John Dempsey believed that "it has had a very good effect in the House, better than any I have seen in the last five years." Dempsey suggested that Roosevelt continue to recommend structural reforms: "It only takes ten days to put those things through and he ought to go ahead and do the job now and not wait until next January!"[41] In July 1939 the President rounded out his implementation of the Reorganization Act by appointing three administrative assistants, one of whom was assigned to work with the Civil Service Commission.[42] Roosevelt's imaginative use of the limited powers granted in 1939 confounded his critics and gave convincing proof of his administrative genius.

# PART FOUR

# Conclusion

# CHAPTER X

# Executive Reorganization and the New Deal

FRANKLIN D. Roosevelt's decision to appoint a committee to reform his administration marked a turning point in the history of the New Deal. In the first years of the New Deal, reorganization had been of slight importance compared with the problems of relief and recovery. From 1933 to 1935, the President and his lieutenants concentrated on the war against hard times, a war that resulted in a proliferation of new government agencies. Unavoidably, this expansion occurred in a helter-skelter fashion. Roosevelt's decision to reorganize the structure of government signified that this mammoth growth was over. By 1936 the President wished to consolidate what had already been done. Having fathered the legislation of the welfare state, Roosevelt now attempted to give order to the structure of that state.

The President's crusade for executive reorganization enlisted the support of a group of professional administrators and political theorists who shared his social philosophy. Louis Brownlow, Charles E. Merriam, and Luther Gulick hoped to remove the administrative obstacles that hindered Roosevelt's efforts to implement the New Deal. They wished to strengthen the Chief Executive and weaken the power of Congressional committees and interest groups to block proposals for federal reorganization. Their conception of the Presidency was thoroughly Hamiltonian. "Energy in the executive is a leading character in the definition of good government," Hamilton had written in *The Federalist*. The report of the President's Committee on Administrative Management was an elaboration of this theme.

Clearly the Committee was justified in its assertion that Congress could not carry out government reorganization. There was little likelihood that hundreds of legislators could formulate a program. Moreover, the powerful pressures that operated upon congressmen would not permit them to undertake the task. Many congressmen were interested less in improving administration than in securing favors for their localities from government bureaus. The individual congressman's demands upon the administrative system predisposed him to want to preserve personal friendships built up over many years with bureau chiefs. Government officeholders who objected to reorganization found congressmen most sympathetic.

But if Congress was subject to pressure, the President was too. Although the President had a much greater stake in improving administration than did a member of Congress, few Chief Executives were prepared to sacrifice political support in order to reform administration. Herbert Hoover had not issued comprehensive plans of reorganization until December 1932; Henry Morgenthau conceded that no President would dare reorganize the government while he sought re-election; the Brownlow Committee withheld its report until after the 1936 election. The President was better equipped than Congress to reorganize the government, but he was not immune from pressure.

Nor was reorganization a scientific process. Should the Forest Service have been transferred to Interior, or should it have remained in Agriculture? The proper position of a government bureau was, ultimately, a matter of judgment, not of scientific certainty. Since the location of a bureau often influenced its policy, the decision involved something more than efficient administration. Again, should a permanent Department of Public Welfare have been created? As Brownlow recognized, this was a question of government philosophy and of constitutional responsibility, and could not be answered by a science of management. Roosevelt's plan of reorganization, which went far beyond bureau reallocation, raised substantive issues of policy that inevitably produced conflict.

The President's plan misfired, in part, because it failed to attract the support of the American people. Roosevelt seemed to be on firm ground when he asserted that reorganization conformed to the American tradition of efficient management. But few felt strongly about reorganization. It appeared to be an abstract subject that promised no tangible benefits. On the other hand, most pressure groups attacked the plan because it threatened their influence over government bureaus. Each successful reform associated with the New Deal had enjoyed the support of some social group or geographic region. Reorganization lacked any such constituency. Those who did not strongly denounce the plan were inclined to be indifferent.

That this indifference gave way to near hysteria was a triumph for conservative opponents of the Roosevelt Administration. Frank Gannett's mailing campaign, William Randolph Hearst's editorials, and Father Coughlin's radio sermons succeeded in frightening many Americans. Unhappily, their attacks upon reorganization distorted the purposes of the bill and prevented a true consideration of its merits. Their ability to manipulate mass attitudes was well demonstrated. Of all New Deal measures, perhaps no other proposal was so little understood by the common man—or so angrily denounced by him—as was executive reorganization.

Those Americans who responded to frenzied attacks upon the measure did so for a number of reasons. In April 1938 the country was reeling under the impact of a sharp recession. For months the President had failed to come forth with a solution, and the Reorganization bill served as a convenient target for resentment born of economic frustration. The measure had come to symbolize New Deal reform at a time when the downturn made men look upon innovation with ill-favor. Moreover, the Nazi victory in Austria in 1938 kindled fears of executive usurpation. The similarity between Roosevelt's and Hitler's call for authority often obscured the fact that they used their power for different purposes. Roosevelt's enemies did their utmost to blur this distinction. Many Americans became obsessed with the dangers inherent in the exercise of power and failed to perceive that power could be directed toward very different ends.

When Roosevelt's critics charged that he sought to establish an executive dictatorship they were following an old tradition. Every strong President had faced a similar accusation. Anti-Federalists asserted that George Washington harbored monarchical ambitions. Whigs claimed that Andrew Jackson worked for "the concentration of all power in the hands of one man." Democrats denounced Abraham Lincoln's personal "despotism." Such attacks seem to have derived their strength from a deep aversion to powerful government; Americans have tended to view authority as alien and arbitrary. In the twentieth century the terms "monarch" and "despot" gave way to "dictator." But the substance of the charge remained the same, and it was not strange that it was employed by Roosevelt's opponents.

When the House of Representatives debated reorganization the voice of reason did not prevail. Congressmen who opposed sacrificing additional authority to the President harshly condemned the bill. An avalanche of protests from individuals, pressure groups, and government bureaus persuaded other legislators to vote to recommit. Conservative Democrats and Republicans snatched at the opportunity to rebuke Roosevelt. The President's political skill momentarily deserted him, and his liberal coalition began to crumble. By voting down the Reorganization bill, Congress struck a powerful blow at the President's prestige. Defeat of the measure both symbolized the decline of New Deal reform and contributed to that decline.

While the battle over reorganization raged, Roosevelt's efforts to clarify his goals had proved futile; his disavowal of dictatorial aims backfired. Only after the bill had been defeated was the President able to reply to his critics effectively. "History proves that dictatorships do not grow out of strong and successful governments, but out of weak and helpless governments," he asserted in a fireside chat on April 14, 1938. Democracy would be secure so long as it provided economic security. Roosevelt went on to draw a deeper lesson from the fight over reorganization. "There is placed on all of us the duty of self-restraint," he said: "That is the duty of a democracy . . . Self-restraint implies restraint by articulate public opinion, trained to distinguish fact from falsehood, trained to believe that bitterness is never a useful instrument in public affairs."

Bibliography

Notes

Index

# Bibliography

MANUSCRIPTS

*1. Papers of Congressmen*

William Bankhead MSS (State of Alabama, Department of Archives and History, Montgomery, Alabama).
Sol Bloom MSS (New York Public Library).
Lyle Boren MSS (University of Oklahoma, Norman, Oklahoma).
Wilburn Cartwright MSS (University of Oklahoma).
Robert Lee Doughton MSS (Southern Historical Collection, University of North Carolina, Chapel Hill, North Carolina).
Joseph Gavagan MSS (Oral History Collection, Columbia University, New York).
Clifford Hope MSS (Kansas State Historical Society, Topeka, Kansas).
Merlin Hull MSS (Wisconsin State Historical Society, Madison, Wisconsin).
Eugene Keogh MSS (Oral History Collection, Columbia University).
John H. Kerr MSS (Southern Historical Collection, University of North Carolina).
Lawrence Lewis MSS (State Historical Society of Colorado, Denver, Colorado).
Jack Nichols MSS (University of Oklahoma).
John J. O'Connor MSS (Indiana University, Bloomington, Indiana).
Henry George Teigan MSS (Minnesota Historical Society, St. Paul, Minnesota).
Lindsay Carter Warren MSS (Southern Historical Collection, University of North Carolina).

*2. Papers of Senators*

Josiah W. Bailey MSS (Duke University, Durham, North Carolina).
William E. Borah MSS (Library of Congress).
Arthur Capper MSS (Kansas State Historical Society).
Carter Glass MSS (University of Virginia, Charlottesville, Virginia).
Theodore Francis Green MSS (Library of Congress).
William G. McAdoo MSS (Library of Congress).
Kenneth McKellar MSS (Memphis Public Library, Memphis, Tennessee).

George Norris MSS (Library of Congress).
Elbert D. Thomas MSS (Franklin D. Roosevelt Library, Hyde Park, New York).
Elmer Thomas MSS (University of Oklahoma).

*3. Papers of Advocates and Opponents of Reorganization*

James Truslow Adams MSS (Columbia University).
Raymond Clapper MSS (Library of Congress).
Joseph B. Eastman MSS (Amherst College, Amherst, Massachusetts).
Herbert Emmerich MSS (privately held, New York City).
Frank E. Gannett MSS (Collection of Regional History, Cornell University, Ithaca, New York).
William B. Greeley MSS (University of Oregon, Eugene, Oregon).
William Green MSS (New York State School of Industrial and Labor Relations, Cornell University).
Alfred M. Landon MSS (Kansas State Historical Society).
Henry Morgenthau Diaries (Franklin D. Roosevelt Library).
Herbert Claiborne Pell MSS (Franklin D. Roosevelt Library).
Amos Pinchot MSS (Library of Congress).
Gifford Pinchot MSS (Library of Congress).
Franklin D. Roosevelt MSS, President's Personal Files (Franklin D. Roosevelt Library).
James Roosevelt MSS (Franklin D. Roosevelt Library).
Harold D. Smith Diaries (Franklin D. Roosevelt Library).
Frank A. Vanderlip MSS (Columbia University).

*4. United States Government Papers*

Records of the Bureau of the Budget (Executive Office Building, Washington, D. C.).
Records of the Bureau of the Budget, Central Files (National Archives).
Department of Agriculture Files, Office of the Secretary (National Archives).
Department of Interior Files, Office of the Secretary (National Archives).
National Resources Planning Board Files, Record Group 187 (National Archives).
Papers of the President's Committee on Administrative Management (Franklin D. Roosevelt Library).
Franklin D. Roosevelt MSS, Official Files (Franklin D. Roosevelt Library).
Records of the Select Committee on Government Reorganization, Records of the House of Representatives, 76th Congress, Record Group 233 (National Archives).

Records of the Special Committee of the U. S. Senate to Investigate Lobbying Activities, Records of the U. S. Senate, 1935-1940, Record Group 46 (National Archives).

PUBLISHED SOURCES:

*1. United States Documents*

U. S., Congress, Joint Committee on Government Organization, *Hearings, Reorganization of the Executive Departments*, 75th Congress, 1st Session, 1937.

U. S., Congress, Senate, Select Committee to Investigate the Executive Agencies of the Government, *Hearings, Investigation of Executive Agencies of the Government*, 75th Congress, 1st Session, 1937.

U. S., Congress, Senate, Select Committee on Government Organization, *Hearings, Reorganization of the Government Agencies*, 75th Congress, 1st Session, 1937.

U. S., Congress, Senate, Special Committee to Investigate Lobbying Activities, *Hearings, pursuant to H. Res. 165*, Part 7, 75th Congress, 3rd Session, 1938.

U. S., Congress, House, Select Committee on Lobbying Activities, *Hearings, pursuant to H. Res. 298*, Part 5, 81st Congress, 2nd Session, 1950.

U. S., Congress, Senate, Committee on Expenditures in the Executive Departments, *Hearings, to Change the Name of the Department of the Interior*, 74th Congress, 1st Session, 1935.

U. S., *Congressional Record*, 1937–1939.

U. S., Bureau of the Budget, *Reorganization of the Executive Branch of the Federal Government 1923–1952: An Annotated Bibliography* (Washington, 1937).

U. S., Civil Service Commission, *Fifty-Fifth Annual Report* (Washington, 1938).

Brookings Institution, *Investigation of Executive Agencies of the Government*, Report to the Select Committee to Investigate the Executive Agencies of the Government (Washington, 1937).

*Report of the President's Committee on Administrative Management*, (Washington, 1937).

*2. Newspapers (1936–1939)*

*C. I. O. News.*
New York *Herald-Tribune.*
New York *Journal-American.*
*Labor.*
Milwaukee *Leader.*
Baltimore *News-Post.*

*New York Times.*
*Wall Street Journal.*
New York *World-Telegram.*

*3. Autobiographies, Memoirs, Letters and Diaries, Speeches, Pamphlets*

Bloom, Sol. *The Autobiography of Sol Bloom.* New York: G. P. Putnam's Sons, 1948.

Brownlow, Louis. *A Passion for Anonymity.* Chicago: University of Chicago Press, 1958.

Byrnes, James F. *All In One Lifetime.* New York: Harper and Bros., 1958.

Committee for Constitutional Government. *Needed Now—Capacity for Leadership, Courage to Lead.* New York, 1944.

Farley, James A. *Behind the Ballots.* New York: Harcourt, Brace and Co., 1938.

———— *Jim Farley's Story.* New York: McGraw-Hill, 1948.

Flynn, Edward J. *You're the Boss.* New York: Viking Press, 1947.

Gannett, Frank E. *What Our New Gold Policy Means.* Address at Rochester Chamber of Commerce, November 3, 1933.

Greeley, William B. *Forests and Men.* New York: Doubleday and Co., 1951.

Ickes, Harold. *The Secret Diary of Harold Ickes.* 3 vols. New York: Simon and Schuster, 1954.

Johnson, Douglas. *The Assault on the Supreme Court.* New York: National Committee to Uphold Constitutional Government, 1937.

Lilienthal, David E. *The Journals of David E. Lilienthal.* 2 vols. New York: Harper and Row, 1964.

Martin, Joseph. *My First Fifty Years in Politics.* New York: McGraw-Hill, 1960.

Merriam, Charles E. *Conflicts in Modern Democracy.* Address at National League of Women Voters National Convention, St. Louis, Missouri, April, 1938.

Moley, Raymond. *After Seven Years.* New York: Harper and Bros., 1939.

Morison, Elting E. (ed.) *The Letters of Theodore Roosevelt.* Cambridge: Harvard University Press, 1954.

National Rivers and Harbors Congress, *Proceedings of the Special "Council of War" Meeting,* Washington, April 26, 1938.

Nixon, Edgar B. (ed.) *Franklin D. Roosevelt and Conservation, 1911–1945.* 2 vols. New York: Franklin D. Roosevelt Library, 1957.

Perkins, Frances. *The Roosevelt I Knew.* New York: The Viking Press, 1946.

Pettengill, Samuel B. *Jefferson, The Forgotten Man.* New York: America's Future, 1938.

Pettengill, Samuel B. *Smoke Screen*. Kingsport, Tennessee: Southern Publishers, 1940.

Pinchot, Amos R. E. *History of the Progressive Party, 1912–1916*. Edited by Helene Maxwell Hooker. New York: New York University Press, 1958.

Roosevelt, Elliott (ed.) *F. D. R.: His Personal Letters*. 4 vols. New York: Duell, Sloan and Pearce, 1948–1950.

Roper, Daniel C. *Fifty Years of Public Life*. Durham: Duke University Press, 1941.

Rosenman, Samuel I. (ed.) *The Public Papers and Addresses of Franklin D. Roosevelt*. 13 vols. New York: Macmillan Co., 1938–1950.

Rosenman, Samuel I. *Working With Roosevelt*. New York: Harper and Bros., 1952.

United States Chamber of Commerce. *Government Reorganization*. Washington: February 1938.

## 4. Books

Beck, James M. *Our Wonderland of Bureaucracy*. New York: Macmillan Co., 1932.

Blaisdell, Donald C. *American Democracy Under Pressure*. New York: Ronald Press Co., 1957.

Brownlow, Louis. *The President and the Presidency*. Chicago: Public Administration Service, 1947.

Burdette, Franklin L. *Filibustering in the Senate*. Princeton: Princeton University Press, 1940.

Burns, James M. *Roosevelt: The Lion and the Fox*. New York: Harcourt, Brace and Co., 1956.

Cantril, Hadley (ed.) *Public Opinion 1935–1946*. Princeton: Princeton University Press, 1951.

Clawson, Marion and Burnell Held. *The Federal Lands: Their Use and Management*. Baltimore: Johns Hopkins Press, 1957.

Corwin, Edward S. *The President: Office and Powers*. New York: New York University Press, 1940.

Crawford, Arthur Whipple. *Monetary Management under the New Deal*. Washington: American Council on Public Affairs, 1940.

Crawford, Kenneth G. *The Pressure Boys*. New York: Julian Messner, 1939.

Cushman, Robert E. *The Independent Regulatory Commissions*. New York: Oxford University Press, 1941.

Dana, Samuel Trask. *Forest and Range Policy*. New York: McGraw-Hill, 1956.

Emmerich, Herbert. *Essays on Federal Reorganization*. Birmingham: University of Alabama Press, 1950.

Foss, Phillip O. *Politics and Grass: The Administration of Grazing on the Public Domain.* Seattle: University of Washington Press, 1960.

Franklin, Jay. *1940.* New York: The Viking Press, 1940.

Gannett, Frank E. and B. F. Catherwood. *Industrial and Labor Relations in Great Britain.* New York: J. J. Little and Ives Co., 1939.

Garrett, Charles. *The LaGuardia Years: Machine and Reform Politics in New York City.* New Brunswick: Rutgers University Press, 1961.

Gaus, John M. *et al. The Frontiers of Public Administration.* Chicago: University of Chicago Press, 1936.

Graves, W. Brooke. *Public Administration in a Democratic Society.* Boston: D. C. Heath and Co., 1950.

————— *Reorganization of the Executive Branch of the Government of the United States.* Washington: Library of Congress, Legislative Reference Service, Public Affairs Bulletin no. 66, February 1949.

Gross, Bertram M. *The Legislative Struggle.* New York: McGraw-Hill, 1954.

Gulick, Luther H. *American Forest Policy.* New York: Duell, Sloan and Pearce, 1951.

————— *The National Institute of Public Administration.* New York: National Institute of Public Administration, 1928.

Gulick, Luther and L. Urwick. (eds.) *Papers on the Science of Administration.* New York: Institute of Public Administration, 1937.

Haines, Charles C. and Marshall E. Dimock (eds.) *Essays on the Law and Practice of Governmental Administration.* Baltimore: Johns Hopkins Press, 1935.

Hardy, Charles O. *The Warren-Pearson Price Theory.* Washington: Brookings Institution, 1935.

Harris, Joseph P. *Congressional Control of Administration.* New York: Doubleday and Co., 1964.

Hays, Samuel P. *Conservation and the Gospel of Efficiency.* Cambridge: Harvard University Press, 1959.

Herring, E. Pendleton. *Public Administration and the Public Interest.* New York: McGraw-Hill, 1936.

High, Stanley. *Roosevelt—And Then?* New York: Harper and Bros., 1937.

Hobbs, Edward H. *Behind the President: A Study of Executive Office Agencies.* Washington: Public Affairs Press, 1954.

————— *Executive Reorganization in the National Government.* University: University of Mississippi Press, 1953.

Hyneman, Charles S. *Bureaucracy in a Democracy.* New York: Harper and Bros., 1950.

Israel, Fred L. *Nevada's Key Pittman*. Lincoln: University of Nebraska Press, 1963.

Jenkin, Thomas Paul. *Reactions of Major Groups to Positive Government in the United States, 1930–1940*. Berkeley: University of California Press, 1945.

Johnson, Gerald W. *Roosevelt: Dictator or Democrat?* New York: Harper and Bros., 1941.

Karl, Barry Dean. *Executive Reorganization and Reform in the New Deal*. Cambridge: Harvard University Press, 1963.

King, Willford I. *The Causes of Economic Fluctuations*. New York: Ronald Press Co., 1938.

Kraines, Oscar. *Congress and the Challenge of Big Government*. New York: Bookman Associates, 1958.

Landis, James M. *The Administrative Process*. New Haven: Yale University Press, 1938.

Laski, Harold J. *The American Presidency*. New York: Harper and Bros., 1940.

Leuchtenburg, William E. *Franklin D. Roosevelt and the New Deal*. New York: Harper and Bros., 1963.

Lyon, Peter. *Success Story: The Life and Times of S. S. McClure*. New York: Charles Scribner's Sons, 1963.

Maass, Arthur. *Muddy Waters: The Army Engineers and the Nation's Rivers*. Cambridge: Harvard University Press, 1951.

McCoy, Donald R. *Angry Voices: Left-of-Center Politics in the New Deal Era*. Lawrence: University of Kansas Press, 1958.

McCune, Wesley. *The Farm Bloc*. New York: Doubleday, Doran and Co., 1943.

McGeary, M. Nelson. *Gifford Pinchot: Forester-Politician*. Princeton: Princeton University Press, 1960.

Mansfield, Harvey C. *The Comptroller General*. New Haven: Yale University Press, 1939.

Marcy, Carl. *Presidential Commissions*. New York: King's Crown Press, 1945.

Meriam, Lewis, and Lawrence F. Schmeckebier. *Reorganization of the National Government: What Does It Involve?* Washington: The Brookings Institution, 1939.

Merriam, Charles E. *On the Agenda of Democracy*. Cambridge: Harvard University Press, 1941.

———— *Prologue to Politics*. Chicago: University of Chicago Press, 1939.

———— *The Role of Politics in Social Change*. New York: New York University Press, 1936.

Milton, George Fort. *The Use of Presidential Power, 1789–1943*. Boston: Little, Brown and Co., 1944.

Peffer, E. Louise. *The Closing of the Public Domain*. Stanford: Stanford University Press, 1951.

Pritchett, C. Herman. *The Tennessee Valley Authority: A Study in Public Administration*. Chapel Hill: University of North Carolina Press, 1943.

Robbins, Roy M. *Our Landed Heritage*. Princeton: Princeton University Press, 1942.

Roose, Kenneth D. *The Economics of Recession and Revival*. New Haven: Yale University Press, 1954.

Rossiter, Clinton. *The American Presidency*. New York: Mentor Books, 1956.

Schattschneider, E. E. *Party Government*. New York: Rinehart and Co., 1942.

Schlesinger, Arthur M., Jr. *The Coming of the New Deal*. Boston: Houghton Mifflin Co., 1959.

——— *The Politics of Upheaval*. Boston: Houghton Mifflin Co., 1960.

Schriftgiesser, Karl. *The Lobbyists: The Art and Business of Influencing Lawmakers*. Boston: Little, Brown and Co., 1951.

Taft, Philip. *The A. F. of L. from the Death of Gompers to the Merger*. New York: Harper and Bros., 1959.

Timmons, Bascom N. *Garner of Texas*. New York: Harper and Bros., 1948.

Tompkins, Dorothy C. *Congressional Investigation of Lobbying*. Berkeley: University of California Press, 1956.

Tugwell, Rexford Guy. *The Democratic Roosevelt*. New York: Doubleday and Co., 1957.

——— *The Enlargement of the Presidency*. New York: Doubleday and Co., 1960.

Tull, Charles J. *Father Coughlin and the New Deal*. Syracuse: Syracuse University Press, 1965.

Waldo, Dwight. *The Administrative State*. New York: Ronald Press Co., 1948.

Wallace, Schuyler C. *Federal Departmentalization: A Critique of Theories of Organization*. New York: Columbia University Press, 1941.

Wengert, Norman. *Natural Resources and the Political Struggle*. New York: Doubleday and Co., 1955.

White, Leonard D. (ed.) *The Future of Government in the United States: Essays in Honor of Charles E. Merriam*. Chicago: University of Chicago Press, 1942.

White, Leonard D. *The Republican Era*. New York: Macmillan Co., 1958.

Williamson, Samuel T. *Frank Gannett*. New York: Duell, Sloan and Pearce, 1940.

Williamson, Samuel T. *Imprint of a Publisher.* (New York?): Robert M. McBride and Co., 1948.

5. *Magazine Articles*

"Administrative Reorganization and Executive Control," *Commercial and Financial Chronical,* 144:333-34 (January 16, 1937).

"Adventure in Blueprints," *The Nation,* 144:116-17 (January 30, 1937).

"A Headless Fourth Branch," *Commercial and Financial Chronicle,* 144:321 (January 16, 1937).

Altman, O. R. "First Session of the Seventy-Fifth Congress," *American Political Science Review,* 31:1071-93 (December 1937).

——— "Second and Third Sessions of the Seventy-Fifth Congress, 1937–1938," *American Political Science Review,* 32:1099-1123 (December 1938).

"American Deadlock," *The (London) Economist,* 131:130-31 (April 16, 1938).

*America's Future* (1938–1940).

Anderson, Paul Y. "Let Gannett Explain," *The Nation,* 146:375-76 (April 2, 1938).

——— "Reorganization and Bunk," *The Nation,* 146:406-7 (April 9, 1938).

"A Needless Defeat," *The (London) Economist,* 131:182-83 (April 23, 1938).

"A New Deal Victory," *New Masses,* 27:12 (April 5, 1938).

"Behind the Reorganization Switch," *Business Week,* April 2, 1938, p. 18.

Beyle, Herman C. "Determining the Effect of Propaganda Campaigns," *Annals of the American Academy of Political and Social Science,* 179:106-113 (May 1935).

Blair, Edson. "Administration Hopes for One Major Triumph Now Pinned to Reorganization Bill," *Barron's* 18:4 (March 21, 1938).

——— "President Now Needs Passage of Reorganization Bill," *Barron's,* 18:4 (April 4, 1938).

——— "Roosevelt, a Reorganization Committee of One," *Barron's,* 17:4 (January 18, 1937).

Bratter, Herbert M. "The Committee for the Nation: A Case Study in Propaganda," *The Journal of Political Economy,* 49:531-53 (August 1941).

"Brookings vs. President," *Business Week,* June 12, 1937, pp. 19-20.

Brownlow, Louis (ed.) "The Executive Office of the President: A Symposium," *Public Administration Review,* 1:101-40 (Winter 1941).

"Bureau Bill Passes Senate," *Nature Magazine,* 31:294 (May 1938).

Butler, Ovid. "The Oregon Checkmate," *American Forests*, 44:157-62, 196-97 (April 1936).

Carroll, R. G. "Pruning and Spraying," *Saturday Evening Post*, January 2, 1937, pp. 24, 50.

Chapman, H. H. "Reorganization and the Forest Service," *Journal of Forestry*, 35:427-34 (May 1937).

———— "Shall the Department of the Interior Become the Department of Conservation and Works," *Science*, 82:101-2 (August 2, 1935).

Cole, Kenneth C. "The 'Merit System' Again," *American Political Science Review*, 31:695-98 (August 1937).

"Concerning Dictators," *The Magazine of Wall Street*, 61:811 (April 9, 1938).

"Conservation," *Nature Magazine*, 30:35-36 (July 1937).

Cooper, Joseph. "The Legislative Veto: Its Promise and Its Peril," *Public Policy; A Yearbook of the Graduate School of Public Administration, Harvard University*, 7:128-74 (1956).

Cooper, Joseph and Ann. "The Legislative Veto and the Constitution," *George Washington Law Review*, 30:467-516 (March 1962).

Corey, Herbert. "Stop, Look, and Listen," *Public Utilities Fortnightly*, 21:707-17 (June 9, 1938).

Corwin, Edward S. "The President as Administrative Chief," *Journal of Politics*, 1:17-61 (February 1939).

Creel, George. "Byrd Song," *Collier's*, 100:21, 30-31 (August 21, 1937).

"Defeat of the Reorganization Bill," New York Chamber of Commerce, *Monthly Bulletin*, 29:395 (April 1938).

Delano, Frederic A. "Shifting Bureaus at Washington," *Review of Reviews and World's Work*, 87:33, 56-58 (May 1933).

"Democracy Must Counter-Attack," *New Masses*, 27:13 (April 19, 1938).

"Departmental Reorganization and Executive Autocracy," *Commercial and Financial Chronicle*, 146:1614-15 (March 12, 1938).

DeVoto, Bernard. "Desertion from the New Deal," *Harper's*, 175:557-60 (October 1937).

"Dictatorship vs. New Deal Technique," *Commercial and Financial Chronicle*, 146:2100 (April 2, 1938).

Dimock, Marshall E. "The Objectives of Government Reorganization," *Public Administration Review*, 11:233-41 (Autumn 1951).

"Editorial," *The Commercial West Weekly*, 75:6 (April 16, 1938).

"Editorial," *The Nation*, 146:231 (February 26, 1938).

E. K. T. "Executive Reorganization," *Magazine of Wall Street*, 61:816 (April 9, 1938).

———— "Reorganization Troubles," *Magazine of Wall Street*, 59:474 (January 30, 1937).

E. K. T. "Roosevelt Defeat," *Magazine of Wall Street,* 62:10 (April 23, 1938).

Emmerich, Herbert. "Personnel Problems in New Federal Agencies," *Annals of the American Academy of Political and Social Science,* 189:119-26 (January 1937).

"F. D. R.'s Reorganizing Job," *Business Week,* January 26, 1937, pp. 26, 28.

"F. D. R. Would Revamp Regulatory Commissions," *Railway Age,* 102:145, 152 (January 16, 1937).

"Federal Department of Conservation and a Clearing House for Federal Public Works Projects," *Bird Lore,* 40:83-85 (January 1938).

"Federal Government Reorganization," New York Chamber of Commerce, *Monthly Bulletin,* 29:312-17 (February 1938).

Fritz, Emanuel. "A Plea for a Fair Appraisal of Federal Forestry Reorganization," *Journal of Forestry,* 36:271-75 (March 1938).

"Ganging Up on the President," *New Republic,* 94:290-91 (April 13, 1938).

Gosnell, Harold F. and Morris H. Cohen. "Progressive Politics: Wisconsin an Example," *American Political Science Review,* 34:920-35 (October 1940).

"Governmental Reorganization," *The Commonweal,* 27:647 (April 8, 1938).

"Government by Men versus Government by Law," *Commercial and Financial Chronicle,* 144:3896-97 (June 12, 1937).

Graham, George A. "Reorganization—A Question of Executive Institutions," *American Political Science Review,* 32:708-18 (August 1938).

———— "The Presidency and the Executive Office of the President," *The Journal of Politics,* 12:599-621 (November 1950).

Greeley, William B. "Common Sense in Conservation," *American Forests,* 44:28 (January 1938).

Gulick, Luther. "Making Democracy Work," *Survey Graphic,* 26:126-28 (March 1937).

———— "Politics, Administration, and the 'New Deal,'" *Annals of the American Academy of Political and Social Science,* 169:55-66 (September 1933).

———— "The Recent Movement for Better Government Personnel," *American Political Science Review,* 31:292-301 (April 1937).

———— "The Scientific Approach to the Problems of Society and Government," *University of Buffalo Studies,* 15:1-8 (March 1938).

Harris, Joseph P. "The Progress of Administrative Reorganization in the Seventy-Fifth Congress," *American Political Science Review,* 21:862-70 (October 1937).

Hayes, Douglas A. "Business Confidence and Business Activity," *Michigan Business Studies,* vol. X (1951).

Helm, William P. "A Blank Check for Mr. Roosevelt?" *California,* 27: 11, 39-40 (March 1937).

Herring, E. Pendleton. "Social Forces and the Reorganization of the Federal Bureaucracy," *Southwestern Social Science Quarterly,* 15: 185-200 (December 1934).

Hurt, Peyton. "Who Should Reorganize the National Administration?" *American Political Science Review,* 26:1082-98 (December 1932).

Hyneman, Charles S. "Administrative Reorganization: An Adventure into Science and Theology," *The Journal of Politics,* 1:62-75 (February 1939).

Ickes, Harold. "Mail-Order Government," *Collier's,* 103:14-15, 53-55 (February 18, 1939).

―――― "My Twelve Years with FDR," *Saturday Evening Post,* July 24, 1948, p. 68.

Kent, Frank R. "Roosevelt's Bid for Dictatorship: Reorganization Bill," *American Mercury,* 43:404-11 (April 1938).

Keyserling, Leon H. "The Wagner Act: Its Origin and Current Significance," *George Washington Law Review,* 29:199-233 (December 1960).

Lasswell, Harold D. "The Person: Subject and Object of Propaganda," *Annals of the American Academy of Political and Social Science,* 179:187-93 (May 1935).

Leach, Henry G. "Not a Dead Issue," *Forum,* 100:49-50 (August 1938).

Leiserson, Avery. "Political Limitations on Executive Reorganization," *American Political Science Review,* 41:68-84 (February 1947).

"Let Mr. Ickes Answer," *American Forests,* 44:23 (January 1938).

Lineweaver, G. W. "Another Job for Hercules," *Public Utilities Fortnightly,* 19:339-49 (March 18, 1937).

"Look Out for the Greased Pig," *Nature Magazine,* 31:45-46 (January 1938).

MacGregor, Donald. "Earthquake in Washington," *Nation's Business,* 25:21-22, 106-8 (February 1937).

"Many Little Bureaucracies," *Banking,* 29:8-10 (February 1937).

McCarl, John R. "Government-Run-Everything," *Saturday Evening Post,* October 3, 1936, pp. 8-9, 52; October 17, 1936, pp. 8-9, 70-76.

―――― "The President's Program for Administrative Management," New York Chamber of Commerce, *Monthly Bulletin,* 28:388-404 (April 1937).

McDiarmid, John. "Reorganization of the General Accounting Office," *American Political Science Review*, 31:508-16 (June 1937).

McKee, Oliver. "A New Deal on the New Deal," *Boston Business*, 29:3 (May 1938).

Merriam, Charles E. "Public Administration and Political Theory," *Journal of Social Philosophy*, 5:293-308 (July 1940).

———— "Putting Politics in its Place," *International Journal of Ethics*, 46:127-50 (January 1936).

———— "The National Resources Planning Board: A Chapter in American Planning Experience," *American Political Science Review*, 38:1075-88 (December 1944).

Millett, John D. and Lindsay Rogers. "The Legislative Veto and the Reorganization Act of 1939," *Public Administration Review*, 1: 176-89 (Winter 1941).

"More Leaders Object," *American Forests*, 44:14-15 (January 1938).

"Mr. Ickes' Answer," *American Forests*, 44:113-15 (March 1938).

Murphy, Robert Cushman. "The President's Page," *Bird Lore*, 40:3 (January 1938).

"Nation Says 'No' to Reorganization Bill," *American Agriculturist*, 135:12 (April 23, 1938).

*Newsweek* (1936–1939).

"New Tools for Uncle Sam," *The New Republic*, 89:371-72 (January 27, 1937).

Phelps, Thomas W. "The Revolt Against Roosevelt," *Barron's*, 18:10 (April 11, 1938).

Pierce, Bessie Louise. "The Political Pattern of Some Women's Organizations," *Annals of the American Academy of Political and Social Science*, 179:50-58 (May 1935).

Pinchot, Gifford. "A Forest Appeal," *Literary Digest*, 120:30 (July 20, 1935).

———— "It Can Happen Here," *American Forests*, 43:282-83 (June 1937).

———— "Save the Forest Service," *California*, 27:21, 39 (November 1937).

Pinkett, Harold T. "The Keep Commission, 1905–1909, A Rooseveltian Effort for Administrative Reform," *Journal of American History*, 52:297-312 (September 1965).

"Press and Reorganization," *Nature Magazine*, 31:105-6 (February 1938).

Price, Don K. "Staffing the Presidency," *American Political Science Review*, 40:1154-68 (December 1946).

"Proposed Reorganization of the Federal Departments," *Science*, 86: 242-43 (September 10, 1937).

"Prospects for Reorganization," *Nature Magazine,* 32:98 (February 1939).

Ray, J. M. "Defeat of the Administration Reorganization Bill," *Southwestern Social Science Quarterly,* 20:115-24 (September 1939).

Reeves, Floyd W. and Paul T. David. "Reorganization in the Federal Government," *Civic Affairs,* 5:1 (September 1937).

"Reorganization Bill Is Turned Back," *American Forests,* 44:207-8 (May 1938).

"Reorganization Bill Passes Senate," *American Agriculturist,* 135:12 (April 9, 1938).

"Reorganization in the Dark," *American Forests,* 43:397 (August 1937).

"Reorganization Jitters," *The New Republic,* 94:263 (April 6, 1938).

"Reorganization Marches On," *The New Republic,* 99:57-58 (May 24, 1939).

"Reorganization—The Transcending Issue," *American Forests,* 43:495 (October 1937).

"Reorganizing Washington," *World's Work,* 61:36-39 (May 1932).

Rogers, Lindsay. "Reorganization: Post-Mortem Notes," *Political Science Quarterly,* 53:161-72 (June 1938).

——— "The Independent Regulatory Commissions," *Political Science Quarterly,* 52:1-17 (March 1937).

Roosevelt, Franklin D. "Results in New York State Vindicate Administrative Reorganization," *National Municipal Review,* 19:223-25 (April 1930).

"Roosevelt Recommends a Department of Conservation," *American Forests,* 43:74, 92 (February 1937).

Schmeckebier, Lawrence F. "Organization of the Executive Branch of the National Government of the United States: Changes between July 16, 1938 and April 25, 1939," *American Political Science Review,* 33:450-55 (June 1939).

"Senator Byrd Talks About 'Presidents I Have Known'," *U. S. News and World Report,* September 10, 1962, pp. 84-85.

"Shadow Boxing," *American Forests,* 44:121-22 (March 1938).

"Shadow Boxing in a Crisis," *The Nation,* 146:400-1 (April 9, 1938).

Short, Lloyd M. "An Investigation of the Executive Agencies of the U. S. Government," *American Political Science Review,* 33:60-66 (February 1939).

——— "Studies of Administrative Management in the Federal Government," *American Political Science Review,* 32:93-103 (February 1938).

"Six Anonymous Sub-Presidents," *Commercial and Financial Chronicle,* 145:825-26 (August 7, 1937).

"So the Government Reorganizes," *Business Week,* April 1, 1939, pp. 15-16.

"The Lower One-Third and the Forest Service," *West Coast Lumberman,* 65:38-39 (June 1938).

"The Press Looks at Reorganization," *American Forests,* 43:545 (November 1937).

*The Progressive and La Follette's Magazine* (1938).

"The Proposed Reorganization of the Federal Government," New York Chamber of Commerce, *Monthly Bulletin,* 29:10-14 (May 1937).

"The Reorganization Bill in Retrospect," *Journal of Forestry,* 36:641-42 (July 1938).

"The Reorganization Quarrel," *The New Republic,* 94:149-50 (March 16, 1938).

"Thomas F. Woodlock on Continued Independence for I.C.C.," *Railway Age,* 102:703 (April 24, 1937).

*Time* (1936–1939).

T. R. B. "Washington Notes: Great Caesar Fell," *The New Republic,* 94:303 (April 13, 1938).

———— "Washington Notes: Rainmaker but No Rain," *The New Republic,* 94:358-59 (April 27, 1938).

———— "Washington Notes: Reorganization," *The New Republic,* 99:18 (May 10, 1939).

"U. S. Forester Silcox Says," *West Coast Lumberman,* 65:9 (March 1938).

"Victory for Hysteria," *The Nation,* 146:427-28 (April 16, 1938).

Weadock, Bernard F. "Fourth Branch of Government," *Edison Electrical Institute,* 5:227-30 (June 1937).

"What Conservation Leaders Say," *American Forests,* 43:588-89 (December 1937).

Wheeler, Burton K. "I.C.C. Should be Independent," *Railway Age,* 102:631-32 (April 10, 1937).

"Whipping a Dead Horse," *The Nation,* 146:317-18 (March 19, 1938).

# Notes

Chapter I. The Origins of Executive Reorganization, 1933–1936

1. Luther Gulick to Franklin D. Roosevelt, September 30, 1937, Roosevelt Papers (Franklin D. Roosevelt Library), Official File (hereafter cited as OF) 285C, Box 16.

2. Leonard D. White, *The Republican Era: 1869–1901* (New York, 1958), p. 84. An account of the Cockrell Committee of 1887 and the Dockery-Cockrell Commission of 1893 may be found in Oscar Kraines, *The Challenge of Big Government* (New York, 1958).

3. Edward Hobbs, *Executive Reorganization in the National Government* (Mississippi, 1953), pp. 10-14; Harold T. Pinkett, "The Keep Commission, 1905–1909: A Rooseveltian Effort for Administrative Reform," *Journal of American History,* 52:297-312 (September 1965). The Keep Commission was named for its chairman, Charles H. Keep, who was Assistant Secretary of the Treasury.

4. Josephus Daniels to Roosevelt, March 29, 1938, Roosevelt Papers, President's Personal File (hereafter cited as PPF) 86.

5. Daniels to Roosevelt, March 29, 1938, Roosevelt Papers, PPF 86; Hobbs, *Executive Reorganization,* pp. 29-34.

6. *New York Times,* February 18, 1932, p. 20. See "Reorganizing Washington," *World's Work,* 61:36-39 (May 1932); James M. Beck, *Our Wonderland of Bureaucracy* (New York, 1932).

7. *New York Times,* December 11, 1932, p. 10. On Hoover's plan, see Lewis Meriam and Lawrence F. Schmeckebier, *Reorganization of the National Government: What Does It Involve?* (Washington, D. C., 1939), pp. 187-96.

8. Roosevelt to Clarence Dill, March 9, 1933, Roosevelt Papers, OF 285C, Box 6; Franklin D. Roosevelt, *Looking Forward* (New York, 1933), p. 71.

9. Daniel Roper, *Fifty Years of Public Life* (Durham, North Carolina, 1941), pp. 267-68; Press Conference, Roosevelt Papers, March 8, 1933, I, 13, 16.

10. Josephus Daniels to Roosevelt, March 29, 1938, Roosevelt Papers, PPF 86; Bernard Baruch to Roosevelt, November 14, 1934, Roosevelt Papers, PPF 88.

11. William McAdoo to Walter P. Jones, April 3, 1938, William G.

McAdoo MSS (Library of Congress), Box 452; J. Warren Davis to Roosevelt, April 6, 1938, Roosevelt Papers, PPF 5310.

12. Samuel I. Rosenman (ed.), *The Public Papers and Addresses of Franklin D. Roosevelt,* 13 vols. (New York, 1938–1950), I, 279-306.

13. W. Brooke Graves, *Reorganization of the Executive Branch of the Government* (Washington, 1949), pp. 381-83.

14. Franklin D. Roosevelt, "Results in New York State Vindicate Administrative Reorganization," *National Municipal Review,* 19:223-25 (April 1930). Roosevelt later said that his Pittsburgh campaign speech promising economy through reorganization was not what he should have said and that he did it only because Baruch and Johnson urged him to do so. Raymond Clapper Diary, April 9, 1938, Raymond Clapper MSS (Library of Congress), Box 8.

15. Louis Brownlow, *A Passion for Anonymity* (Chicago, 1958), p. 382.

16. Press Conference, Roosevelt Papers, May 31, 1933, I, 333-34; June 2, 1933, I, 335-40A.

17. In one sense, the creation of New Deal emergency agencies "reorganized" the Executive Branch. Roosevelt, however, took the term to refer to reshuffling bureau functions in order to reduce duplication of effort and improve government operations.

18. Graves, *Reorganization of the Executive Branch,* pp. 111-29; Meriam and Schmeckebier, *Reorganization of the National Government,* pp. 197-215.

19. See Pendleton Herring, "Social Forces and the Reorganization of the Federal Bureaucracy," *Southwestern Social Science Quarterly,* 15:186 (December, 1934).

20. Press Conference, Roosevelt Papers, March 22, 1933, I, 62; March 31, 1933, I, 104; May 5, 1933, I, 228-29; May 19, 1933, I, 280-81; May 24, 1933, I, 294.

21. Frances Perkins, *The Roosevelt I Knew* (New York, 1946), pp. 359-60. Roosevelt told this to Miss Perkins during World War II, but there is reason to believe that it fairly reflected his earlier outlook. See Arthur M. Schlesinger, *The Coming of the New Deal* (Boston, 1959), p. 534; Brownlow, *Passion for Anonymity,* pp. 318-21.

22. Harold D. Smith Diary, July 31, 1939, Harold D. Smith MSS (Franklin D. Roosevelt Library).

23. Press Conference, Roosevelt Papers, October 31, 1939, XIV, 266; May 31, 1933, I, 333.

24. Henry Morgenthau Diary, December 8, 1936, Henry Morgenthau MSS (Franklin D. Roosevelt Library), Book 47.

25. Dan Roper to Edward M. House, January 9, 1933, Roosevelt Papers, OF 46; Dan Roper memorandum to Roosevelt, June 7, 1933, Roosevelt Papers, OF 285C, Box 6.

26. Herbert Emmerich, *Essays on Federal Reorganization* (Birmingham, Ala., 1950), p. 37; Brownlow, *Passion for Anonymity*, p. 392.

27. Brownlow, *Passion for Anonymity*, p. 239.

28. *Ibid.*, pp. 277, 284, 287; Brownlow to Louis Howe, April 27, 1933, Roosevelt Papers, OF 285C, Box 6.

29. Barry Dean Karl, *Executive Reorganization and Reform in the New Deal* (Cambridge, 1963), chap. 2. The three members of the President's Research Committee on Social Trends were Merriam, Wesley C. Mitchell, an economist, and William F. Ogburn, a sociologist.

30. Charles E. Merriam, "Proposed Study of Management in the Federal Government," October 1935, President's Committee on Administrative Management Files (Franklin D. Roosevelt Library), Box 1. [Cited hereafter as PCAM Files.]

31. Brownlow, *Passion for Anonymity*, pp. 299-301, 329-31; F. A. Delano to Harold Ickes, October 30, 1935, PCAM Files, Box 1. Frederick A. Delano, the President's uncle, was chairman of the NRC.

32. "Summary of a Meeting Held Between Lewis Meriam, Charles Ascher, Louis Brownlow and Joseph P. Harris," December 16, 1935, PCAM Files, Box 1.

33. Brownlow, *Passion for Anonymity*, pp. 332-33.

34. Merriam to Brownlow, February 20, 1936, PCAM Files, Box 1. Ickes, Delano, and Charles W. Eliot II were also present at the meeting.

35. Charles Eliot II, "Notes on a conference with the President," February 20, 1936, PCAM Files, Box 1; Brownlow, *Passion for Anonymity*, pp. 333-34.

36. Merriam to Brownlow, February 20, 1936, PCAM Files, Box 1.

37. Charles Eliot II, "Notes on a conference with the President," February 20, 1936, PCAM Files, Box 1.

38. Third draft of Louis Brownlow, "Management Study," February-March 1936, PCAM Files, Box 1.

39. Brownlow to Roosevelt, March 6, 1936, Roosevelt Papers, OF 285C, Box 6; Brownlow, *Passion for Anonymity*, p. 337.

40. Karl, *Executive Reorganization*, chap. 3.

41. Charles E. Merriam, "Conflicts in Modern Democracy," Address to the National League of Women Voters, St. Louis, Missouri, April, 1938, pp. 10-12; Brownlow, *Passion for Anonymity*, pp. 353, 371.

42. Interview with Louis Brownlow, September 4, 1962.

43. Karl, *Executive Reorganization*, p. 212.

44. On the role of the President, see: Brownlow, *Passion for Anonymity*, p. 336; Louis Brownlow, *The President and the Presidency* (Chicago, 1949), pp. 110-11, 129; statement of Charles Merriam, *Hearings before the Joint Committee on Government Organization*, 75th Cong., 1st sess. (Washington, 1937), p. 130.

45. On the need for planning see: Charles E. Merriam, *The Role of Politics in Social Change* (New York, 1936), pp. 123-43; *On the Agenda of Democracy* (Cambridge, 1941), pp. 50, 73-97; "Putting Politics in Its Place," *International Journal of Ethics*, 46:149 (January 1936); "The National Resources Planning Board: A Chapter in American Planning Experience," *American Political Science Review*, 38: 1086-87 (December 1944). See also Luther Gulick, "Politics, Administration and the 'New Deal'," *Annals of the American Academy of Political and Social Science*, 169:55-56 (September 1933).

46. On the importance of administrative management see: Charles E. Merriam, *On the Agenda of Democracy*, pp. 26-51; "Public Administration and Political Theory," *Journal of Social Philosophy*, 5:295 (July 1940); *Prologue to Politics* (Chicago, 1939), p. 54. Also, Luther Gulick, "Notes on the Theory of Organization," in L. Gulick and L. Urwick (eds.), *Papers on the Science of Administration* (New York, 1937), pp. 1-46.

47. On the scientific approach, see: Luther Gulick, "The Scientific Approach to the Problems of Society and Government," *The University of Buffalo Studies*, 15:27-34 (March 1938); *The National Institute of Public Administration* (New York, 1928), pp. 52, 101-2, 105.

The ideas of Brownlow, Merriam, and Gulick were not carbon copies of one another; certain differences existed. Nevertheless, these seem to be mainly differences in emphasis. A complete study of the background and ideas of the three men may be found in Karl, *Executive Reorganization*, especially chaps. 2, 3, 4.

48. Harris to Brownlow, April 20, 1936, PCAM Files, Box 18. Harris had been employed by the Public Administration Committee of the Social Science Research Council.

49. Harris memorandum to Brownlow, Merriam, and Gulick, February 25, 1937, PCAM Files, Box 1; Emmerich, *Federal Reorganization*, pp. 67-68.

50. "Minutes of the New York Conference," May 9–10, 1936, PCAM Files, Box 1. Two sets of minutes were kept, and this account is based upon both versions. Although the distinction between "top management" and departmental reorganization appeared obvious to Committee members, the line of demarcation was not always clear to the staff.

51. "Minutes of the New York Conference," May 9–10, 1936, PCAM Files, Box 1; Herbert Emmerich memorandum to Harris, May 6, 1936, *ibid*.

52. "Minutes of the New York Conference," May 9–10, 1936, PCAM Files, Box 1. See J. P. Harris memorandum on conference with Emmerich, Brownlow and Reeves, May 6, 1936, *ibid*.

53. In February the Senate had created a committee to study reorganization; in March the House had created a similar committee.

54. Statement of A. E. Buck, "Minutes of the New York Conference," May 9–10, 1936, PCAM Files, Box 1.

55. Brownlow, *Passion for Anonymity*, pp. 338-42. The relationship between Brownlow's committee and the Senate Committee under Senator Byrd will be considered in Chapter 2.

56. Brownlow to F. A. Delano, March 5, 1936, Roosevelt Papers, OF 285C, Box 6.

57. Brownlow to Roosevelt, March 6, 1936, Roosevelt Papers, OF 285C, Box 6.

58. Buchanan, who was also Chairman of the Appropriations Committee, had refused to approve a grant for Brownlow unless he agreed to investigate ways to achieve savings. When White House pressure to bring Buchanan "back into the channel" proved unsuccessful, a compromise had been reached: the appropriation act directed the President's Committee to study overlapping of functions, but Buchanan agreed that it might fulfill this obligation by turning over a portion of its funds to the Brookings Institution which had been commissioned by the Senate to report on the problem. Memorandum for Charles West from White House Assistant Kannee, "Description of Interview Between Harris and Gulick and Buchanan," May 23, 1936, Roosevelt Papers, OF 285C, Box 6; Harris to Gulick, May 18, 1936, *ibid*.

59. Buchanan to Clark Wren, November 25, 1936, Records of the Select Committee on Government Reorganization (Records of the House of Representatives, Record Group 233, National Archives), Box 1. [Cited as Reorganization Committee Files.]

60. Wren to Buchanan, November 14, 1936, Reorganization Committee Files, Box 1.

61. Wren to Buchanan, November 14, 1936, Reorganization Committee Files, Box 1.

62. Clark C. Wren, "Historical Investigation in Connection with the Mission Contemplated by House Res. 460," Reorganization Committee Files, Box 1.

63. Harris memorandum to staff, August 31, 1936, PCAM Files, Box 1.

64. Wren to Buchanan, November 14, 1936, Reorganization Committee Files, Box 1; Clark C. Wren, "First Supplement for Report of Committee," December 21, 1936, *ibid*.

65. Brownlow memorandum on contents of report, November 5, 1936, PCAM Files, Box 1; Brownlow, *Passion for Anonymity*, pp. 378-82.

66. Roosevelt's marginal comments on tentative short summary report, December 18, 1936, PCAM Files, Box 2.

67. *Report of the President's Committee on Administrative Management* (Washington, 1937), pp. 4, 51-53. [Cited as PCAM *Report*.]

68. PCAM *Report*, passim.

69. Herbert Emmerich, "Personnel Problems in New Federal Agencies," *Annals of the American Academy of Political and Social Science*, 189:119-25 (January 1937). See Civil Service Commission to Roosevelt, December 15, 1936, Roosevelt Papers, OF 2, listing New Deal agencies exempt from the merit system.

70. Paul David memorandum (undated) for Senator LaFollette, PCAM Files, Box 12.

71. Tugwell cited in Schlesinger, *Coming of the New Deal*, p. 534; Gulick to Herbert Hoover, February 1, 1937, PCAM Files, Box 16.

72. Draft letter to William Green (undated), PCAM Files, Box 12; John Miller and J. P. Harris draft of a reply to speech by Representative Ramspeck, April 1938, *ibid.*

73. Gulick to Hoover, February 1, 1937, PCAM Files, Box 16.

74. Harvey Mansfield, *The Comptroller-General* (New Haven, 1939), pp. 187-92.

75. John R. McCarl, "Government Run-Everything," *Saturday Evening Post*, October 3, 1936, pp. 8-9, 52; October 17, 1936, pp. 8-9, 70, 73, 74, 76.

76. Mansfield, *The Comptroller-General*, is an excellent critique, especially pp. 2-4, 70-73, 176, 190-92, 254, 266, 274-77. Beck, *Wonderland of Bureaucracy*, pp. 189-90 defends McCarl.

77. Fred A. Ironside, Jr., memorandum for Donald R. Richberg, September 18, 1934, PCAM Files, Box 9; Harold Ickes, *The Secret Diary of Harold Ickes*, 3 vols. (New York, 1954), II, 354; David E. Lilienthal, *The Journals of David E. Lilienthal*, 2 vols. (New York, 1964), I, 345.

78. Henry Morganthau Diaries, June 3, 1936, Morgenthau MSS, Book 26; Rexford G. Tugwell, *Enlargement of the Presidency* (New York, 1960), p. 399.

79. Charles Eliot II, "Notes on a conference with the President," February 20, 1936, PCAM Files, Box 1; Brownlow to Roosevelt, April 11, 1938, Roosevelt Papers, OF 285C, Box 7.

80. Gulick explained his ideas in "Fundamental Considerations Concerning the Place of Control and Audit in Administration," March 5, 1937, PCAM Files, Box 8. Gulick held that control and audit must be separate; if combined, control would destroy audit because it is "psychologically impossible" for the same person who makes advance decisions to consider impartially his actions.

81. Roper, *Fifty Years of Public Life*, pp. 267-68; Roosevelt to Baruch, September 12, 1934, Roosevelt Papers, PPF 88. (Baruch de-

clined because he feared that his differences with Roosevelt might turn
a "trusted friend" into an "inside critic.")

82. Roosevelt, *Public Papers and Addresses,* VII, 184.

83. Gulick to Hoover, February 1, 1937, PCAM Files, Box 16.

84. Confidential studies of agency transfers were prepared for the
Committee, but the Committee recommended only that the President
be permitted to make the transfers he considered necessary. Plans for
departmental transfers were prepared for the Committee by Professor
Schuyler Wallace, "Administrative Reorganization in Relation to Administrative Management," PCAM Files, Box 4.

85. Brownlow notation on Homer Cummings letter to Roosevelt,
January 4, 1937, Roosevelt Papers, OF 285C, Box 16.

86. PCAM *Report,* pp. 39-42.

87. *Ibid.,* pp. 27, 51.

88. Joseph P. Harris, "Outline for the New York Conference," May
9, 10, 1936, PCAM Files, Box 1. See Charles E. Merriam memorandum on National Resources Planning Board, March 23, 1938, PCAM
Files, Box 13.

89. "Minutes of the New York Conference," May 9-10, 1936,
PCAM Files, Box 1. See Roosevelt memorandum to Daniel Bell, February 17, 1937, Roosevelt Papers, OF 79, for the President's conception of planning.

90. PCAM *Report,* p. 5. Brownlow has described the origin of this
phrase in *Passion for Anonymity,* p. 357. For a slightly different version see "Minutes of P.C.A.M.," August 17, 1936, PACM Files, Box
1, p. 20.

91. PCAM *Report,* pp. 11, 18, 19, 29, 30.

92. See Avery Leiserson, "Political Limitations on Executive Reorganization," *American Political Science Review,* 41:69-70 (February
1947).

93. Dwight Waldo, *The Administrative State* (New York, 1948),
pp. 66ff discusses the ambitions of professional administrators in these
terms.

94. Eugene S. Leggett Memorandum for Roosevelt, December 29,
1936, Roosevelt Papers, OF 285C, Box 6.


### Chapter II: The Progress of Reorganization during 1937

1. *New York Times,* January 17, 1937, IV, 7. For other reports on
Congressional reaction, see: "FDR's Reorganizing Job," *Business
Week,* January 16, 1937, p. 26; "2nd Objective," *Time,* January 25,
1937, pp. 9-11; "Reorganization," *Newsweek,* January 23, 1937, p. 7;
*Washington Post,* January 17, 1937, Herbert Emmerich MSS (New
York City), Scrapbook.

2. J. R. Wiggins of the St. Paul *Pioneer Press* won a contest among reporters for a poem lampooning the proposal for six assistants with "a passion for anonymity." The poem was printed in the *New York Times,* January 13, 1937, p. 13:

| | |
|---|---|
| Send a scout to far Valhalla | And remember if you find him |
| With an order that he wait | Whom you go afar to seek |
| At five thousand doors of Odin | Just in closing please remind him |
| For a likely candidate. . . | That his job may last a week. |

3. Roosevelt worked out this illustration in a note he marked: "Not for press beforehand but for my use in answering questions," January 16, 1937, Roosevelt Papers, OF 285C, Box 7.

4. Press Conference, January 11, 1937, Roosevelt Papers, IX, 50-51.

5. *Ibid.,* IX, 66, 64; Press Conference, December 22, 1936, Roosevelt Papers, VIII, 194.

6. Press Conference, January 11, 1937, Roosevelt Papers, IX, 70, 94-95.

7. *Ibid.,* IX, 66-68, 87.

8. *Ibid.,* IX, 74-76, 79, 84.

9. *Ibid.,* IX, 93.

10. *Ibid.,* IX, 92. See Raymond Clapper's notes on press conference, Clapper MSS, Box 207.

11. National League of Women Voters to Roosevelt, February 16, 1937, Roosevelt Papers, PPF 1439; Will Hays to Roosevelt, January 12, 1937, Roosevelt Papers, PPF 1945; Lowden statement in *New York Times,* January 24, 1937, p. 27.

12. Nicholas M. Butler to Roosevelt, January 13, 1937, Roosevelt Papers, PPF 445.

13. Irving Fisher to Roosevelt, January 14, 1937, Roosevelt Papers, PPF 431; Lindsay Rogers, "The Independent Regulatory Commissions," *Political Science Quarterly,* 52:1-5 (March 1937); John McDiarmid, "Reorganization of the General Accounting Office," *American Political Science Review,* 31:516 (June 1937).

However, many political scientists later took exception to some of the Committee's proposals. Such criticism may be found in: Kenneth G. Cole, "The 'Merit System' Again," *American Political Science Review,* 31:695-98 (August 1937); James M. Landis, *The Administrative Process* (New Haven, 1938), pp. 4-5, 28, 88, 111-13, 116; Charles S. Hyneman, "Administrative Reorganization: An Adventure into Science and Theology," *Journal of Politics,* 1:62-75 (February 1939); Harold Laski, *The American Presidency* (New York, 1940), pp. 260-62; Edward S. Corwin, *The President: Office and Powers* (New York, 1940), pp. 96-110, esp. p. 101.

14. *New York Times,* January 13, 14, 1937. Newspaper editorials

commenting on the plan may be found in PCAM Files, Box 2, and in Reorganization Committee Files, Box 13.

15. Roosevelt to Gulick, January 16, 1937, Roosevelt Papers, PPF 4307.

16. "Reorganization," *Newsweek*, January 23, 1937, p. 9.

17. Harry Byrd to Carter Glass, September 21, 1937, Carter Glass MSS (University of Virginia), Box 380.

18. George W. Spicer, "From Political Chief to Administrative Chief," in Charles G. Haines and Marshall E. Dimock (eds.), *Essays on the Law and Practice of Governmental Administration* (Baltimore, 1935), p. 103. See A. E. Buck, *The Reorganization of State Governments in the United States* (New York, 1938), pp. 240-46.

19. Brownlow Diary, March 4, 1936, PCAM Files, Box 1.

20. Brownlow, *Passion for Anonymity*, pp. 349-50.

21. Drafts of letters appointing President's Committee, March 15-17, 1936, Roosevelt Papers, OF 285C, Box 6; Harris to Gulick, May 18, 1936, PCAM Files, Box 18.

22. Brownlow memorandum for F. A. Delano, March 5, 1936, OF 285C, Box 6.

23. Gulick to Roosevelt, November 23, 1936, PCAM Files, Box 1.

24. Gulick to Roosevelt, *ibid.*

25. Brownlow telegram to Roosevelt, November 25, 1936, Roosevelt Papers, OF 285C, Box 6; Gulick to Roosevelt, November 23, 1936, PCAM Files, Box 1.

26. R. G. Carroll, "Pruning and Spraying," *Saturday Evening Post,* January 2, 1937, pp. 24, 50; *New York Times,* January 2, 1937, p. 4.

27. *Congressional Record,* 75th Cong., 3rd sess., App., pp. 26-28.

28. Byrd to Roosevelt, January 13, 1937, Roosevelt Papers, OF 285C, Box 7.

29. Brownlow Diary, March 4, 1936, PCAM Files, Box 1. Brownlow thought that the difference was that Byrd sought "Simplification–Efficiency–Economy," whereas his group wanted "Management–Administration–Saving," March 14, 1936, PCAM Files, Box 1.

30. George Creel, "Byrd Song," *Colliers,* August 21, 1937, pp. 21, 30, 31; *New York Times,* December 27, 1937, p. 3.

31. Press Conference, December 22, 1936, Roosevelt Papers, VIII, 188-91; *ibid.,* January 11, 1937, IX, 44-48.

32. Roosevelt memorandum for Daniel Bell, February 17, 1937, Roosevelt Papers, OF 79; James Roosevelt memorandum for Roosevelt, May 28, 1937, and Roosevelt reply, May 29, 1937, Records of the Bureau of the Budget, Central Files (National Archives), Box 192 (7).

33. Brownlow to McIntyre, January 9, 1937, Roosevelt Papers, OF 285C, Box 7.

34. Byrd to Roosevelt, January 13, 1937, Roosevelt Papers, OF 285C, Box 7.

35. Roosevelt memorandum for Marvin McIntyre, January 18, 1937, Roosevelt Papers, OF 285C, Box 7; Ickes, *Secret Diary,* II, 55. Garner, Farley, and Ickes agreed that Byrd should be on the Committee, and persuaded Roosevelt to leave the decision up to Garner.

36. Gulick to Byrd, January 11, 1937, PCAM Files, Box 18.

37. *Congressional Record,* 79th Cong., 1st sess., November 9, 1945, pp. 10571-72.

38. "Senator Byrd Talks About 'Presidents I Have Known,' " *U. S. News and World Report,* September 10, 1962, pp. 84-85.

39. Brownlow, *Passion for Anonymity,* p. 375. It was Lewis Meriam who drafted the memorandum which Charles E. Merriam used as a basis for his own presentation of the need for a study of reorganization.

40. Meriam memorandum for Harris, October 1936, PCAM Files, Box 19; Meriam memorandum on W. Y. Elliott's study, 1936, *ibid.,* Box 13; Harris progress report, August 15, 1936, *ibid.,* Box 1.

41. Brownlow, *Passion for Anonymity,* p. 375.

42. Harris to Fred Powell, June 30, 1936, PCAM Files, Box 1; Harris to Byrd, July 10, 1936, *ibid.;* Powell to Harris, July 6, 1936, *ibid.,* Box 16.

43. The position of the President's Committee is put forth in: Brownlow, *Passion for Anonymity,* pp. 345-46; Emmerich, *Federal Reorganization,* pp. 65-66. Brookings' point of view is stated in: Fred Powell to Byrd, March 26, 1936, Reorganization Committee Files, Box 1; Byrd to Harold G. Moulton, June 12, 1936, *ibid.*

44. Harold G. Moulton memorandum for Stacy May of the Rockefeller Foundation, April 3, 1937, PCAM Files, Box 2. Moulton, President of Brookings, wrote this ten-page memorandum for May in order to justify his course of action.

45. Harris note on Moulton memorandum, April, 1937, PCAM Files, Box 2.

46. John Miller, Journal of the P.C.A.M., PCAM Files, Box 2.

47. Powell to James Buchanan, September 28, 1936, Reorganization Committee Files, Box 1.

48. Miller, Journal of the P.C.A.M., PCAM Files, Box 2; Moulton memorandum for May, April 3, 1937, *ibid.*

49. Powell to Buchanan, September 28, 1936, Reorganization Committee Files, Box 1.

50. Moulton memorandum for May, April 3, 1937, PCAM Files, Box 2. According to Moulton, Gulick saw Powell late in October to arrange for a meeting, and "for about twenty minutes they spoke generalities."

51. Moulton memorandum for Stacy May, April 3, 1937, PCAM

Files, Box 2; Gulick to F. A. Delano, January 12, 1937, *ibid.;* Gulick to Moulton, January 13, 1937, *ibid.* Gulick informed Moulton that the Committee's final position was "very much more nearly in line with that suggested by Lewis Meriam" than Brookings might have expected.

52. Moulton memorandum for Brownlow, January 19, 1937, PCAM Files, Box 2.

53. Moulton memorandum for May, April 3, 1937, PCAM Files, Box 2.

54. Moulton memorandum for May, April 3, 1937, PCAM Files, Box 2; Moulton to Brownlow, February 26, 1937, *ibid.*

55. Moulton memorandum for May, April 3, 1937, PCAM Files, Box 2; Moulton to John Cochran, March 3, 1937, Reorganization Committee Files, Box 3; Moulton to Brownlow, March 4, 1937, PCAM Files, Box 2.

56. Moulton to Brownlow, March 4, 1937, PCAM Files, Box 2; Moulton memorandum for Stacy May, April 3, 1937, *ibid.;* Brownlow memorandum for Moulton, March 11, 1937, *ibid.*

57. Moulton memorandum for Stacy May, April 3, 1937, PCAM Files, Box 2.

58. U. S. Congress, Joint Committee on Government Organization, *Hearings, Reorganization of the Executive Departments,* 75th Cong., 1st sess., 1937, passim. [Cited as Joint Committee, *Hearings.*] For Gulick's position see p. 401; for Meriam's position, see p. 281.

59. *Ibid.,* pp. 277, 283, 284, 302-8. Cf. Brookings Institution, "Financial Administration of the Federal Government," Report no. 5, *Investigation of Executive Agencies of the Government* (Washington, 1937), pp. 93-94.

60. Cf. Moulton to Brownlow, March 24, 1937, PCAM Files, Box 2; Gulick to F. A. Delano, January 12, 1937, *ibid.;* Harris note on Moulton memorandum for Stacy May, April 1937, *ibid.*

61. Meriam and Schmeckebier, *Reorganization of the National Government,* pp. 24, 32-35, 41, 169-71, and esp. p. 86.

62. *Ibid.,* pp. 147, 150. Meriam thought this staff should be made up of men "totally devoid of will-power," an unhappy substitute for Brownlow's phrase "a passion for anonymity."

63. *Ibid.,* p. 168; Brookings, "Financial Administration," p. 103. See Lloyd M. Short, "Investigation of the Executive Agencies of the Government," *American Political Science Review,* 33:60-66 (February 1939).

64. Meriam and Schmeckebier, *Reorganization of the National Government,* pp. 161, 183.

65. Joint Committee, *Hearings,* p. 316.

66. Powell to Byrd, March 26, 1936, Reorganization Committee Files, Box 1.

67. Waldo, *The Administrative State,* pp. 118-20; Carl Marcy, *Presidential Commissions* (New York, 1945), pp. 81-82.

68. Meriam memorandum for Harris, 1936, PCAM Files, Box 7.

69. Leverett S. Lyon to Clark C. Wren, November 2, 1936; Wren to Lyon, November 3, 1936, Reorganization Committee Files, Box 1.

70. Brownlow memorandum for Moulton, March 11, 1937, PCAM Files, Box 2.

71. In the House were 328 Democrats, 90 Republicans, 5 Farmer-Laborites, and 8 Progressives. In the Senate were 76 Democrats, 16 Republicans, 2 Farmer-Laborites, 1 Progressive, and 1 Independent.

72. This account of the meeting is based on: Brownlow, *Passion for Anonymity,* pp. 386-96; Miller, Journal of the P.C.A.M., PCAM Files, Box 2; interview with Herbert Emmerich, April 10, 1963; Ickes, *Secret Diary,* II, 46; Steve Early memorandum for McIntyre, January 8, 1937, Roosevelt Papers, OF 285C, Box 7.

73. Edwin E. Witte interview with Middleton Beaman, September 2, 1936, PCAM Files, Box 16.

74. Roosevelt, *Public Papers and Addresses,* V, 668-74.

75. *Washington Post,* January 17, 1937, Herbert Emmerich MSS, Scrapbook; *New York Times,* January 13, 1937, p. 17; transcript of James Byrnes telephone conversation with Henry Morgenthau, January 13, 1937, Morgenthau MSS, Book 51.

76. "Reorganization Act, 1937," James Roosevelt MSS (Franklin D. Roosevelt Library), Box 36; James Roosevelt memorandum for McIntyre, February 5, 1937, Roosevelt Papers, OF 285C, Box 7.

77. Press Conference, February 26, 1937, Roosevelt Papers, IX, 188-89.

78. Arthur Krock in *New York Times,* March 9, 1937, p. 22.

79. Roosevelt memorandum for Brownlow, February 19, 1937, PCAM Files, Box 11; Roosevelt memorandum for Acting Director of the Budget, March 29, 1937, Roosevelt Papers, OF 285C, Box 16; Press Conference, *ibid.,* April 6, 1937, IX, 248.

80. Joint Committee, *Hearings,* p. 22. See n.58 above.

81. Brownlow, *Passion for Anonymity,* p. 391.

82. Joint Committee, *Hearings,* pp. 8-13; *Congressional Record,* 75th Cong., 1st sess., Appendix, pp. 271-72.

83. Miller, Journal of the P.C.A.M., PCAM Files, Box 2.

84. Harris to James Roosevelt, January 29, 1937, PCAM Files, Box 19.

85. On February 2 James Roosevelt informed Harris that "it had been decided not to use the amendments concerning the independent regulatory commissions unless they were insisted upon later on," Miller, Journal of the P.C.A.M., PCAM Files, Box 2.

86. Joint Committee, *Hearings,* pp. 52, 265.

87. *Ibid.,* pp. 55-56.

88. *Ibid.,* p. 411.

89. *Ibid.,* pp. 8, 23, 170-71, 174, 180.

90. *Ibid.,* pp. 182, 179.

91. Charles West memorandum for Roosevelt, February 20, 1937, Roosevelt Papers, OF 285C, Box 7. An official of the Interior Department learned that McNary "accused the President of attempting to deprive Congress of many of its prerogatives," Rufus C. Poole memorandum for Harold Ickes, March 5, 1937, Department of the Interior Files, Office of the Secretary (National Archives), Box 2564.

92. Joint Committee, *Hearings,* pp. 87-88, 80, 74-75.

93. *Ibid.,* pp. 6, 175, 179, 89, 9, 79, 140.

94. *Ibid.,* pp. 179, 25-26, 76-77.

95. Cochran to Roosevelt, July 24, 1937, Roosevelt Papers, OF 285C, Box 7; Press Conference, June 22, 1937, *ibid.,* IX, 457; *New York Times,* May 28, 1937, p. 14.

96. Press Conference, June 22, 1937, Roosevelt Papers, IX, 457; Ickes, *Secret Diary,* II, 54-55, 59, 152; *New York Times,* August 10, 1937, p. 3.

97. Robinson was quoted as saying that the failure of reorganization would not be a great "public calamity," *New York Times,* May 27, 1937, p. 14.

98. Senators Robinson (Arkansas) and Pat Harrison (Mississippi) had an abiding interest in flood control projects and wanted these two agencies exempted.

99. U. S. Congress, Senate, Select Committee on Government Organization, *Hearings, Reorganization of the Government Agencies,* 75th Cong., 1st sess., 1937, pp. 52-57. [Cited as Select Committee, *Hearings.*]

100. Bell memorandum for Roosevelt, June 18, 1937, Bureau of the Budget Files, Box 192 (12).

101. Roosevelt to Byrnes, July 26, 1937, Elliott Roosevelt, *F.D.R.: His Personal Letters, 1928–1945,* 2 vols. (New York, 1950), I, 696.

102. Minutes of Caucus of Democratic Members of House Select Committee on Government Reorganization, April 26, 1937, Reorganization Committee Files, Box 1.

103. *New York Times,* May 21, 1937, p. 10; Press Conference, May 21, 1937, Roosevelt Papers, IX, 383.

104. Minutes of Meeting of House Select Committee on Government Reorganization, June 1, 1937, June 15, 1937, Reorganization Committee Files, Box 1.

105. Hester to Cochran, June 21, 1937, Reorganization Committee Files, Box 12.

106. Pencil notation on draft of H.R. 7730, June 29, 1937, Reorganization Committee Files, Box 3. Cf. Clark C. Wren to Fred Vinson, July 1, 1937, *ibid.*, Box 2. Cochran explained that Hester's drafts came from an official who probably was in a position to know the desires of the President, James Mead to Cochran, August 12, 1937, *ibid.*, Box 12.

107. Cochran to Roosevelt, July 24, 1937, Roosevelt Papers, OF 285C, Box 7.

108. *Ibid.*

109. *Congressional Record*, 75th Cong., 1st sess. [cited as *CR* below] pp. 7682, 7691-92, 7684.

110. *CR*, pp. 7694, 7697-98.

111. *CR*, pp. 7681-82, 7685-86, 7693-94, 7696-97.

112. *CR*, pp. 8850-53, 8871-72.

113. *CR*, pp. 8852, 8859-61, 8864-65, 8874.

114. *CR*, pp. 8859, 8861-62, 8863, 8854-55.

115. *CR*, pp. 8859, 7691-92, 7698-99.

116. *CR*, pp. 7695, 7692-93, 8857.

117. Eighteen Democrats voted against the Robinson bill, twenty-eight against the Warren bill.

118. On August 18 the House Committee reported favorably the Mead bill to expand the civil service and the Vinson bill to reform the General Accounting Office. See Minutes of Meeting of House Select Committee on Government Organization, August 18, 1937, Reorganization Committee Files, Box 1; James Mead to Cochran, August 5, 1937, *ibid.*, Box 12; John Taber to Mead, August 4, 1937, *ibid.*

119. Cochran to McIntyre, November 10, 1937, November 16, 1937, Roosevelt Papers, OF 285C, Box 7.

120. *Congressional Record,* 75th Cong., 2nd sess., pp. 33-35; Joseph P. Harris, "The Progress of Administrative Reorganization in the Seventy-Fifth Congress," *American Political Science Review,* 21:862-70 (October 1937).

121. Clifford Hope to L. H. Houdyshell, November 24, 1937, Clifford Hope MSS (Kansas State Historical Society), Legislative Correspondence, 1937–38.

122. Gulick to Roosevelt, September 30, 1937, Roosevelt Papers, OF 285C, Box 16.

123. *New York Times,* April 22, 1937, p. 13; August 9, 1937, p. 18.

124. Bernard DeVoto, "Desertion from the New Deal," *Harpers,* 175:557-60 (October 1937).

125. Delano to James Roosevelt, January 22, 1938, James Roosevelt MSS, Box 7.

Chapter III: The National Committee to Uphold Constitutional Government

1. G. M. Titus of Muscatine, Iowa to Hatton Sumners, April, 1938, Department of Agriculture Files, Office of the Secretary (National Archives), Correspondence, 1938 (283); Gannett mailing sent to Roosevelt by an Iowa lawyer, March 1938, Roosevelt Papers, OF 285C, Box 7.

2. Frank Gannett, "History of the Formation of the NCUCG and the Supreme Court Fight," [August] 1937, Frank Gannett MSS (Cornell University), Box 16; Samuel D. Williamson, *Frank Gannett* (New York, 1940), pp. 175-80.

3. Amos Pinchot to Oswald Garrison Villard, February 19, 1937, Amos Pinchot MSS (Library of Congress), Box 61; Gannett, "History of the Formation of the NCUCG," Gannett MSS, Box 16.

4. See Gannett to James Truslow Adams, February 22, 1937, James Truslow Adams MSS (Columbia University). Adams was a prominent historian; Coburn an actor; Holmes the minister of the Community Church in New York, and a noted liberal; Dorothy Thompson a prominent journalist. McClure was founder of *McClure's Magazine,* an early muckraking journal; Louis Taber was head of the National Grange; Vanderlip was a former president of the National City Bank of New York; Gerard was a New York businessman, whose brother, James Gerard, had been Treasurer of the Democratic Party and Wilson's ambassador to Germany.

5. Pinchot to Rumely, June 10, 1940, Pinchot MSS, Box 67.

6. Ford's nephew attended Rumely's Interlaken School. In 1917 Rumely attempted to secure a draft exemption for Edsel Ford who, he thought, could better serve his country in a civilian capacity organizing production of tractors. Rumely to Gifford Pinchot, May 15, 1917, October 15, 1917, Gifford Pinchot MSS (Library of Congress), Box 2078.

7. Rumely, "The Interlaken School" [1910], Gifford Pinchot MSS, Box 2078.

8. Rumely to Charles Evans Hughes, October 13, 1916, Gifford Pinchot MSS, Box 2078; Rumely to Theodore Roosevelt, February 23, 1917, *ibid.*

9. Rumely to William R. Willcox, October 12, 1916, Gifford Pinchot MSS, Box 2078; Rumely to Gifford Pinchot, February 19, 1917, *ibid.*

10. Rumely to Gifford Pinchot, October 7, 1915, Gifford Pinchot MSS, Box 2078; Pinchot to Rumely, September 18, 1915, *ibid.*

11. Rumely to Gifford Pinchot, October 11, 1915, October 5, 1916, Gifford Pinchot MSS, Box 2078. On Rumely's business connections

with Germany, see Peter Lyon, *Success Story: The Life and Times of S. S. McClure* (New York, 1963), pp. 382-83, 354-60.

12. Rumely insisted that his newspaper served as an organ for Theodore Roosevelt, and hoped that his personal association with Roosevelt would exonerate him. Several of Roosevelt's letters commending Rumely were printed by the NCUCG; but cf. Elting E. Morison (ed.), *The Letters of Theodore Roosevelt* (Cambridge, 1954), VIII, 1339, 1002, for letters by the former President criticizing Rumely.

13. Arthur W. Crawford, *Monetary Management Under the New Deal* (Washington, 1940), pp. 69-75, 337-38; Charles O. Hardy, *The Warren-Pearson Price Theory* (Washington, 1935).

14. Frank E. Gannett, "What Our New Gold Policy Means," Address at Rochester Chamber of Commerce, November 3, 1933, p. 15. See Rumely to William Hard, May 20, 1938, Pinchot MSS, Box 65.

15. Rumely to Frank A. Vanderlip, January 9, 1933, Frank A. Vanderlip MSS (Columbia University). On the founding of the Committee see Rumely to Vanderlip, October 1, 1932, November 9, 1932, and Rumely to Vincent Bendix, December 20, 1932, Vanderlip MSS. See Herbert M. Bratter, "Committee for the Nation: A Case Study in Propaganda," *The Journal of Political Economy,* 49:531-53 (August 1941).

16. Backers included: J. H. Rand, Jr., president of Remington Rand, Inc.; Lessing J. Rosenwald and Robert E. Wood, directors of Sears, Roebuck, and Co.; and Vincent Bendix, chairman of the Bendix Aviation Corporation. A report on contributions may be found in Rumely to Wood, July 23, 1935, and Rumely to Vanderlip, January 29, 1936, Vanderlip MSS.

17. Rumely to Wood, November 4, 1936, Vanderlip MSS.

18. Gannett, "What Our New Gold Policy Means," p. 5.

19. Rumely to Vanderlip, June 1, 1935, Vanderlip MSS; Gannett to Robert A. Taft, April 2, 1936, Gannett MSS, Box 16.

20. Pinchot to Samuel B. Pettengill, January 5, 1938, Pinchot MSS, Box 65; Pinchot to Roy Howard, May 18, 1938, *ibid.,* Box 64.

21. Rumely to Marvin McIntyre, April 5, 1938, Roosevelt Papers, OF 3220.

22. Gannett to Henry H. Stebbins, Jr., November 13, 1936, Gannett MSS, Box 16.

23. *Ibid.;* Frank E. Gannett, *Industrial and Labor Relations in Great Britain* (New York, 1939), pp. 2-11.

24. Pinchot to Gannett, April 21, 1937, Pinchot MSS, Box 61.

25. Pinchot to Roy Howard, February 5, 1937, Pinchot MSS, Box 61.

26. Gannett to Alex Falck, March 7, 1936, Gannett MSS, Box 16.

27. Pinchot to Lincoln Colcord, April 28, 1937, Pinchot MSS, Box 61.

28. Rumely to Pinchot, December 18, 1937, Pinchot MSS, Box 61.

29. Pinchot to Ben Lindsay, March 22, 1939, Pinchot MSS, Box 63; Pinchot to Roy Howard, July 21, 1937, *ibid.*, Box 60; Pinchot to Marion Murphy, August 5, 1941, *ibid.*, Box 70.

30. Pinchot to Ezra Pound, January 26, 1937, Pinchot MSS, Box 60.

31. Gannett to Pinchot, May 4, 1939, Pinchot MSS, Box 66.

32. *America's Future,* II (Fall 1939), p. 2.

33. Pinchot to John T. Flynn, August 8, 1941, Pinchot MSS, Box 69. See Minutes of the Executive Committee of the New York chapter of America First, November 25, 1941, *ibid.*, Subject File 88.

34. Samuel B. Pettengill to Gannett, September 27, 1939, Pinchot MSS, Subject File 136; Pinchot to Randolph Walker, September 29, 1939, *ibid.*, Box 66.

35. Pinchot to Rumely, June 9, 1937, Pinchot MSS, Box 60; Pinchot to Burton Wheeler, April 27, 1937, *ibid.*, Box 61.

36. Pinchot to Gannett, October 18, 1937, Pinchot MSS, Box 61. "The Republican Party," asserted Gannett in the fall of 1937, "is dying of dry rot," Gannett to William A. Eddy, October 5, 1937, Gannett MSS, Box 16.

37. Pinchot to Burton Wheeler, April 27, 1937, Pinchot MSS, Box 61. See Pinchot to Gannett, May 3, 1937, *ibid.; * Gannett to John Hamilton, April 28, 1937, *ibid.*

38. Pinchot to William Hard, April 27, 1937, Pinchot MSS, Box 61.

39. Gannett, "History of the Formation of the NCUCG," Gannett MSS, Box 16.

40. Contributors report, April 1938, Adams MSS. Critics of the Committee pointed out that fourteen persons donated $1000 each, and that only 850 contributions accounted for 40 per cent of its funds. Rumely received $15,000 annually.

41. Rumely draft of letter for Pinchot to send to Henry and Edsel Ford, March 18, 1937, Pinchot MSS, Box 60.

42. Notes of a conference between Rumely and Mr. Nahm, June 9, 1938, Pinchot MSS, Box 65; Rumely to Sumner Gerard, June 10, 1938, *ibid.*

43. One automobile executive said: "I personally regard such contributions in the nature of insurance for the future," letter to Pinchot, February 26, 1937, Pinchot MSS, Box 61.

44. Gannett to Pinchot, July 17, 1939, Pinchot MSS, Box 66.

45. Gannett to Henry H. Kleinpell, September 27, 1937, Gannett MSS, Box 16.

46. Williamson, *Frank Gannett,* pp. 182-94.

47. Gannett to Douglas Johnson, April 30, 1937, Pinchot MSS, Box

60; Rumely to Adams, June 15, 1937, Adams MSS; Gannett letter to contributors, April 3, 1937, National Committee to Uphold Constitutional Government Literature (New York Public Library). The Committee distributed 250,000 copies of Douglas Johnson's *The Assault on the Supreme Court* (New York, 1937).

48. Gannett, "History of the Formation of the NCUCG," Gannett MSS, Box 16. Burke's tabulation showed 52 senators for the Hatch-Logan compromise (which would have permitted Roosevelt to add one justice each year when a member of the Court reached the age of seventy-five), and 44 opposed. The eight senators won over were: Clyde C. Herring, John H. Overton, Alva B. Adams, Edwin C. Johnson, Charles O. Andrews, Prentice M. Brown, Richard B. Russell, and William J. Bulow. Once a clear majority opposed the bill, others were willing to take a stand.

49. Gannett to Pinchot, July 27, 1937, Pinchot MSS, Box 60.

50. Pinchot to Samuel Untermeyer, February 15, 1937, Pinchot MSS, Box 61.

51. In 1940 the Committee's president, Samuel Pettengill, said the Supreme Court was "no longer a predictable body," *Smoke Screen* (New York, 1940), pp. 122-23. In 1948 the Committee violently attacked the Court's tideland oil decision.

52. Gannett open letter, July 31, 1937, Pinchot MSS, Box 60; Pinchot open letter to Roosevelt, July 26, 1937, *ibid.* See James T. Adams to Edward R. Burke, July 30, 1938, Adams MSS.

53. Rumely to William E. Borah, August 7, 1937, Pinchot MSS, Box 60.

54. Gannett to Mark Sullivan, August 17, 1937, Pinchot MSS, Box 60. See Aled Davies to Rumely, August 18, 1937, *ibid.*

55. Pinchot to Lincoln Colcord, September 23, 1937, Pinchot MSS, Box 61.

56. Secretary's minutes of NCUCG meeting, October 1, 1937, Pinchot MSS, Box 61; Pinchot to Gannett, October 18, 1937, *ibid.*

57. Gannett open letters, October 16, 1937, October 30, 1937, Pinchot MSS, Box 61.

58. Gannett to Alva Adams, October 20, 1937, Gannett MSS, Box 16. The same letter was also sent to Senators Tydings, McCarran, Lonergan, Clark, George, Gillette, and Wheeler.

59. Gannett to William A. Eddy, October 5, 1937, Gannett MSS, Box 16.

60. Gannett to James Donovan, October 6, 1937, Gannett MSS, Box 16; Gannett to Pinchot, October 28, 1937, Pinchot MSS, Box 62.

61. Rumely to Pinchot, June 10, 1937, Pinchot MSS, Box 61.

62. Rumely to Gannett, October 24, 1937, Pinchot MSS, Box 61.

63. *Ibid.*

64. Pinchot to Rumely, June 4, 1940, Pinchot MSS, Box 67. On Gannett's aspirations, see: Gannett to Thomas H. Moore, April 15, 1938, Gannett to Pinchot, July 5, 1939, Pinchot MSS, Box 66; Gannett to L. Pulsifier, August 10, 1939, Gannett MSS, Box 16.

65. See George H. Moses to Carter Glass, November 1, 1937; Glass to Moses, November 8, 1937, Carter Glass MSS (University of Virginia), Box 380.

66. Gannett to C. G. Welch, January 10, 1938, Gannett MSS, Box 16.

67. Gannett to W. A. Shaeffer, March 1, 1938, Gannett MSS, Box 16.

68. Pinchot to Hiram Johnson, October 2, 1940, Pinchot MSS, Box 68.

69. Pinchot to Rumely, June 4, 1940, Pinchot MSS, Box 67.

70. Pinchot to Gannett, May 12, 1937, Pinchot MSS, Box 61; Pinchot to Lincoln Colcord, May 7, 1937, *ibid.*

71. Amos Pinchot to Gifford Pinchot, May 21, 1937, Gifford Pinchot MSS, Box 356; Pinchot to Samuel D. Williamson, February 23, 1940, Pinchot MSS, Box 67.

72. Draft of bill with comments, Pinchot MSS, Subject File 95.

73. Pinchot to Charles E. Roos, May 24, 1937, Pinchot MSS, Box 62; Pinchot to F. Van Nuys, May 27, 1937, *ibid.*, Box 60.

74. Gannett to Adams, July 22, 1937, Adams MSS.

75. Pinchot to Roosevelt, July 26, 1937, Roosevelt Papers, PPF 1677. Douglas Johnson's *The Assault on the Supreme Court,* p. 62, attacks reorganization.

76. Gannett to NCUCG supporters, May 27, 1937, Pinchot MSS, Box 61; Samuel B. Pettengill to Adams, August 18, 1937, Adams MSS; Gannett to NCUCG contributors, September 15, 1937, Adams MSS.

77. Gannett to H. D. Howard, September 18, 1937, Gannett MSS, Box 16; Gannett to Grenville Clark, October 5, 1937, *ibid.*

78. Gannett to Mrs. E. F. Dunbar, August 4, 1937, Gannett MSS, Box 3a, Scrapbook 5.

79. Adams to Gannett, May 29, 1937, Adams MSS.

80. Gannett to Harper Sibley, April 13, 1938, Gannett MSS, Box 6a, Scrapbook 1; Gannett to Adams, April 12, 1938, Adams MSS; Gannett to L. M. Champaign, April 15, 1938, Gannett MSS, Box 6a, Scrapbook 1.

81. Discussing Adams's misgivings, Rumely said that his name could be dropped from the Committee if necessary, Rumely to Gannett, August 2, 1937, Pinchot MSS, Box 60. Cf. Adams to Rumely, May 25, 1937, *ibid.*, Box 61.

82. Pinchot to Roosevelt, January 29, 1938, Roosevelt Papers, PPF 1677. Roosevelt replied: "I can only say that I have never yet read a

letter so full of complete misstatements and perversions of fact as yours," Marvin McIntyre to Pinchot, February 2, 1938, *ibid.*

83. Rumely to Pinchot, January 28, 1938, Pinchot MSS, Box 64.

84. Joint Committee, *Hearings,* especially pp. 72, 137, 95, 21. The text of the Brownlow bill may be found on pp. 26-44.

85. Samuel Pettengill to Pinchot, February 1, 1938, Pinchot MSS, Box 64.

86. Pinchot to Charles Merz, January 31, 1938, Pinchot MSS, Box 64. Cf. John Cochran to Louis Ludlow, February 16, 1939, Reorganization Committee Files, Box 13, for a different view.

87. Rumely to Gannett, February 4, 1938, Pinchot MSS, Box 65.

88. Gannett to Charles McNary, March 17, 1938, *Congressional Record,* 75th Cong., 3rd sess., pp. 3891-92.

89. Gannett mailing sent by Judge Alfred D. Riess to Roosevelt, February 28, 1938, Roosevelt Papers, OF 285C, Box 7. The two other crises, according to Gannett, had been the Revolution and the Civil War.

90. Gannett mailing sent by an Iowa lawyer to Roosevelt, March 25, 1938, Roosevelt Papers, OF 285C, Box 7. The Senator's name was filled in differently in each state.

91. Williamson, *Frank Gannett,* pp. 200-5.

92. Pinchot to Rumely, May 31, 1938, Pinchot MSS, Box 63; Rumely to Pinchot, June 2, 1938, *ibid.*

93. Rumely to Sumner Gerard, April 24, 1937, Pinchot MSS, Box 61.

94. Gannett letter to a reader, *America's Future,* November 1938, p. 31; editorial, *ibid.,* January 1939, p. 26. The Committee began publishing this magazine in the fall of 1938.

95. *America's Future,* Mid-Spring 1939, p. 32.

96. Rumely to Douglas Johnson, September 12, 1938, Pinchot MSS, Box 65; this letter describes the views of various Committee members with whom Rumely had spoken.

97. Rumely to Gannett, September 29, 1938, Pinchot MSS, Box 65.

98. Rumely to William R. Willcox, October 12, 1916, Gifford Pinchot MSS, Box 2078.

99. Rumely to Samuel Williamson, September 12, 1938, Pinchot MSS, Box 65. The Committee played up the word "purge" in connection with the elections of 1938.

100. Rumely to Gannett, September 29, 1938, Pinchot MSS, Box 65.

101. Photograph, *America's Future,* Summer 1939, p. 29.

102. Rumely to Gannett, March 31, 1938, Adams MSS; Rumely to Coughlin, December 18, 1937, Pinchot MSS, Box 64.

103. Pinchot to Rt. Rev. Edward Mooney, November 8, 1937, Pinchot MSS, Box 61; Pinchot to Coughlin, January 3, 1938, *ibid., Box 65.

104. Gannett to W. A. Sheaffer, March 1, 1938, Gannett MSS, Box 16; Gannett to James T. Wilson, March 9, 1938, *ibid.* See also Rumely to Josiah W. Bailey, March 9, 1938, Josiah W. Bailey MSS (Duke University).

105. Gannett to Claude Ashbrook, March 26, 1938, Gannett MSS, Box 16. See Rumely to Adams, March 24, 1938, Adams MSS; Gannett to Adams, March 26, 1938, *ibid.;* Rumely to Gannett, March 31, 1938, *ibid.*

106. Gannett to W. Allen Underhill, April 19, 1938; Gannett to John A. Slattery, April 15, 1938; Gannett to Thomas H. Moore, April 15, 1938, Gannett MSS, Box 6a, Scrapbook 1.

107. Gannett to Miss E. B. Ripley, April 15, 1938, Gannett MSS, Box 6a, Scrapbook 1.

108. Herbert A. Blomquist memorandum (six pages) for Sherman Minton, March 24, 1938, Records of the Special Committee of the United States Senate to Investigate Lobbying Activities (National Archives), Box 106 (Office memoranda, 45.1). [Cited as Lobby Committee Files.] Attached to this memorandum are the notes the investigators took on Rumely's stationery of the letters they saw, including several from Irene DuPont and Pierre DuPont accompanying contributions.

109. United States Senate, Special Committee to Investigate Lobbying Activities, *Hearings* (1938), pt. 7, pp. 2139, 2147-48, 2102-5. [Cited as Lobby Committee, *Hearings.*]

110. Pinchot to Geoffrey Parsons, March 21, 1938, Pinchot MSS, Box 63. Gerald Nye was a Republican senator from North Dakota.

111. Lobby Committee, *Hearings,* pp. 2119-25, 2133-35.

112. Herbert A. Blomquist to Sherman Minton, March 16, 1938, Lobby Committee Files, Box 246. Blomquist hoped that the "rapid fire procedure" would give Minton the "first inning on publicity." Much of the Lobby Committee's information on Rumely came from a memorandum submitted by one Lewis E. Myers, Box 106 (E. A. Rumely, 50.4).

113. Lobby Committee, *Hearings,* pp. 2106-7, 2115.

114. Notes on a conference between Rumely and Mr. Nahm, June 9, 1938, Pinchot MSS, Box 65. On the distinction between education and propaganda, see: Harold D. Lasswell, "The Person: Subject and Object of Propaganda," *Annals of the American Academy of Political and Social Science,* 179:187-93 (May 1935); Donald Blaisdell, *American Democracy Under Pressure* (New York, 1957), pp. 82-98.

115. Proposed outline for questioning of Sumner Gerard, April 1938, Lobby Committee Files, Box 246.

116. Lobby Committee, *Hearings,* pp. 2151-53, 2169-74, 2156-58, 2166.

117. Gannett to John L. Griffith, March 22, 1938, Gannett MSS,

Box 16; Gannett to M. M. Odil, March 28, 1938, *ibid.; New York Times,* March 23, 1938, p. 15. Minton's activities drew many protests; see, for example, American Civil Liberties Union to Minton, May 27, 1938, Lobby Committee Files, Box 106 (Office Files, 45).

118. Paul Y. Anderson, "Let Gannett Explain," *Nation,* April 2, 1938, pp. 375-76. Senator Lewis Schwellenbach asserted: "The Du Ponts apparently have decided that they cannot succeed through organizations which they openly direct and control. Instead of using the word 'Liberty,' we now find a new committee using the word 'Constitutional,' " *Congressional Record,* 75th Cong., 3rd sess., pp. 1181-82.

119. Harold Ickes, "Mail Order Government," *Colliers,* February 18, 1939, pp. 14-15, 53. This article was written shortly after the Reorganization bill of 1938 was defeated; Michael Straus to Steve Early, July 25, 1938, Roosevelt Papers, OF 6.

120. Minton to Clarence F. Merrell, March 12, 1937, Lobby Committee Files, Box 106.

## Chapter IV: Bureaucracy and the Special Interest Groups

1. Roosevelt, *Public Papers and Addresses,* VI, 179.

2. For a discussion of the New Deal and pressure groups, see William E. Leuchtenburg, *Franklin D. Roosevelt and the New Deal* (New York, 1963), p. 88.

3. *Congressional Record,* 75th Cong., 3rd sess., p. 3820.

4. Select Committee, *Hearings,* p. 162.

5. John T. Taylor to James Mead, June 29, 1937, Reorganization Committee Files, Box 12.

6. Gulick to Herbert Hoover, February 1, 1937, PCAM Files, Box 16.

7. Thomas Kirby to John Cochran, March 10, 1937, Reorganization Committee Files, Box 13.

8. Select Committee, *Hearings,* pp. 160-62. The influence of veterans' groups on the Veterans Administration is discussed in Andrew Ten Eyck to Roosevelt, April 23, 1938, Roosevelt Papers, OF 285C, Box 7.

9. Nebraska American Legion to George Norris, March 21, 1938, George Norris MSS (Library of Congress), Tray 33, Box 6.

10. *Congressional Record,* 75th Cong., 3rd sess., pp. 4490-91; Baltimore *News-Post,* April 4, 1938, p. 2.

11. *Congressional Record,* 75th Cong., 3rd sess., pp. 3822-27; New York *Herald-Tribune,* March 23, 1938, p. 13.

12. *Congressional Record,* 75th Cong., 3rd sess., pp. 4796, 4802, 5012.

13. Virginia E. Jenckes to Roosevelt, February 2, 1937, Roosevelt Papers, OF 21-L.

14. Dr. Edward A. McLaughlin to Aime J. Forand, Reorganization Committee Files, Box 13; Select Committee, *Hearings*, pp. 126-28.

15. Medical Society of Virginia to Roosevelt, February 10, 1937, Roosevelt Papers, OF 21-L; Select Committee, *Hearings*, pp. 124-25.

16. Cleveland County Medical Society, Shelby, North Carolina, to Roosevelt, February 23, 1937, Roosevelt Papers, OF 21-L; Select Committee, *Hearings*, p. 124.

17. *Congressional Record*, 75th Cong., 3rd sess., pp. 5019-20; Cochran to Dr. William C. Woodward, May 4, 1939, Reorganization Committee Files, Box 13.

18. Robert Catherwood to Merriam, March 20, 1937, PCAM Files, Box 12.

19. Gulick to Roosevelt, July 9, 1937, Roosevelt Papers, PPF 4307.

20. *New York Times*, July 19, 1937, p. 2; National Civil Service Reform League to Senate Select Committee, July 14, 1937, PCAM Files, Box 12; Select Committee, *Hearings*, pp. 157-59, 139-46.

21. For examples of opposition by local Leagues of Women Voters, see Mrs. F. E. Wilson to Merlin Hull, April 2, 1938, Merlin Hull MSS (Wisconsin State Historical Society), and Mrs. Catherine Gardiner to Theodore Francis Green, July 8, 1937, Theodore Francis Green MSS (Library of Congress), Box 19. *Good Government* (March–April 1938) contains Kaplan's statement supporting the Reorganization bill.

22. Walter White to Roosevelt, March 4, 1938, Roosevelt Papers, OF 285C, Box 12.

23. National Consumer's League to Roosevelt, February 10, 1937, Roosevelt Papers, OF 15-E. See Msgr. Robert F. Keegan to Roosevelt, January 21, 1937, *ibid.*, PPF 3539; memorandum on Children's Bureau, February 19, 1937, PCAM Files, Box 6.

24. *New York Times*, November 10, 1937, p. 5; November 21, 1937, p. 26; February 25, 1938, p. 8; Green to George Norris, March 7, 1938, March 21, 1938, Norris MSS, Tray 33, Box 6 (File 2).

25. Green to E. Lloyd Whitner, March 30, 1938, William Green MSS (Cornell University), Reel 25, #211.

26. Green to Roosevelt, May 11, 1939, Roosevelt Papers, OF 15-H; Green to Roosevelt, December 13, 1939, *ibid.*, OF 15-E.

27. Select Committee, *Hearings*, p. 147; Charles I. Stengle to George Norris, March 22, 1938, Norris MSS, Tray 33, Box 6 (File 2); Stengle to Josiah W. Bailey, April 26, 1938, Josiah W. Bailey MSS (Duke University), "Political—1938."

28. Green to labor leaders, March 21, 1938, Green MSS, Reel 25, #548.

29. *Congressional Record*, 75th Cong., 3rd sess., pp. 4506-7.

30. Green to labor leaders, March 21, 1938, Green MSS, Reel 25, #548; Green to labor leaders, March 28, 1938, *ibid.,* #24-29.

31. E. E. Vandeleur to B. W. Gearhart, *Congressional Record,* 75th Cong., 3rd sess., p. 4658.

32. *Ibid.,* p. 4365.

33. Green to [illegible], March 28, 1938, Green MSS, Reel 25, #23.

34. *Labor,* January 19, 1937, August 17, 1937. See Select Committee, *Hearings,* pp. 253-55.

35. *Labor,* April 5, 1938, April 12, 1938.

36. A. Johnston, D. B. Robertson, A. F. Whitney to McAdoo, March 27, 1938; J. W. Buzzell to McAdoo, March 28, 1938; McAdoo to Byrnes, March 29, 1938, McAdoo MSS, Box 452.

37. *New York Times,* March 26, 1938, p. 1; McAdoo draft of reply to unions, March 29, 1938, McAdoo MSS, Box 452. See Amos Pinchot to Roy Howard, April 4, 1938, Pinchot MSS, Box 64.

38. Jacob Baker to Roosevelt, January 19, 1937, Roosevelt Papers, OF 2923; Select Committee, *Hearings,* pp. 155-57, 165-67; postcards from "non-classified" employees to Lindsay Warren, February 1938, Warren MSS, Box 19.

39. *The C.I.O. News,* April 9, 1938.

40. *New York Times,* January 20, 1937, p. 10. The Chamber withheld comment on the proposed new departments and the plan for the independent regulatory commissions.

41. "Reorganization Troubles," *Magazine of Wall Street,* January 30, 1937, p. 474; "F.D.R.'s Reorganizing Job," *Business Week,* January 16, 1937, p. 26.

42. "Administrative Reorganization," *Commercial and Financial Chronicle,* January 16, 1937, pp. 333-34.

43. W. P. Helm, "Blank Check for Mr. Roosevelt?" *California: The Magazine of Pacific Business,* 27:11, 39-40 (March 1937); Thomas F. Woodlock, "Hands Off Both!" *Railway Age,* April 24, 1937, p. 703.

44. "The Proposed Reorganization of the Federal Government," New York Chamber of Commerce *Monthly Bulletin,* 29:10-14 (May 1937).

45. J. J. Keon to Roosevelt, April 6, 1938, Roosevelt Papers, OF 285C, Box 8; Milwaukee Association of Commerce to Merlin Hull, March 31, 1938, Hull MSS.

46. "Defeat of the Reorganization Bill," New York Chamber of Commerce *Monthly Bulletin,* 29:395 (April 1938); "A New Deal on the New Deal," *Boston Business,* 29:3 (May 1938).

47. *The Commercial West Weekly,* 75:6 (April 16, 1938); *Boston Business,* 29:3 (May 1938).

48. *The Commercial West Weekly,* 75:6 (April 16, 1938). But cf.

"Roosevelt Defeat," *The Magazine of Wall Street,* April 23, 1938, p. 10, for the view that defeat was "not a rout" for the President.

49. United States Chamber of Commerce, *Government Reorganization* (Washington, 1938), p. 16.

50. Herbert Corey, "Stop, Look, and Listen," *Public Utilities Fortnightly,* 21:716-17 (June 9, 1938).

51. "Federal Government Reorganization," New York Chamber of Commerce *Monthly Bulletin,* 29:313 (February 1938); Winthrop Aldrich to James F. Byrnes, February 21, 1938, PCAM Files, Box 16. Cf. Thomas Paul Jenkin, *Reactions of Major Groups to Positive Government in the United States, 1935–40* (Berkeley, 1945), pp. 301-5, 322, for another view.

52. Gulick to Brownlow, February 5, 1937, PCAM Files, Box 2.

53. Joseph O'Mahoney to Harry Illsley, March 30, 1958, Joseph O'Mahoney MSS (University of Wyoming). I am indebted to Professor William E. Leuchtenburg for the use of his notes on the O'Mahoney Papers.

54. Memorandum on the nature of reorganization, April 16, 1939, Roosevelt Papers, OF 285C, Box 8.

55. Cliff Scott to Donald Richberg, February 15, 1935, Roosevelt Papers, OF 1-Misc.

56. Brownlow, *Passion for Anonymity,* pp. 346-48, 372-73; Harold D. Smith Diary, September 5, 1939, Smith MSS.

57. Harold D. Smith Diary, May 6, 1939, April 27, 1939, Smith MSS. See Smith's diary entries for April 21, May 4, and June 26, 1939, *ibid.;* Roper, *Fifty Years of Public Life,* pp. 347-48.

58. Select Committee, *Hearings,* pp. 202-8, 257-63; *New York Times,* August 10, 1937, p. 4; H. A. Morgan to Roosevelt, September 23, 1939, Roosevelt Papers, OF 42.

59. Eastman to Henry W. Anderson, January 27, 1937, Joseph B. Eastman MSS (Amherst College), Reading File, 1937.

60. Eastman speech, January 21, 1937, Eastman MSS, Addresses, 1936–41; Eastman to R. V. Fletcher, January 27, 1937, *ibid.,* Reading File, 1937.

61. Eastman memorandum to ICC, July 1, 1937, Eastman MSS, Reading File, 1937; Select Committee, *Hearings,* pp. 177-78, 184.

62. Select Committee, *Hearings,* p. 220.

63. A. L. Reed to Clark C. Wren, March 27, 1937, Reorganization Committee Files, Box 12. It was generally believed that if the Brownlow plan went through, the ICC would come under the Department of Commerce.

64. Select Committee, *Hearings,* pp. 287-88, 290.

65. Mitchell to Roosevelt, January 12, 1937, February 11, 1937, Roosevelt Papers, OF 2.

66. Brownlow to Roosevelt, February 22, 1937, Roosevelt Papers, OF 2; Select Committee, *Hearings*, pp. 271-75.

67. Gulick to Brownlow and Merriam, September 14, 1937, PCAM Files, Box 11.

68. Ordway to Brownlow, October 19, 1937, PCAM Files, Box 11.

69. Gulick to Brownlow and Merriam, September 14, 1937; Guy Moffett to Brownlow, October 18, 1937, PCAM Files, Box 11; *New York Times,* February 25, 1938, p. 6.

70. See Beck, *Our Wonderland of Bureaucracy,* pp. 205-6, 228-39, 260-63.

71. Cochran to Clark Wren, August 25, 1937, Reorganization Committee Files, Box 12; *Congressional Record,* 75th Cong., 3rd sess., p. 4488.

72. Ickes, *Secret Diary,* II, 47, 157.

73. Select Committee, *Hearings,* p. 265.

74. John J. Keegan to Norris, March 18, 1939, Norris MSS, Tray 33, Box 6 (File 2).

75. James F. Byrnes, *All In One Lifetime* (New York, 1958), p. 107.

76. T. F. Thomas to Elbert D. Thomas, March 2, 1938, Elbert D. Thomas MSS (Franklin D. Roosevelt Library), Box 14.

77. Joint Committee, *Hearings,* p. 154.

78. Henry Morgenthau Diaries, December 8, 1936, Morgenthau MSS, Book 47.

79. *Congressional Record,* 75th Cong., 3rd sess., pp. 33-35; Select Committee, *Hearings,* pp. 277, 289.

80. See Emmerich, *Essays on Federal Reorganization,* pp. 33-49; Norman Wengert, *Natural Resources and the Political Struggle,* p. 53.

81. Select Committee, *Hearings,* p. 290.

82. "The Reorganization Quarrel," *New Republic,* March 16, 1938, pp. 149-50; Avery Leiserson, "Political Limitations on Executive Reorganization," *American Political Science Review,* 41:71-74, 79, 83 (February 1947).

83. Lawrence Lewis Diary, March 22, 1938, Lawrence Lewis MSS (State Historical Society of Colorado).

84. Byrnes, *All In One Lifetime,* pp. 105-6. A full account of the role of the Engineers may be found in Arthur Maass, *Muddy Waters* (Cambridge, 1951).

85. Cochran to Roosevelt, November 10, 1939, Roosevelt Papers, OF 285C, Box 8.

86. Harold D. Smith Diary, July 19, 1939, Smith MSS.

87. Cochran to P. H. Elwood, January 31, 1939, cited in Maass, *Muddy Waters,* p. 95. See Samuel P. Hays, *Conservation and the Gos-*

*pel of Efficiency* (Cambridge, 1959), pp. 198-218; Maass, *Muddy Waters*, pp. 72-95.

88. Ickes, *Secret Diary*, II, 151-52.

89. Charles W. Eliot to Merriam, March 25, 1938, National Resources Planning Board Papers (National Archives), Box 47 (070.3). Emphasis added.

90. *Congressional Record*, 75th Cong., 3rd sess., pp. 3837, 3999-4013.

91. National Rivers and Harbors Congress, *Proceedings of the Special 'Council of War' Meeting* (Washington, April 26, 1938), pp. 7-8, 26. Nine of seventeen Democrats on the House Committee on Rivers and Harbors voted against the Reorganization bill, including its chairman.

92. Interview with Louis Brownlow, September 4, 1962.


## Chapter V: The Forest Service Lobby

1. Byrnes, *All In One Lifetime*, p. 106.

2. Ickes, *Secret Diary*, I, 151, 601-6; Harold Ickes, "My Twelve Years with FDR," *Saturday Evening Post* (July 24, 1948), p. 68.

3. Ickes, *Secret Diary*, I, 24; Ickes to Gifford Pinchot, April 20, 1933, Gifford Pinchot MSS (Library of Congress), Box 1905.

4. Wallace to Roosevelt, June 27, 1934, in Edgar B. Nixon (ed.), *Franklin D. Roosevelt and Conservation*, 2 vols. (New York, 1957), I, 307; Ickes, *Secret Diary*, I, 169-70. A discussion of the Taylor Grazing Act may be found in Phillip O. Foss, *Politics and Grass: The Administration of Grazing on the Public Domain* (Seattle, 1960), pp. 39-72.

5. Ickes, *Secret Diary*, I, 250, 259; Schlesinger, *Coming of the New Deal*, p. 347.

6. Ickes, *Secret Diary*, I, 258, 328, 343-44, 350. See Schlesinger, *Coming of the New Deal*, pp. 343-49; E. Louise Peffer, *The Closing of the Public Domain* (Stanford, 1951), pp. 232-46.

7. U. S. Senate, Committee on Expenditures in the Executive Department, *Hearings*, 74th Cong., 1st sess., 1935, pp. 10-16; Ickes, *Secret Diary*, I, 386.

8. Silcox to Regional Foresters, July 31, 1935, Pinchot MSS, Box 1904. See Tugwell memorandum for Roosevelt, August 3, 1935, Roosevelt Papers, OF 1-C.

9. Ickes, *Secret Diary*, I, 417-19, 601-2, 604-6.

10. Peffer, *Public Domain*, pp. 235-37; Ickes to Roosevelt, August 19, 1936; Wallace to Ickes, November 13, 1936, in Nixon (ed.), *Roosevelt and Conservation*, I, 550-55, 595, 606.

11. David J. Speck memorandum for Solicitor Margold, November 24, 1939, Department of Interior Files, Office of the Secretary (Na-

tional Archives), Box 296; J. D. Wolfsohn memorandum for Solicitor Margold describing a meeting of the Interior Department reorganization committee, November 22, 1939, *ibid.*

12. Ickes to Roosevelt, February 7, 1940, in Nixon (ed.), *Roosevelt and Conservation,* II, 420-21; Ickes to Roosevelt, April 1, 1939, Roosevelt Papers, OF 6.

13. Roosevelt to Pinchot, January 15, 1940; Roosevelt to Edward A. O'Neal, February 1, 1940, Roosevelt Papers, OF 1-C.

14. Ickes, *Secret Diary,* I, 601; II, 624.

15. M. Nelson McGeary, *Gifford Pinchot: Forester-Politician* (Princeton, 1960), pp. 235, 257, 390, 409; Ickes to Pinchot, April 20, 1933, Pinchot MSS, Box 1905.

16. Ickes to Pinchot, July 15, 1935; Pinchot to Ickes, July 18, 1935, Pinchot MSS, Box 1904; Pinchot to Warren Jones, November 4, 1936, *ibid.*

17. *New York Times,* May 1, 1937, p. 8; Ickes to Roosevelt, May 3, 1937, Roosevelt Papers, PPF 289; Pinchot to Herbert A. Smith, July 3, 1937, Pinchot MSS, Box 352; Ickes radio address, November 1, 1937 and Pinchot reply, November 4, 1937, Pinchot MSS, Box 1903.

18. Pinchot to William F. Finley, March 29, 1940, Pinchot MSS, Box 1901; McGeary, *Gifford Pinchot,* pp. 411-13.

19. Ickes, *Secret Diary,* I, 584; II, 7-8, 20-21.

20. Wallace to Roosevelt, December 22, 1936, PCAM Files, Box 6.

21. A discussion of forestry pressure groups may be found in: Luther Gulick, *American Forest Policy* (New York, 1951), pp. 40-44; Marion Clawson and Burnell Held, *The Federal Lands* (Baltimore, 1957), pp. 136-41.

22. Select Committee, *Hearings,* p. 112.

23. "The Reorganization Bill in Retrospect," *Journal of Forestry,* 36:641-42 (July 1938).

24. H. H. Chapman, "Reorganization and the Forest Service," *Journal of Forestry,* 35:427-34 (May 1937). For an attack on the entire program, see "Reorganization in the Dark," *American Forests,* 43: 397 (August, 1937).

25. Gifford Pinchot to Amos Pinchot, January 21, 1937, Gifford Pinchot MSS, Box 356; Pinchot to Mrs. L. E. Van Etten, March 29, 1937, *ibid.,* Box 358. Gifford Pinchot's reaction to the Brownlow report was much milder than was Amos's. Gifford said, "It is not a bad document," but he thought it showed a lack of experience in "actual administration," Pinchot Diary, January 27, 1937, Pinchot MSS, Box 3322.

26. Pinchot to Secretary of Agriculture, October 21, 1911, Pinchot MSS, Box 1855.

27. Henry A. Wallace to John Cochran, December 11, 1935, Bureau

of the Budget Files, Box 191; Letter to Editor, *Science,* 86:242-43 (September 10, 1937); "Conservation," *Nature,* 30:35-36 (July 1937).

28. Gifford Pinchot, "Save the Forest Service," *California,* 27:39 (November 1937).

29. H. H. Chapman to Roosevelt, October 26, 1934, Roosevelt Papers, OF 1-C; Select Committee, *Hearings,* p. 42.

30. Interview with Henry Wallace, January 25, 1963.

31. Ickes to L. L. MacBride, December 16, 1937, Department of Interior, Secretary's File, Box 2565; Select Committee, *Hearings,* pp. 353-58.

32. Roosevelt to Ickes, July 8, 1941, Roosevelt Papers, OF 149.

33. C. M. Brown to Roosevelt, June 4, 1934, Roosevelt Papers, OF 1-C; R. Y. Stuart to Pinchot, April 21, 1933, Pinchot MSS, Box 1905.

34. Pinchot to Roosevelt, April 18, 1933, Roosevelt Papers, PPF 289.

35. The complicated history of the Oregon and California lands, and the conflict between Interior and Agriculture over jurisdiction, is discussed in Clawson and Held, *Federal Lands,* pp. 32, 82-84.

36. Ovid Butler, "Oregon Checkmate," *American Forests,* 42:157-62, 197 (April 1936). Butler, of the American Forestry Association, was a prominent conservationist.

37. Pinchot speech to the American Forestry Association, May 31, 1937, Roosevelt Papers, PPF 289. For the Administration's attitude toward the dispute, see memoranda of August 1937 by Harold Ickes and Daniel Bell, Roosevelt Papers, OF 633.

38. Select Committee, *Hearings,* pp. 45-46; Emanuel Fritz to H. H. Chapman, January 13, 1937, PCAM Files, Box 6.

39. Pinchot, "Save the Forest Service," *California,* 27:21 (November 1937). See Ralph S. Hosmer to John J. Cochran, May 3, 1937, Reorganization Committee Files, Box 12.

40. Ed I. Kotok to William B. Greeley, July 17, 1935, William B. Greeley MSS (University of Oregon).

41. Pinchot to H. W. Carroll, September 7, 1937, Pinchot MSS, Box 1903.

42. McGeary, *Gifford Pinchot,* pp. 23-24, 87; Hays, *Conservation and the Gospel of Efficiency,* pp. 1-4, 28, 127, 141-46; Wengert, *Natural Resources,* p. 52.

43. Ickes, *Secret Diary,* II, 438; Irving Brant to Harold Ickes, February 13, 1936, Roosevelt Papers, OF 1-C.

44. Chapman to Roosevelt, February 23, 1937, Roosevelt Papers, OF 1-C.

45. H. H. Chapman, "Reorganization and the Forest Service," *Journal of Forestry,* 35:427-34 (May 1937).

46. William B. Greeley, *Forests and Men* (New York, 1951), pp. 111-12, 77.

47. Letter to Charles Dunwoody, October 1, 1937, Lobby Committee Files, Box 254.

48. On the relationship between lumbermen and the Forest Service, see Hays, *Conservation and the Gospel of Efficiency,* pp. 30, 41, 57, 65, 71, 141-46.

49. President of Dude Ranchers Association to Joseph O'Mahoney, December 28, 1937, Lobby Committee Files, Box 254.

50. Wyoming Livestock Association outline of National Woolgrowers' Association brief opposing transfer of the Forest Service (n.d.), Lobby Committee Files, Box 254.

51. "Mr. Ickes' Answer," *American Forests,* 44:113-15, 142 (March 1938). One Democratic congressman complained of collusion between the special timber interests and forestry officials, Compton I. White to James A. Farley, November 2, 1933, Roosevelt Papers, OF 1-C.

52. Greeley, *Forests and Men,* pp. 210, 212, 101-14; McGeary, *Gifford Pinchot,* pp. 84, 331, 334-36, 408.

53. "U. S. Forester Silcox Says—'Public Regulation of Private Forests is Essential,'" *West Coast Lumberman,* 65:9 (March 1938); "The Lower One Third and the Forest Service," *ibid.* (June 1938), 38-39; Kenneth G. Crawford, *The Pressure Boys* (New York, 1939), p. 199.

54. James McClure, for example, was president of both the Farmers' Federation and the American Forestry Association.

55. Bailey to Edward A. O'Neal, April 6, 1938, Bailey MSS, "General, 1938." Bailey was a strong opponent of reorganization.

56. For a discussion of such "catalytic pressure group" techniques, see Blaisdell, *American Democracy under Pressure,* pp. 113-14.

57. R. G. Poole memorandum for Ickes, March 5, 1937, Department of Interior, Office of the Secretary, Box 2564.

58. Butler to John Baker, January 26, 1937, Department of Interior, Office of the Secretary, Box 2564.

59. Pinchot Diary, February 26, April 30, May 3, May 31, 1937, Pinchot MSS, Box 3322.

60. Pinchot to James McClure, June 4, 1937, Pinchot MSS, Box 1903.

61. "Report on Status of Government Reorganization," June 11-14, 1937, Pinchot MSS, Box 1903.

62. Collingwood to Pinchot, June 24, 1937, Pinchot MSS, Box 1903; "Meeting at A.F.A. offices," June 24, 1937, *ibid.*

63. "Meeting at A.F.A. offices," *ibid.*

64. Dunwoody to Pinchot, May 6, 1937, Pinchot MSS, Box 352. On Dunwoody's activities, see material in Lobby Committee Files, Box 254

(Current Tax Folder), especially Charles Dunwoody to W. L. Connolly, February 18, 1938.

65. Pinchot to Dunwoody, September 10, 1937, Pinchot MSS, Box 352.

66. "Report on Status of Government Reorganization," October 27, 1937, Pinchot MSS, Box 1904; Butler to James McClure, October 30, 1937, *ibid.,* Box 1903.

67. The names of all contributors and the amounts given were subpoenaed by the Senate Lobby Committee, and may be found in Box 254 (Charles Dunwoody Envelope). The largest contributors were: Ogden (Utah) Chamber of Commerce—$2796; A. R. Watzek (Portland)—$2200; Knapp Fund (Santa Barbara)—$2000; Gifford Pinchot —$1500.

68. Daily expense accounts of Charles Dunwoody, April 1937–March 1938, Lobby Committee Files, Box 254.

69. Dunwoody to W. L. Connolly, November 23, 1937, Lobby Committee Files, Box 254.

70. Dunwoody to cooperators, November 10, 1937, Lobby Committee Files, Box 254.

71. "Master Key List—Reorganization," Lobby Committee Files, Box 107.

72. Dunwoody to supporters, December 3, 1937, Lobby Committee Files, Box 254.

73. Dunwoody to W. L. Connolly, November 13, 1937, November 23, 1937, Lobby Committee Files, Box 254; Pinchot Diary, November 25, 1937, Pinchot MSS, Box 3322.

74. Dunwoody memorandum for Norman Sloane, November 26, 1937, Lobby Committee Files, Box 254.

75. Bessie L. Pierce, "The Political Pattern of Some Women's Organizations," *Annals of the American Academy of Political and Social Science,* 179:50-58 (May 1935).

76. Crawford, *Pressure Boys,* p. 197.

77. Emily Bogert to Pinchot, October 19, 1937; Emily Bogert to Dunwoody, October 25, 1937; Pinchot to Emily Bogert, November 3, 1937, Pinchot MSS, Box 1903.

78. Emily Bogert to Pinchot, November 10, 1937, Pinchot MSS, Box 1903.

79. Emily Bogert letters to G.F.W.C. state presidents, November 8, 1937, November 10, 1937, Roosevelt Papers, OF 285C, Box 7; Emily Bogert to Dunwoody, March 3, 1938, Lobby Committee Files, Box 254.

80. Pinchot Diary, November 20–26, 1937, December 3, 15, 1937, Pinchot MSS, Box 3322.

81. Pinchot to Gifford B. Pinchot, November 17, 1937, Pinchot MSS, Box 356; Pinchot Diary, November 17, 1937, *ibid.*, Box 3322.

82. Bureau chief notice re: "President's report submitting report of President's Committee on Administrative Management," January 13, 1937, Department of Agriculture, Office of the Secretary (National Archives), Correspondence, 1937, Acc. 1074, Drawer 1.

83. Pinchot Diary, February 28, 1937, Pinchot MSS, Box 3322.

84. Paul Appleby to Ovid Butler, March 6, 1937, Department of Agriculture, Secretary's File, Acc. 1074; Appleby to T. G. Woolford, March 9, 1937, *ibid.*

85. Pinchot to Emily Bogert, November 17, 1937, Pinchot MSS, Box 1903; J. D. LeCron to E. J. Fjeldstad, December 15, 1937, Department of Agriculture, Secretary's File, Acc. 1074.

86. Aled Davies to Edward A. Rumely, February 14, 1938, Amos Pinchot MSS, Box 63.

87. Lieber to Harry Slattery, November 4, 1937, Department of Interior, Secretary's File, Box 2564.

88. Lieber to Roosevelt, November 17, 1937; Ickes to Roosevelt, December 20, 1937, Roosevelt Papers, Official File 177-A. For an estimate of the extent of pro-Ickes sentiment among conservationists, see Paul A. Herbert to Ickes, March 14, 1940, Department of Interior, Secretary's File.

89. "President's Page," *Bird Lore*, 40:3, 82-83 (January 1938); Ickes to James Roosevelt, February 4, 1938, PCAM Files, Box 6.

90. Cf. T. G. Woolford to Dunwoody, November 19, 1937; Earl L. Hockett to Dunwoody, September 15, 1937, Lobby Committee Files, Box 254.

91. Scrugham to Ickes, November 17, 1937, Department of Interior, Secretary's File, Box 2565. Cf. John Dempsey to Ickes, January 8, 1938; M. M. Logan to Ickes, January 31, 1938, *ibid.*

92. Voorhis to Roosevelt, November 28, 1937, Roosevelt Papers, OF 1-C.

93. Warren to Clarence Poe, January 10, 1938, Lindsay Carter Warren MSS (University of North Carolina), Box 19.

94. Memorandum on Rep. Gehrmann, March 2, 1938, Lobby Committee Files, Box 254.

95. Dunwoody letter to supporters, December 27, 1937, January 5, 1938, Lobby Committee Files, Box 254.

96. Dunwoody to cooperators, February 14, 1938, Lobby Committee Files, Box 254.

97. Fred Brenckman to state Grange officers, March 2, 1938, Lobby Committee Files, Box 254; Butler letter, March 2, 1938, Warren MSS, Box 19.

98. Dunwoody to Lloyd Wentworth, March 7, 1938, Lobby Committee Files, Box 254.

99. *Congressional Record,* 75th Cong., 3rd sess., pp. 2626-27, 3466.

100. Wallace to Byrnes, February 8, 1938, Department of Agriculture, Secretary's File, Box 65.

101. J. D. LeCron form letters, March, 1938, Department of Agriculture, Secretary's File, Correspondence, 1938.

102. Dunwoody to Lloyd Wentworth, March 7, 1938, Lobby Committee Files, Box 254.

103. Dunwoody to Pinchot, May 5, 1938, Pinchot MSS, Box 1903.

104. Dunwoody to Pinchot, May 21, July 3, August 24, December 8, 1939, Pinchot MSS, Box 1903. Dunwoody believed that Ickes brought pressure upon his employers to have him fired.

105. Dunwoody to Pinchot, February 1, 4, 10, and 16, March 18 and 28, April 7, 1940, Pinchot MSS, Box 1901; Dunwoody to Pinchot, November 21, December 8, 1940, *ibid.,* Box 1900.

## Chapter VI: The Senate Approves

1. Ickes, *Secret Diary,* II, 319; *Congressional Record,* 75th Cong., 3rd sess. [cited below as *CR*], p. 2517.

2. Bailey to J. G. Merrimon, March 7, 1938, Bailey MSS, "General, 1938."

3. Glass to George H. Moses, November 8, 1937, Glass MSS, Box 380.

4. *CR,* p. 3231 (Burke), 3463 (Johnson), 3924 (Hale), 2740 (Bailey).

5. *CR,* pp. 3235 (Clark), 3462 (Johnson), 3931-34 (Davis).

6. *CR,* p. 2829.

7. *CR,* p. 3386.

8. *CR,* p. 3020.

9. *CR,* p. 2831.

10. *CR,* pp. 3178-79, 3230, 3258, 3261.

11. *CR,* p. 3657.

12. *CR,* pp. 2682-88, 2815, 3303-4, 3364.

13. *CR,* p. 3299.

14. *CR,* pp. 3307-8, 2807-13, 3362-65, 3372.

15. *CR,* p. 3404.

16. *CR,* pp. 3018-23.

17. *CR,* pp. 3472-73.

18. *CR,* pp. 3034, 3038.

19. One of Brownlow's associates said later: "If an amendment similar to the Wheeler amendment is adopted, we may as well say

goodby to reorganization," Joseph P. Harris, Memorandum on Reorganization, 1939, PCAM Files, Box 2.

20. *CR*, pp. 3479-84, 3559; New York *Herald-Tribune*, March 17, 1938, p. 1.

21. New York *Herald-Tribune*, March 18, 1938, p. 12.

22. *CR*, pp. 3640-41, 3644-45.

23. *CR*, p. 3819.

24. Robert Wagner of New York and Charles Andrews of Florida, who were paired against the Wheeler amendment, voted against the bill.

25. Ickes, *Secret Diary*, II, 338-39, 344-46. On the influence of public opinion on Lundeen, see Henry G. Teigan to H. C. Rowbert, April 7, 1938, Henry George Teigan MSS (State Historical Society of Minnesota).

26. *CR*, pp. 2502, 2505.

27. Edward R. Burke to James T. Adams, March 25, 1938, Adams MSS.

28. *CR*, pp. 3840, 3743.

29. *CR*, pp. 2594-96. Byrd now claimed that the Comptroller-General exercised pre-control through his power to countersign warrants, rather than through the preaudit.

30. See *CR*, pp. 2604-5 for views of Lewis Schwellenbach, the only accountant in the Senate, who supported Byrnes.

31. *CR*, p. 2600.

32. *New York Times*, March 7, 1938, p. 5; *CR*, Appendix, pp. 986-87.

33. *CR*, pp. 3749, 3459-61.

34. *CR*, p. 3815.

35. Elmer Thomas to American Legion, Oklahoma City, April 9, 1938, Thomas MSS.

36. *CR*, pp. 3466, 2626-27. See James Murray to Gifford Pinchot, February 6, 1940, Pinchot MSS, Box 1902.

37. *CR*, pp. 3467, 3469.

38. *CR*, pp. 3645-48, 3999-4013.

39. In 1939 a planning advocate complained about such restrictions to a Senate leader. "I don't think we should quarrel about an academic question," replied the senator; "Remember I'm the one who has to get the votes." Gerald Egan memorandum for Charles W. Eliot on a conversation with Senator Carl Hayden, June 17, 1939, National Resources Planning Board Papers, Box 47 (070.3).

40. Edward R. Burke to James T. Adams, March 25, 1938, Adams MSS.

41. James A. Farley, *Behind the Ballots* (New York, 1938), p. 362;

Ickes, *Secret Diary*, II, 349; James Roosevelt to J. Hamilton Lewis, March 27, 1938, Roosevelt Papers, PPF 1707.

42. Borah to Mrs. Edwin Snow, March 29, 1938, William E. Borah MSS (Library of Congress), Box 421.

43. New York *Herald-Tribune*, March 28, 1938, p. 1; Gannett to Claude Ashbrook, March 26, 1938, Gannett MSS, Box 16. Borah, however, thought that the chances were "very slim" that the bill could be beaten, Borah to W. C. Geddes, March 28, 1938, Borah MSS, Box 421.

44. Ickes, *Secret Diary*, II, 349; New York *Herald-Tribune*, March 28, 1938, pp. 1-2.

45. Telegrams were identified as forgeries when replies to the "sender" were not deliverable, or when the "sender" denied having sent the telegram upon receipt of a reply. Some examples of such telegrams may be found in Lobby Committee Files, Box 107.

46. *CR*, pp. 4191 (Vandenberg), 4193 (Capper), 4201 (Walsh). In March, 1932, Vandenberg had said: "This process of reorganizing the fundamental structure never in the world is going to be achieved by Congressional effort . . . It must be an executive function." (Cited in Pendleton Herring, *Public Administration and the Public Interest* [New York, 1936], p. 346.)

47. *CR*, pp. 4192-93 (McAdoo), 4187-88 (Green), 4195-96 (LaFollette). See Theodore F. Green to James L. Jenks, March 25, 1938, Green MSS, Box 40.

48. *CR*, pp. 4186-87.

49. *CR*, pp. 4190-92.

50. *CR*, pp. 4198-4201.

51. *CR*, p. 4204; *New York Times*, March 29, 1938, p. 1; New York *Herald-Tribune*, March 29, 1938, p. 1; Bailey to E. Hervey Evans, March 29, 1938, Bailey MSS, "General, 1938"; transcript of Wayne Taylor telephone conversation with Henry Morgenthau, March 28, 1936, Morgenthau MSS, Book 117.

52. "Reorganization Renaissance," *Time*, March 28, 1938, p. 9.

53. Gannett to Claude Ashbrook, March 26, 1938, Gannett MSS, Box 16; Marvin McIntyre to Roosevelt, January 11, 1939, Roosevelt Papers, OF 285C, Box 8.

54. For Pittman's attitude to Ickes, see Fred Israel, *Nevada's Key Pittman* (Lincoln, 1963).

55. *CR*, pp. 3999-4001; *New York Times*, March 25, 1938, p. 1; Ickes, *Secret Diary*, II, 499.

56. Pinchot to Homer Bone, November 14, 1938, Amos Pinchot MSS, Box 63; Ickes, *Secret Diary*, II, 416.

57. Ickes, *Secret Diary*, II, 349; *CR*, pp. 3844-45.

58. George Meany and John O'Hanlon to Robert Wagner,

March 21, 1938; William Green to Wagner, March 21, 1938, Robert Wagner MSS (Georgetown University); Raymond Clapper to Alfred M. Landon, March 30, 1938, Clapper MSS, Box 48; Ickes, *Secret Diary*, II, 349-50. I am indebted to Professor William E. Leuchtenburg for the use of his notes on the Wagner Papers.

59. New York *Herald-Tribune*, March 30, 1938, p. 6.

60. Ickes, *Secret Diary*, II, 184; Leon Keyserling, "The Wagner Act: Its Origin and Current Significance," *George Washington Law Review*, 29:203, 207-8, 210-12 (December 1960).

61. McAdoo to Edward M. Swasey, April 3, 1938, McAdoo MSS, Box 452.

62. Pinchot Diary, November 26, 1937, Gifford Pinchot MSS, Box 3322. See Green to Robert Palmer, March 25, 1938, Green MSS, Box 40.

63. *New York Times*, March 29, 1938, p. 20.

64. New York *Herald-Tribune*, March 22, 1938, p. 1. Berry and Gillette had voted for the Wheeler amendment; Brown thought a majority vote should be able to override an Executive order.

65. *Ibid.*, March 19, 1938, p. 1.

66. Anonymous resident in Kearney, Nebraska, to George Norris, March 19, 1938, Norris MSS, Tray 33, Box 6 (File 2). See M. T. McShane to Norris, April 9, 1938, *ibid.*

67. *CR*, p. 3477.

68. *CR*, p. 3473. See Pinchot Diary, January 28, 1937, April 26, 1937, Gifford Pinchot MSS, Box 3322 for Norris's attitude on Forestry.

69. *CR*, p. 3475.

70. *CR*, p. 3823.

71. *CR*, pp. 3539, 3560.

72. Norris to Herbert A. Lien, April 14, 1938, Norris MSS, Tray 96, Box 5. I have found no other evidence to support the contention that power companies opposed reorganization.

73. John P. Robertson to resident of Christine, North Dakota, April 21, 1938, Norris MSS, Tray 33, Box 6 (File 2).

74. Norris to Roosevelt, September 9, 1939, Roosevelt Papers, OF 42.

75. Bailey to Mrs. Earl Bishopric, March 30, 1938, Bailey MSS, "Political, 1938."

76. Clifford Hope to A. H. Heaps, February 23, 1938, Clifford Hope MSS, Legislative Correspondence, 1937-38. See "Confidential memo concerning . . . Congressman Cochran's attitude on procedure to be followed in Congress," October 22, 1937, Roosevelt Papers, OF 285C, Box 16.

77. *CR*, pp. 4014-17.

78. *CR*, pp. 4204-5.

79. *CR*, p. 4205.

80. This version was reported by Louis Brownlow, Interview, September 4, 1962.

81. *CR*, p. 4205.

82. New York *Herald-Tribune*, March 29, 1938, pp. 1-2. See O. R. Altman, "Second and Third Sessions of the Seventy-fifth Congress," *American Political Science Review*, 32:1111-12 (December 1938); Memorandum for C. M. Hester on the history of Reorganization bills in the 75th Congress, August 5, 1938, PCAM Files, Box 6.

83. Bailey to E. Hervey Evans, March 29, 1938, Bailey MSS, "General, 1938."

## Chapter VII: Roosevelt, Reorganization, and the Public

1. Hadley Cantril (ed.), *Public Opinion 1935–1946* (Princeton, 1951), p. 756; Burns, *Roosevelt: The Lion and the Fox*, p. 338. The Gallup and Roper polls should be used with caution; they do, however, indicate a trend which cannot be ignored.

2. Letter to Roosevelt, April 7, 1938, Roosevelt Papers, PPF 1820.

3. John Haynes Holmes to Amos Pinchot, March 4, 1938, Amos Pinchot MSS, Box 65.

4. Letter to Merlin Hull, April 7, 1938, Hull MSS.

5. Letter to Henry George Teigan, April 5, 1938, Teigan MSS.

6. W. H. Gruel to Roosevelt, April 1, 1938, Roosevelt Papers, OF 285C, Box 7. See W. A. Cochrane to John O'Connor, April 6, 1938, John J. O'Connor MSS (Indiana University): "I have noticed for months Mr. Roosevelt gets no applause in the News Reels showing."

7. Cantril, *Public Opinion*, p. 759.

8. John Dewey to Amos Pinchot, March 11, 1938, Amos Pinchot MSS, Box 65.

9. Cantril, *Public Opinion*, p. 404. These results were obtained in a Gallup Poll taken on March 30, 1938; a Fortune Poll in July 1938 showed 22.3 per cent for the bill, 38.3 per cent against, and 39.4 per cent undecided or uninformed.

10. Cantril, *Public Opinion*, p. 760. Sampling those who *opposed* the President, Roper reported that 49 per cent also disliked his Wages and Hours bill, 32 per cent disliked his international policy, 62 per cent disliked his attitude toward labor, 71 per cent disliked his attitude toward big business, but that 74 per cent disliked the Reorganization bill.

11. Cantril, *Public Opinion*, p. 404.

12. Ida Bergh to Roosevelt, April 9, 1938, Roosevelt Papers, OF 285C, Box 8. See Jay Franklin, *1940* (New York, 1940), pp. 42-43.

13. *New York Times*, March 12-14, 1938.

14. Letter to William E. Borah, March 23, 1938, Borah MSS, Box 421.

15. Letter to Merlin Hull, March 28, 1938, Hull MSS. See G. C. Jefferson to John O'Connor, April 5, 1938, O'Connor MSS.

16. John J. O'Brien to Roosevelt, April 7, 1938, Roosevelt Papers, PPF 1820.

17. Douglas A. Hayes, "Business Confidence and Business Activity," *Michigan Business Studies*, 10:11-12, 15, 35-37 (1951); Kenneth D. Roose, *The Economics of Recession and Revival* (New Haven, 1954), pp. 22-26, 37-38, 55.

18. Letter to Merlin Hull, April 6, 1938, Hull MSS.

19. Letter to Roosevelt, April 6, 1938, Roosevelt Papers, OF 285C, Box 13.

20. Letter to William E. Borah, March 25, 1938, Borah MSS, Box 421. See Harold Pickering to Elbert D. Thomas, March 23, 1928, Thomas MSS, Box 25.

21. Letter to Merlin Hull, April 7, 1938, Hull MSS.

22. Cantril, *Public Opinion*, p. 404. A poll showed 56.3 per cent of the unemployed opposed to the bill.

23. Letter to Merlin Hull, April 4, 1938, Hull MSS.

24. Letter to John O'Connor, April 4, 1938, O'Connor MSS.

25. Letter to Merlin Hull, April 6, 1938, Hull MSS. See also F. D. Lisle to Theodore F. Green, April 11, 1938, Green MSS, Box 40.

26. Letter to Lyle Boren, April 2, 1938, Lyle Boren MSS (University of Oklahoma), Box 248.

27. Letter to Josiah W. Bailey, April 5, 1938, Bailey MSS, "Political, 1938." See Clifford Hope to B. T. Robinson, April 6, 1938, Hope MSS, Legislative Correspondence, 1937–38; H. H. Buffett to George Norris, March 21, 1938, Norris MSS, Tray 33, Box 6 (File 2); M. MacLennan to the Joint Committee on Reorganization, March 31, 1938, Reorganization Committee Files, Box 13.

28. Letters to John O'Connor, April 5, 1938, O'Connor MSS; to Henry George Teigan, April 2, 1938, Teigan MSS. A correspondent wrote to Theodore F. Green, March 21, 1938, Green MSS, Box 40: "There are more persons unemployed today than when he [Roosevelt] took office. . . His experiments have not turned out well. . . Yet we are asked after five years of this to give him almost absolute and unlimited power to do with us . . . as he pleases . . ."

29. Letter of a constituent to Merlin Hull, April 6, 1938, Hull MSS.

30. Gannett to W. A. Shaeffer, March 1, 1938, Gannett MSS, Box 16.

31. Kenneth Romney to Bankhead, November 17, 1938, William Bankhead MSS (State of Alabama, Archives), Box 13. Romney was sergeant-at-arms of the House of Representatives.

32. *Congressional Record*, 75th Cong., 3rd sess., pp. 4806-7.

33. *Ibid.*, p. 4808.

34. Letter to Merlin Hull, April 2, 1938, Hull MSS.

35. New York *Journal-American*, April 4, April 5, 1938.

36. New York *World-Telegram*, April 7, 1938, p. 4; James F. O'Kelly to John O'Connor, April 6, 1938, O'Connor MSS.

37. Accounts of the rally may be found in the New York *Journal-American*, April 6, 1938, and the New York *Herald-Tribune*, April 6, 1938. The *Journal* estimated that 3000 attended; the *Tribune* said 2000.

38. Baltimore *News-Post*, April 7, April 8, 1938.

39. New York *Journal-American*, April 7, 1938.

40. New York *Herald-Tribune*, April 10, 1938.

41. Ickes, *Secret Diary*, II, 325-26, 339-40; Clapper to Alfred M. Landon, March 30, 1938, Clapper MSS, Box 48.

42. Charles A. LeBounty to Roosevelt, March 4, 1938, Roosevelt Papers, OF 285C, Box 7. Emphasis added. Roosevelt had a copy of the Report of the Brownlow Committee sent to him.

43. Donald Wilhelm to Roosevelt, April 1, 1938; H. H. Clark to Roosevelt, April 2, 1938, Roosevelt Papers, OF 285C, Box 7; Roosevelt to Arthur B. Sherman, April 6, 1938, Elliott Roosevelt (ed.) *F.D.R.: His Personal Letters*, II, 774. Boake Carter was a radio commentator who had attacked reorganization.

44. Ickes, *Secret Diary*, II, 317. For a comment on Roosevelt's attitude toward deficit spending, see Harold D. Smith Diary, June 12, 1939, Smith MSS.

45. Thomas R. Amlie in *The Progressive*, March 19, 1938, p. 7. Amlie was a Progressive from Wisconsin.

46. Schlesinger, *Coming of the New Deal*, pp. 327-33.

47. C. Herman Pritchett, *The Tennessee Valley Authority: A Study in Public Administration* (Chapel Hill, 1943), pp. 186-211.

48. Lilienthal, *Journals of David E. Lilienthal*, I, 69-76.

49. New York *Herald-Tribune*, March 23, 1938, p. 1. Those politicians most hostile to the principle represented by the TVA seized upon the Morgan affair to attack the President.

50. Allan Nevins to James Truslow Adams, March 20, 1938, Adams MSS.

51. Letter of resident of Vandergrift, Pennsylvania, to Roosevelt, March 31, 1938, Roosevelt Papers, OF 285C.

52. Harry P. Grier to Robert Lee Doughton, April 8, 1938, Robert Lee Doughton MSS (University of North Carolina), Drawer 10. See Florence Keen to John O'Connor, April 5, 1938, O'Connor MSS.

53. *Congressional Record*, 75th Cong., 3rd sess., p. 4368.

54. Lawrence Lewis Diary, March 30, 1938, Lewis MSS.

55. Hope to Harry Sharp, March 31, 1938, Hope MSS, Legislative Correspondence, 1937-38. See Josiah Bailey to William H. Harrison,

April 4, 1938, Bailey MSS, "General, 1938"; Lindsay Warren to R. H. Gregory, April 5, 1938, Warren MSS, Box 19.

56. Press Conference, March 29, 1938, Roosevelt Papers, XI, 260. The joking references to a reporter, Fred Storm, were typical of the press conference.

57. Arthur Krock in the *New York Times*, March 30, 1938, p. 22.

58. Roosevelt, *Public Papers and Addresses*, VII, 179-81.

59. Charles Gifford in the *Congressional Record*, 75th Cong., 3rd sess., p. 4583.

60. *New York Times*, April 1, 1938, p. 3.

61. Lawrence Lewis Diary, March 31, 1938, Lewis MSS.

62. *New York Times*, April 10, 1938, IV, p. 6. The cartoon had appeared originally in *The Chicago News*.

63. Some newspapers reported that the letter had been written at the request of House Democratic leaders who thought it would aid the Reorganization bill; some hinted that the Congressional leaders had actually drafted the letter, although this seems unlikely. See memorandum on conversation with Roosevelt, March 31, 1938, Morgenthau MSS, Book 117.

64. This account of the evening of March 30 is based upon a story filed by one of the reporters in Warm Springs: Claude A. Mahoney, "Washington Windmill," *Wall Street Journal*, April 9, 1938, p. 4. Cf. the report by Arthur Krock in the *New York Times*, April 4, 1938, p. 20, which agrees in most respects, but holds that the President was asleep throughout the evening, and that McIntyre agreed to release the story because he thought it was too late to make the morning editions anyhow.

65. Press Conference, March 11, 1938, Roosevelt Papers, XI, 221-23.

66. Interview with Herbert Emmerich, April 10, 1963.

67. Press Conference, April 8, 1938, Roosevelt Papers, XI, 302-3.

68. Not until Roosevelt decided to resume pump-priming did his lassitude give way to renewed confidence. See his fireside chat on economic conditions of April 14, 1938, in which he replied to critics of reorganization in sure tones, Roosevelt, *Public Papers and Addresses*, VII, 242, 247.

69. Roosevelt to J. David Stern, April 12, 1938, Roosevelt Papers, PPF 5310.

### Chapter VIII: Defeat in the House

1. Henry Morgenthau Diaries, April 11, 1938, Morgenthau MSS, Book 118; Lindsay Warren to Julia Jones, April 7, 1938, Warren MSS, Box 19.

2. "Minutes of House Select Committee on Government Reorganization," March 30, 1938, Reorganization Committee Files, Box 1; John Cochran to Lindsay Warren, March 23, 1938, *ibid.*, Box 12.

3. Both the House bill and the Senate bill created an Auditor-General to carry out a postaudit; the Senate version gave the comptroller's functions to the Bureau of the Budget; the House bill left these functions with the Comptroller-General, who was made removable at the will of the President (rather than serving a fifteen-year term).

4. Warren to Wade Marr, April 4, 1938, Warren MSS, Box 19. Cochran agreed with Warren, *Congressional Record*, 75th Cong., 3rd sess. [cited below as *CR*], Appendix, pp. 1449-50.

5. Ickes, *Secret Diary*, II, 350; Pinchot to Gifford Pinchot, Jr., March 31, 1938, Gifford Pinchot MSS, Box 362; Hope to E. E. Lake, March 31, 1938, Hope MSS, Legislative Correspondence, 1937–38.

6. *New York Times*, April 1, 1938, p. 1; *CR*, pp. 4483-84, 4491.

7. The Administration rejected a sixteen-hour limitation which would have been acceptable to the opposition. It appears that the Republican members on the Cochran Committee had agreed to a six-hour debate, but the House would not accept the agreement, "Minutes of House Select Committee," March 30, 1938, Reorganization Committee Files, Box 1.

8. Lawrence Lewis Diary, April 1, 1938, Lewis MSS; *CR*, pp. 4616-17.

9. Bailey to Samuel Pettengill, April 2, 1938, Bailey MSS, "Political, 1938."

10. Hull to Mr. Heller, April 5, 1938, Hull MSS; *New York Times*, April 7, 1938, p. 1. The motion to strike out the enacting clause was offered by John O'Connor.

11. O'Connor to George D. Riley, November 4, 1938, O'Connor MSS; O'Connor to E. V. Stebbins, February 15, 1938, *ibid.;* transcript of telephone conversation between Father Coughlin and O'Connor, March 29, 1938, *ibid.*

12. Maurice P. Mahoney to O'Connor, March 29, 1938, O'Connor MSS; O'Connor to Mahoney, April 4, 1938, *ibid.*

13. *CR*, pp. 4871-72; Hope to B. P. Griffith, April 4, 1938, Hope MSS, Legislative Correspondence, 1937–38.

14. *CR*, pp. 5121-24. Bankhead said that he could allow a recount only if two, three, or four votes separated the two sides; in this case he did not consider a recapitulation justified. New York *Herald-Tribune*, April 9, 1938, reported the vote as 191-182 for recommittal; the call of absentees and some switching made the final tally 204-196.

15. Baltimore *News-Post*, April 9, 1928, p. 2; New York *Herald-Tribune*, April 9, 1938, p. 2. See John S. McGroarty to John O'Connor,

April 9, 1938, O'Connor MSS; Compton I. White to O'Connor, April 9, 1938, *ibid.*

16. Lawrence Lewis Diary, April 8, 1938, Lewis MSS.

17. Discussions of the defeat of the bill may be found in: Lindsay Rogers, "Reorganization: Post Mortem Notes," *Political Science Quarterly*, 53:161-72 (June 1938); J. M. Ray, "Defeat of the Administration Reorganization Bill," *Southwestern Social Science Quarterly*, 20:115-24 (September 1939); Mansfield, *The Comptroller-General*, pp. 283-84.

18. *CR*, pp. 4864, 4494-95.

19. Eugene Keogh, Columbia Oral History Collection, p. 48; Lawrence Lewis Diary, April 7, 1938, Lewis MSS. See Finly H. Gray to William Bankhead, November 14, 1938, Bankhead MSS, Box 13.

20. *CR*, pp. 5021-24. For the most part, debate on these topics repeated what was said in the Senate. Opposition to the civil service features of the bill was led by Robert Ramspeck of Georgia, chairman of the House Civil Service Committee and a noted friend of the merit system; for his views, see *ibid.*, pp. 4614, 4796-4800.

21. See Ickes, *Secret Diary*, II, 357; Edward J. Flynn, *You're the Boss* (New York, 1947), p. 156.

22. *CR*, p. 4762.

23. Lawrence Lewis Diary, April 4, 1938, Lewis MSS; *CR*, pp. 4654-55.

24. Boren to Mrs. J. Reed Moore, April 12, 1938, Boren MSS, Box 248; Mack M. Brady to Boren, April 12, 1938, *ibid.*

25. Ickes, *Secret Diary*, II, 357. Representative John Dempsey told Ickes that Representative Hatton Sumners told this to Bankhead.

26. Harold Ickes was told that the Catholic church feared Hopkins and his social workers because they looked with favor on birth control, *Secret Diary*, II, 356. Lutherans also feared the effect of a transfer on their schools; see John W. Boehne to Roosevelt, March 23, 1938, Roosevelt Papers, PPF 5310.

27. *CR*, pp. 4595, 4873.

28. Roosevelt to John Boehne, March 26, 1938, Roosevelt Papers, PPF 5310; Press Conference, April 20, 1938, in Roosevelt, *Public Papers and Addresses*, VII, 251.

29. *New York Times*, April 2, 1938, p. 3; Cardinal Mundelein to Roosevelt, April 7, 1938, Roosevelt Papers, PPF 5310.

30. Kniffin explained his proposal in *CR*, pp. 5004-6. The substance of the Wheeler amendment was introduced in the House by Gerald Boileau of Wisconsin, and defeated, 104–121.

One other important amendment was adopted shortly before the final vote was taken. Claude Fuller of Arkansas offered an amendment restoring patronage over first-, second-, and third-class postmasters to members of the House ("by the eternal, we want them back and we are going to have them back," he promised). Everyone recognized the perversity of attaching this proposal to the Reorganization bill, but it was accepted by a vote of 123–103. It is not clear whether this amendment had the approval of the House leadership. Although a vote for the bill with the Fuller amendment was a vote for the spoils system, it seems not improbable that the amendment would have been eliminated in conference with the Senate had the bill passed; see *CR*, pp. 5103-5, 5121.

31. Josiah Bailey to Amos Pinchot, April 5, 1938, Amos Pinchot MSS, Box 64; Kerr to George A. Moore, April 9, 1938, Kerr MSS, Box 12.

32. James A. Farley, *Jim Farley's Story* (New York, 1948), p. 129.

33. *CR*, pp. 4635, 5009. William Barry (D-N.Y.) claimed that he voted against the bill because he believed that this amendment was unconstitutional, New York *Journal-American,* April 8, 1938, p. 2.

34. *CR*, p. 4995.

35. *CR*, p. 4911; Hope to Roy Painter, April 4, 1938, Hope MSS, Legislative Correspondence, 1937–38; Merlin Hull to C. G. Pearse, April 6, 1938, Hull MSS.

36. Joseph Martin, *My First Fifty Years in Politics* (New York, 1960), p. 90. For comments on the insincerity of the opposition to reorganization, see: Paul Y. Anderson, "Reorganization and Bunk," *Nation,* 146:406-7 (April 9, 1938); Aime J. Forand to Herbert C. Pell, May 26, 1938, Herbert C. Pell MSS (Franklin D. Roosevelt Library); Adolph J. Sabath to Amos Pinchot, August 11, 1937, Amos Pinchot MSS, Box 60.

37. Elbert D. Thomas to Frank Jonas, April 26, 1938, Thomas MSS, Box 24; Henry G. Teigan news-letter, April 14, 1938, Roosevelt Papers, OF 285C, Box 12. See Teigan to Fred F. Werstlein, April 8, 1938, Teigan MSS.

38. Warren to John R. Wheeler, April 8, 1938, Warren MSS, Box 19.

39. Cochran to Pinchot, May 17, 1938, Amos Pinchot MSS, Box 64. See Theodore F. Green to Harold A. Waterworth, April 20, 1938, Green MSS, Box 40.

40. Interview with Louis Brownlow, September 4, 1962. See Ickes, *Secret Diary,* II, 354; "Shadow Boxing in a Crisis," *Nation,* 146:400-1 (April 9, 1938); "Ganging Up on the President," *New Republic,* 94:290-91 (April 13, 1938); Heywood Broun, "It Seems to Me," *The Progressive,* April 23, 1938, p. 3; H. G. Leach, "Not a Dead Issue," *Forum,* 100:49-50 (August 1938).

41. Boren to Ross Porter, April 11, 1938, Boren MSS, Box 248.

42. Lawrence Lewis Diary, March 31, April 8, 1938, Lewis MSS.

43. *CR*, Appendix, pp. 1612-13. See Ernest J. Bohn to Martin Sweeney, April 2, 1938, National Resources Planning Board Files, Box 47.

44. Resident of Shawnee, Oklahoma, to Lyle Boren, April 5, 1938, Boren MSS, Box 248.

45. Letter to Merlin Hull, April 5, 1938, Hull MSS.

46. Pinchot memorandum for Roy Howard, March 28 or 29, 1938, Amos Pinchot MSS, Box 64.

47. A citizen of Broken Arrow, Oklahoma, to Lyle Boren, April 2, 1938, Boren MSS, Box 248.

48. Henry G. Teigan to Peter Morell, April 4, 1938, Teigan MSS; Blanche Childress to Roosevelt, April 14, 1938, Roosevelt Papers, OF 285C, Box 8; *New York Times*, May 5, 1938, p. 1.

49. Warren to author, July 21, 1962. See Joseph E. Casey to Sherman Minton, enclosing petition from Gardner, Massachusetts, Lobby Committee Files, Box 107.

50. *CR*, Appendix, p. 1488.

51. Doughton to K. S. Tanner, April 1, 1938, Doughton MSS, Drawer 10; Doughton to H. N. Williams, March 26, 1938, *ibid*.

52. Byron B. Harlan, of Ohio, in *CR*, pp. 4503-04.

53. Kerr to Rev. Arthur J. Barton, February 19, 1938, Kerr MSS, Box 11; Kerr to R. H. Bennett, April 4, 1938, *ibid*.

54. *CR*, pp. 4989, 4626-28.

55. Flannagan to Roosevelt, April 9, 1938, Roosevelt Papers, PPF 5310. See Memorandum for Steve Early on telephone call from Wright Patman, April 9, 1938, *ibid*., OF 285C, Box 8.

56. *CR*, pp. 5094 (Drew); 4626 (Starnes); 4883, Appendix, pp. 1249-50, 1358-59 (Eberharter).

57. Clifford Hope to R. M. Skidmore, April 13, 1938, Hope MSS, Legislative Correspondence, 1937-38.

58. Farley, *Jim Farley's Story*, p. 130; Lawrence Lewis Diary, April 8, 1938, Lewis MSS.

59. Coffee to Gifford Pinchot, November 24, 1937, Gifford Pinchot MSS, Box 1903; Ickes, *Secret Diary*, II, 366.

60. See the discussion of these points in Chapter VII.

61. Elbert Thomas to Frank Jonas, April 26, 1938, Thomas MSS, Box 24; *CR*, p. 4636.

62. *The Progressive*, April 2, 1938, p. 7; Farley, *Jim Farley's Story*, p. 128. Democrats from the eleven southern states cast 51 votes for the bill, and 35 against (12 did not vote). However, four southern states—Tennessee, Louisiana, North Carolina, and Alabama—provided a 25–3 margin for the bill. Most of the others divided evenly, except for Florida and Virginia, which voted overwhelmingly against the measure.

63. Ickes, *Secret Diary*, II, 357; Robert Lee Doughton to C. L. Shuping, April 8, 1938, Doughton MSS, Drawer 10.

64. Ickes, *Secret Diary*, II, 368.

65. *New York Times*, April 9, 1938, p. 2.

66. New York *World-Telegram*, April 9, 1938, p. 20; Gannett to William J. Weller, April 25, 1938, Gannett MSS, Box 6a, Scrapbook 1.

67. Thomas W. Phelps, "The Revolt Against Roosevelt," *Barron's* 18:10 (April 11, 1938). See "A Needless Defeat," *The (London) Economist*, 131:182-83 (April 23, 1938); "American Deadlock," *ibid.* (April 16, 1938), 130-31; "Revolt," *Newsweek*, April 18, 1938, p. 14; Peter A. Odegard, *Prelude to November, 1940* (New York, 1940), pp. 16-19; Bascom N. Timmons, *Garner of Texas* (New York, 1948), p. 232.

68. James J. Coke to Jack Nichols, April 1, 1938, Jack Nichols MSS (University of Oklahoma), General Correspondence.

69. Martin to Alfred M. Landon, April 12, 1938, Landon MSS. Martin thought that the Republicans would make important gains in Congress; "That is, of course, if the business picture remains poor."

70. Henry G. Teigan to Edward Prochaska, April 10, 1938, Teigan MSS. Two of the five Farmer-Labor delegates from Minnesota also voted to recommit.

71. Donald R. McCoy, *Angry Voices* (Lawrence, 1958), pp. 163-66; *The Progressive*, April 30, 1938.

72. *New York Times*, April 26, 1938, p. 20. See Franklin, *1940*, p. 94.

73. Hull to C. W. Berthiaume, April 5, 1938; Hull to J. A. Amacker, April 1, 1938, Hull MSS.

74. Hull to D. Whelan, April 11, 1938, Hull MSS.

75. On Progressive opposition to Administration measures, see: Hull to Al C. Anderson, April 14, 1938, Hull MSS; *The Progressive*, March 19, 1938: Milwaukee *Leader*, March 23, 1938; *CR*, Appendix, pp. 2798-99. The Ludlow war referendum was a proposed Constitutional amendment that would have required a national referendum before war could be declared, unless the United States was invaded.

76. Hull to J. W. McCauley, April 8, 1938; Hull to Ed J. Scott, April 5, 1938, Hull MSS.

77. *The Progressive*, March 19, 1938, pp. 7-8. Gehrmann offered an explanation of his vote against the bill in *ibid.*, April 9, 1938, p. 7.

78. Statement of Merlin Hull before Committee considering Canadian reciprocity, April 5, 1938, Hull MSS; Hull to A. F. Ender, April 5, 1938, *ibid.*; Lawrence Lewis Diary, March 23, 1938, Lewis MSS. See Harold F. Gosnell and Morris H. Cohen, "Progressive Politics: Wisconsin an Example," *American Political Science Review*, 34:925 (October 1940).

79. *CR*, p. 4897; Warren to Raymond S. McKeough, April 9, 1938, Warren MSS, Box 19.

80. Five of the seven Brooklyn congressmen voted for the bill; all three Bronx Democrats voted for it. On Tammany opposition, see *New York Times*, April 10, 1938, p. 2; Walter Hurley to Rev. E. L. Curran, April 8, 1938, O'Connor MSS.

81. Charles Garrett, *The LaGuardia Years: Machine and Reform Politics in New York City* (New Brunswick, 1961), pp. 91, 336, 105; Flynn, *You're the Boss*, pp. 94, 102-4; Interview with Jeremiah T. Mahoney, June 4, 1962. On Tammany leadership in this period, see Herbert C. Pell to Robert F. Wagner, July 22, 1938, and Herbert C. Pell to Jeremiah T. Mahoney, May 9, 1938, Pell MSS.

82. Interview with James A. Farley, May 19, 1962; *New York Times*, April 6, 1938, p. 12.

83. Joseph A. Gavagan, Columbia Oral History Collection, p. 53.

84. Gannett to Frantz Haverstick, April 15, 1938, Gannett MSS, Box 6a, Scrapbook 1.

85. Ramspeck and Allen objected to the civil service features of the bill, *CR*, p. 5107. Hamilton was an anti-Byrd Democrat; he voted with the Administration to close debate on April 1, but voted to recommit on April 8. For a conservative Virginian's estimate of Hamilton, see Carter Glass to Colgate Darden, August 5, 1938, Glass MSS, Box 398.

86. *CR*, p. 4871, Appendix, pp. 1537-38; Vincent F. Harrington to Roosevelt, April 12, 1938, Roosevelt Papers, OF 285C, Box 8.

87. T. R. B., "Washington Notes: Rainmaker But No Rain," *New Republic*, 94:358-59 (April 27, 1938).

88. Keller to Roosevelt, April 18, 1938, Roosevelt Papers, OF 119.

89. Fries to Roosevelt, April 5, 1938, Roosevelt Papers, PPF 5310; "W. D. H." memorandum for Steve Early, April 11, 1938, *ibid.*

90. Hull to F. D. Calway, April 9, 1938; Hull to Al C. Anderson, April 14, 1938, Hull MSS. In fact, of 39 Democratic committee chairmen, 13 voted to recommit and 2 abstained.

91. Crawford, *The Pressure Boys*, p. 207; *New York Times*, April 9, 1938, pp. 1-2.

92. Thomas to Charles H. Hatfield, April 9, 1938, Elmer Thomas MSS, Legislation—Correspondence and Papers, 75th Congress.

93. Marvin McIntyre memorandum for Steve Early, April 6, 1938, reporting a conversation with Martin Dies, Roosevelt Papers, PPF 3458.

94. New York *World-Telegram*, April 9, 1938, p. 5. Hamilton Fish had said during the debate: "The defeat of the reorganization bill will also put an end to any third-term movement," *CR*, p. 5114.

95. See Ickes, *Secret Diary*, II, 358; Farley, *Jim Farley's Story*, p. 130; Tugwell, *The Democratic Roosevelt*, p. 468.

Chapter IX: The Reorganization Act of 1939

1. Brownlow to Roosevelt, April 11, 1938, Roosevelt Papers, OF 285C.

2. Press Conference, July 5, 1938, Roosevelt Papers, XII, 11-12.

3. John Miller, "Journal of the President's Committee," July 5, 1938, PCAM Files, Box 2. See Joseph P. Harris to F. A. Bland, June 21, 1938, *ibid.*, Box 12.

4. Several officials who opposed the new spending program believed that the defeat of the Reorganization bill caused Roosevelt to adopt pump-priming as a way to recoup his prestige. It appears, however, that the President had come to a decision a few days before the vote was taken. See Henry Morgenthau Diaries, April 5, 6, and 11, 1938, Morgenthau MSS, Book 118. On congressional support for the spending program, see Sol Bloom to Leonard A. Hollander, April 15, 1938, Sol Bloom MSS (New York Public Library).

5. Cantril, *Public Opinion*, p. 756; Gannett to Elisha Hanson, April 15, 1938, Gannett MSS, Box 6a, Scrapbook 1.

6. H. V. Thornton to Marvin McIntyre, June 14, 1938, Roosevelt Papers, PPF 5310; "Reorganization Backfire," *Newsweek*, April 25, 1938, p. 7. See letters from constituents to Lyle Boren, April 15, 1938: "If you are going to join the reactionaries against the President, then we are off of you forever," Boren MSS, Box 248.

7. Cochran to Roosevelt, April 20, 1938, Roosevelt Papers, PPF 4694.

8. Landon to R. W. Babson, May 14, 1938, Landon MSS.

9. Arthur Krock in the *New York Times*, June 5, 1938, IV, p. 3.

10. Roosevelt, *Public Papers and Addresses*, VII, 206. This may have been meant to prevent opposition to the spending program.

11. Sabath to Roosevelt, April 9, 1938, Roosevelt Papers, PPF 955.

12. Lee to Roosevelt, June 22, 1938, Roosevelt Papers, PPF 1820.

13. The decision to embark upon the purge is described in: Samuel Rosenman, *Working with Roosevelt* (New York, 1952), pp. 176-77, and Flynn, *You're the Boss*, p. 149. Roosevelt endorsed Robert Bulkley, who voted to recommit the bill, and opposed Cotton Ed Smith and Guy Gillette, who supported it.

14. Speech at Barnesville, Georgia, Roosevelt, *Public Papers and Addresses*, VII, 469-70.

15. Ickes, *Secret Diary*, II, 359; Cooke to Roosevelt, April 19, 1938, Roosevelt Papers, PPF 940.

16. Adolph J. Sabath to Roosevelt, May 5, 1938, Roosevelt Papers, PPF 955; Ickes, *Secret Diary*, II, 378-79.

17. Gulick to Brownlow and Merriam, May 27, 1938, PCAM Files, Box 18.

18. *New York Times*, June 1, 1938, p. 1; Roosevelt to Morris Cooke, April 22, 1938, Roosevelt Papers, PPF 940.

19. Owen Johnson to James Roosevelt, April 11, 1938, James Roosevelt MSS, Box 14.

20. Ickes, *Secret Diary*, II, 390.

21. *New York Times*, May 15, 1938, p. 6. One report claimed that the Administration promised not to reintroduce the bill in return for Senator Byrd's promise not to begin a filibuster on the spending bill, *ibid.*, June 1, 1938, p. 1.

22. Daniel Bell memorandum for Bureau of the Budget, April 19, 1938, Bureau of the Budget Files, Box 192 (91); see United States Civil Service Commission, *Fifty-Fifth Annual Report* (Washington, 1938). Although defeat of the bill had denied Harry Hopkins a Cabinet post, Roosevelt asked Hopkins to sit in on Cabinet meetings anyway.

23. Sam Rayburn to Lindsay Warren, November 11, 1938, Warren MSS, Box 20.

24. Warren to Roosevelt, November 14, 1938; Warren to John Cochran, November 23, 1938, Warren MSS, Box 20; Warren to William Bankhead, December 3, 1938, Bankhead MSS, Box 13.

25. "Memorandum concerning conversation on Reorganization," December 8, 1938, Roosevelt Papers, OF 285C, Box 16. Brownlow could not attend the meeting due to illness. The conferees hoped to be able to introduce bills relating to the civil service and accounting later. See Brownlow to Roosevelt, November 2, 1938, *ibid.*

26. Byrnes to Warren, December 20, 1938, Warren MSS, Box 20.

27. Warren to John Cochran, December 17, 1938, Warren MSS, Box 20. When Roosevelt asked if his Committee should attend the meeting on December 20, Warren demurred: "I made no mention of it." For Warren's view of the Congressional temper, see Warren to Byrnes, December 22, 1938, *ibid.*

28. Byrd to Amos Pinchot, March 28, 1939, Amos Pinchot MSS, Box 66; Cochran to Gulick, March 15, 1939, Reorganization Committee Files, Box 13.

29. Aled Davies to Pinchot, December 9, 1938, Amos Pinchot MSS, Box 64; "Where Do We Go From Here?" *America's Future*, 1:25 (January 1939).

30. Pinchot to Gannett, March 17, 1939; Pinchot to John O'Connor, March 3, 1939, Amos Pinchot MSS, Box 66.

31. Sumner's amendment was accepted on a teller vote in Committee of the Whole, 176–156; it was later defeated on a roll call vote, 209–193. The bill passed by a vote of 246–153.

32. Warren to Ed Flanagan, March 18, 1939, Warren MSS, Box

20; Hope to S. R. Stebbins, March 14, 1939, Hope MSS, Legislative Correspondence, 1938–39.

33. *New York Times,* March 21-23, 1939; Harry Byrd to Pinchot, March 28, 1939, Amos Pinchot MSS, Box 66; Ickes, *Secret Diary,* II, 602-3. The bill passed by a vote of 63–23.

A significant feature of the Reorganization Act of 1939 was its use of the technique of the legislative veto; on this point, see: John D. Millett and Lindsay Rogers, "The Legislative Veto and the Reorganization Act of 1939," *Public Administration Review,* 1:176-89 (Winter 1941); Joseph Cooper, "The Legislative Veto: Its Promise and Its Perils," *Public Policy; A Yearbook of the Graduate School of Public Administration, Harvard University,* VII (1956), 128-74; Joseph P. Harris, *Congressional Control of Administration* (New York, 1964), chap. 8.

34. Roosevelt to Gulick, March 20, 1939, Roosevelt Papers, PPF 4307.

35. Gulick to Brownlow and Merriam, March 21, 1939, PCAM Files, Box 18; memorandum for Roosevelt from Kannee, March 29, 1939, Roosevelt Papers, OF 285C, Box 8; Brownlow to Roosevelt, April 2, 1939, *ibid.*

36. The drafting of these plans is discussed in: Roosevelt memorandum on a meeting with Brownlow, Merriam, and Bell, April 13, 1939, PCAM Files, Box 24; Notes of conferences held between Brownlow and the Bureau of the Budget, April–May, 1939, Bureau of the Budget Records (F2-82).

37. Harold D. Smith Diary, April 23, April 26, 1939, Smith MSS.

38. On the Executive Office of the President, see: Clinton Rossiter, *The American Presidency* (New York, 1956); Edward H. Hobbs, *Behind the President* (Washington, 1954); George A. Graham, "The Presidency and the Executive Office of the President," *Journal of Politics,* 12:599-621 (November 1950); Don K. Price, "Staffing the Presidency," *American Political Science Review,* 40:1154-68 (December 1946).

39. Ickes, *Secret Diary,* II, 623. On the Congressional outlook, see: James F. Byrnes to Roosevelt, April 29, 1939, Roosevelt Papers, OF 285C, Box 8; John Cochran to Roosevelt, May 1, 1939, *ibid.*

40. Harold D. Smith Diary, April 11, August 10, 1939, Smith MSS.

41. Memorandum for Watson from Kannee describing telephone conversation with John Dempsey, May 10, 1939, Roosevelt Papers, OF 285C, Box 8.

42. The three presidential assistants were: Lauchlin Currie, William H. McReynolds, and James H. Rowe. In 1940 Lindsay Warren became Comptroller-General.

# Index